OXFORD READINGS IN PHILOSOPHY

PROPERTIES

D0140971

PROPERTIES

edited by
D. H. MELLOR
and
ALEX OLIVER

OXFORD
UNIVERSITY PRESS

OXFORD
UNIVERSITY PRESS

Great Clarendon Street, Oxford OX2 6DP

Oxford University Press is a department of the University of Oxford.
It furthers the University's objective of excellence in research, scholarship,
and education by publishing worldwide in

Oxford New York

Auckland Bangkok Buenos Aires Cape Town Chennai
Dar es Salaam Delhi Hong Kong Istanbul Karachi Kolkata
Kuala Lumpur Madrid Melbourne Mexico City Mumbai Nairobi
São Paulo Shanghai Taipei Tokyo Toronto

Oxford is a registered trade mark of Oxford University Press
in the UK and in certain other countries

Published in the United States
by Oxford University Press Inc., New York

Introduction and selection © Oxford University Press 1997

The moral rights of the author have been asserted
Database right Oxford University Press (maker)

First published 1997
Reprinted in paperback 1999, 2002 Twice, 2004

British Library Cataloguing in Publication Data
Data available

Library of Congress Cataloging in Publication Data
Data available
ISBN 0-19-875177-X
ISBN 0-19-875176-1 (Pbk)

7 9 10 8

Typeset in Times
Printed in Great Britain by
Biddles Ltd., King's Lynn
www.biddles.co.uk

CONTENTS

INTRODUCTION

D. H. MELLOR AND ALEX OLIVER

1. PROPERTIES

Particular objects have *properties*, respects in which they may be alike or differ. People running are alike in motion, if not in shape or size, and differ in that respect from people standing still; spheres are alike in shape, if not in size or motion, and differ in that respect from cubes; and so on.

Similarly with *relations*. Take Don and his son Bill, and Kim and her daughter Ann. Don's parent–child relation to Bill holds also between Kim and Ann. In this respect these so-called *ordered pairs*—written ⟨Don,Bill⟩ and ⟨Kim,Ann⟩—are like all other parent–child pairs, and differ from any other pair, like ⟨Don,Ann⟩ or the child–parent pair ⟨Bill,Don⟩, whose first member is not a parent of the second.

Similarly with relations of three or more particulars. These are respects in which ordered triples, quadruples etc. (*n*-tuples in general) may be alike or differ. Suppose Don is older than Kim, who is older than Bill, who is older than Ann. Then ⟨Don,Kim,Bill⟩ and ⟨Ann,Bill,Don⟩ are alike in that the middle member of each triple is *between* the other two in age—if not perhaps in height or weight—and differ in this respect from triples, like ⟨Don,Bill,Kim⟩, whose members are not ordered by age.

Describing relations in this way, as properties of *n*-tuples of particulars, is of course artificial, but the artifice has a point. The point is to remind us that properties and relations raise similar questions, about what it is for particulars and groups of particulars to differ or to be alike, questions that are best tackled together. And the answers to these questions matter both in themselves and in their implications, e.g. for *change*: since to change in some respect is just to differ in that respect at different times. Thus a particular that differs in colour but not in shape at different times thereby changes its colour but not its shape, just as Bill's outgrowing his father

We would like to thank the members of a reading group at Cambridge for their helpful discussion of the papers included in this volume, and Hallvard Lillehammer for cross-referencing and indexing it. Some material from Oliver (1996) has, with the permission of Oxford University Press, been incorporated into this introduction.

is ⟨Don,Bill⟩ changing by ceasing to be an instance of the *taller than* relation. In what follows, we shall usually work with properties for ease of presentation. When what we say about properties does not apply to relations we shall say so and when there is something distinctive to be said about relations we shall say it.

The most important questions about the kinds of sameness, difference and change that properties embody concern their reality and objectivity. Do particulars change or stay the same, resemble or differ from each other, independently of how we think of or describe them? That is, do properties exist in their own right—and if so which?

But if these are the important questions about properties, they can hardly be our first ones. For just as we cannot know that unicorns do not exist (but that if they did they would do so independently of our thinking so) without knowing what unicorns are, so we cannot know whether and which properties exist without knowing what properties are. So our first question is this: what sort of entities are properties like running and relations like being taller than?

This question involves at least two comparisons. First, how do properties relate to the predicates that apply to the particulars (and *n*-tuples of particulars) which have those properties: how are running and being taller than related to what 'runs' and 'is taller than' mean? And second, how do properties differ from and relate to the particulars that have them?

These questions would be hard enough to answer if everyone agreed on the meanings of predicates, on what fixes their meanings and on the nature of the particulars they apply to. But these too are contentious matters, a fact which complicates our questions by making answers to them parts of semantic and metaphysical package deals, which need to be assessed *en bloc*. This fact, and the long history of the subject, also makes different writers use different terms for what we are calling 'properties', 'predicates' and 'particulars'—and also use these terms to mean different things. So to help readers understand the readings that follow and relate them to each other, we shall note in passing some of these other uses.

Before introducing the readings we have chosen, we should say something about why we have chosen them and not others. First, with limited space, we have tried not to duplicate other collections. Hence our omission of all work before Frege, well covered by Schoedinger (1992), and on Wittgenstein's notion of family resemblance, also well covered by Schoedinger and by Loux (1970). (We have included Quine's 'On What There Is', despite its occurring in these collections, because we think its importance and influence makes it essential reading for all students of the subject.) Hence also our omission of easily available work on Wittgenstein's remarks on following a rule, to which however we refer in § 15 in asking how properties relate to predicates. Finally, despite Frege's example, we have omitted recent work on properties in the metaphysics of mathematics, most of which is too specialized to be suitable for this volume. (We list some references under 'Properties and the Metaphysics of Mathematics' in our Select Bibliography.)

2. FREGE: PROPERTIES AS FUNCTIONS

We start with four selections, from Frege, Russell and Ramsey, which are both important in themselves and also provide a self-contained background to the pieces that follow. In our chapter I, an abridgement of his 'Function and Concept', Frege uses mostly mathematical examples to give an account of properties, which he calls 'concepts', and of how they differ from the particulars that have ('fall under') them. He starts by distinguishing a *function*, like $2x^3+x$, from its *arguments* (e.g. the number 2) and corresponding *values* (the number 18). The difference, he says (p. 36), is that a function is 'incomplete' or 'unsaturated', since it needs supplementing by one object (an argument) to make up another (its value for that argument). He then applies this distinction to functions, like $x^2 = 1$, whose values are not numbers but the *truth values*: (the) True and (the) False. These functions he identifies with concepts, i.e. properties, in this case 'the property that its square is 1': 'a concept is a function whose value is always a truth value' (p. 41). Relations similarly are functions whose values are truth values but which, like $x > y$, have more than one argument (p. 44).

The values and arguments of functions are not restricted to numbers and truth values. They can be objects of any kind (e.g. Berlin, the value of the function expressed by 'the capital of x' when its argument is Germany), where 'an object is anything that is not a function, so that an expression for it does not contain any empty place' (p. 43). In particular, what Frege calls the 'graph' of a function—which if the function is a concept is its *extension*—is an object, even though the function (concept, property) is not. So while for Frege the property of being a square root of 1 is not an object, its extension, comprising the numbers, -1 and 1, that have this property, is.

Frege thus draws a sharp distinction between objects, including particulars—numbers like 1, cities like Berlin, countries like Germany—and their properties. The former are complete, the latter are not. Properties are the essentially incomplete functions whose value, when the particulars that have them are their arguments, is the truth-value True. On this view, moreover, there are as many properties as there are (possible) predicates with different extensions, since any true sentence 'φa' about a particular a states a property of a, namely the function φx from any particular x to the truth value of 'φx'.

The function φx is however rarely if ever what, in any non-Fregean sense, the predicate 'φ' means, since Frege (1892–5, p. 120) takes predicates that are coextensive, i.e. apply to the very same particulars, to correspond to the same concept. For suppose, to take a well-worn example, all and only animals with hearts have kidneys. Then if 'has a heart' and 'has kidneys' are coextensive, they express the same function from particulars to truth values. Yet in no normal sense would anyone say that these predicates had the same meaning, expressed the same concept or ascribed the same property.

Frege's theory of properties therefore yields both too many properties and too few. Too few, by identifying coextensive properties; too many, by letting *every* predicate express a property, thus obliterating the general distinction between differing and being alike and hence between changing and staying the same. Take the variant of Goodman's (1965) notorious predicate 'grue' that for some time t_1 means 'green and $t < t_1$ or blue and $t \geq t_1$'. This expresses a function from particulars at times to truth values and so, for Frege, a property, *being grue*: a respect in which any particular a that is green before t_1 is like anything blue after t_1 (including a if it changes colour at t_1) and hence different from anything green after t_1 (including a if it does *not* change colour). But this is absurd: so we need a way of excluding 'gruesome' properties, which Frege himself does not provide.

3. RUSSELL: PROPERTIES AS UNIVERSALS

We might exclude improper properties by excluding improper predicates —*if* we can say what makes predicates 'proper' without a viciously circular appeal to properties. But that, by reducing properties to mere shadows of (proper) predicates, prompts the nominalist question: why postulate properties at all? Why not let our predicates define the respects in which the particulars they apply to are alike, and different from those they do not apply to? One answer is that we do not apply proper predicates to particulars arbitrarily. Given what 'runs', 'is a square root' and 'is taller than' mean, it is usually a matter of perceptible or provable fact, not of arbitrary decision, whether these predicates apply to any given particular or ordered pair of particulars. But what then makes such predicates apply to some particulars and not others, if not that particulars have or lack corresponding properties?

One nominalist answer to that question, that of the *resemblance nominalist*, is attacked by Russell in chapter II, 'The World of Universals'. Russell starts with Plato's idea of a property like being just, or white, as a *universal*, something shared by certain particulars: all just acts, white things. After noting, like us, that we must include both the *qualities* of particulars and *relations* between two or more particulars, he remarks that

if we wish to avoid the universals *whiteness* and *triangularity*, we shall choose some particular patch of white or some particular triangle, and say that anything is white or a triangle if it has the right sort of resemblance to our chosen particular. But then the resemblance required will have to be a universal. Since there are many white things, the resemblance must hold between many pairs of particular white things; and this is the characteristic of a universal (p. 48).

But nominalists can no more admit a universal *resembles in colour* than the universal colour, whiteness, which they invoked the resemblance to replace.

This objection to resemblance nominalism may not be fatal, as we shall see when considering the *trope theory* of Williams and Campbell, whose resembling objects are not particulars like Russell's white patch but property-instances (called *tropes*) like the patch's whiteness. But it does show that predicates provide no easy or automatic substitute for properties.

Russell meanwhile, rejecting nominalism, claims that universals, being common to all their instances, cannot be located within space or time, not even by being in our minds: there is nothing mental about the universal constituent (*north of*) in the fact that Edinburgh is north of London. So since 'universals do not exist in this sense [of being in time], we shall say that they *subsist* or *have being*, where "being" is opposed to "existence" as being timeless' (p. 50). But this restriction on 'exists' is misplaced; for as Quine remarks in 'On What There Is' (our chapter V),

if spatio-temporal reference is lacking when we affirm the existence of the cube root of 27, this is simply because a cube root is not a spatio-temporal kind of thing, and not because we are being ambiguous in our use of 'exist' (p. 76).

The fact that universals, unlike many particulars (but not numbers, if numbers are particulars), lack a restricted space-time location is no reason to deny that, if any exist, they do so in the same sense as the particulars whose properties and relations they are.

In chapter III, 'On Our Knowledge of Universals', Russell attacks another source of scepticism about universals. The problem here is that our senses seem only to show us objects which, unlike universals, are located within space and time. How then can our senses tell us what universals there are, when they are instantiated, how they are related, and so on? The answer, Russell says, is that

when we see a white patch, we are acquainted, in the first instance, with the particular patch; but by seeing many white patches, we easily learn to abstract the whiteness which they all have in common, and in learning to do this we are learning to be acquainted with whiteness (p. 51).

Similarly, for other universals, including relations like *before*, and relations between universals, as when we see that 'the resemblance between two shades of green is greater than the resemblance between a shade of red and a shade of green' (p. 52).

This answer will not do. That we can 'learn to abstract the whiteness which [many white patches] have in common' is, if true, the very fact that needs explaining. To explain it would be to show how our eyes can make the whiteness of patches cause us to see that they have that very property; but Russell does not do this. Nor could he if, as many argue, colours and other so-called secondary qualities are properties, not of the particulars we ascribe them to, but of our perceptions of them. For then all Russell's story says is that even an untutored eyesight will make the so-called primary qualities of white particulars cause them to look alike to those who see them. But all this shows, if true, is how we can get and apply a mental *concept* of whiteness, not how we can gain knowledge of any *property* of white particulars.

Russell's positive argument for universals is that they explain how we can have *a priori* knowledge, all of which he claims 'deals exclusively with the relations of universals' (p. 52). For example, even when we interpret the proposition that $2+2=4$

as meaning 'any collection formed of two twos is a collection of four' . . . we can see what it is that it asserts, as soon as we know what is meant by 'collection' and 'two' and 'four'. It is quite unnecessary to know all the couples in the world: if it were necessary, obviously we could never understand the proposition. . . . Thus the statement 'two and two are four' deals exclusively with universals and therefore may be known by anybody who is acquainted with the universals concerned and can perceive the relation between them which the statement asserts (p. 53).

This too will hardly do. For first, if, as Russell says, '$2+2=4$' 'fails to make any statement whatever about any actual particular couple' (p. 53), how can it contradict a statement which says that two such couples do *not* make four? And second, to say we 'perceive the relation' between 2 and 4 that makes $2+2=4$ hardly explains our *a priori* knowledge of this fact without an account of *how* we perceive it, which Russell does not give. In short, Russell's theory of properties as universals is as incomplete as Frege's theory of them as functions.

4. RAMSEY ON THE PARTICULAR/UNIVERSAL DISTINCTION

Frege's and Russell's theories face a more serious charge than incompleteness. This is Ramsey's objection in chapter IV, 'Universals', to a basic assumption made by Frege, Russell and almost all others: namely that particulars and properties differ in kind. For even nominalists, in order to deny the existence of universals, must distinguish them from particulars, whose existence they accept. Yet Ramsey argues that this distinction entails no real difference of kind between the entities, particulars and universals, so distinguished.

First, Ramsey notes that we cannot base our distinction on a merely grammatical difference between subject and predicate: e.g. between 'Socrates' and 'is wise' in 'Socrates is wise'. For in the equivalent proposition, 'Wisdom is a characteristic of Socrates', the subject is wisdom, which is not a particular. Also, in *molecular* sentences (i.e. ones that contain other sentences) like 'Socrates is wise or Plato is foolish', the subject-predicate distinction generates *complex universals*, like being wise-unless-Plato-is-foolish. Despite these being perfectly good functions and concepts (i.e. properties) in Frege's sense (chapter I), Ramsey argues that no such entities can exist. For if they did, then, to take his other example, that a universal R relates a to b, that a has the complex property Rb and that b has the property aR would

be three different propositions because they have different sets of constituents, and yet they are ... but one ... namely that a has R to b. So the theory of complex universals is responsible for an incomprehensible trinity, as senseless as that of theology (p. 61).

Similarly with Socrates's apparent property of being wise-unless-Plato-is-foolish and Plato's of being foolish-unless-Socrates-is-wise. If, as Ramsey assumes, the proposition that Socrates is wise or Plato is foolish can have only one set of constituents, there can be no such complex properties.

The weakness in this argument is its assumption that a proposition (and so, if the proposition is true, the corresponding fact) cannot have different sets of constituents. Whether this is so depends on what the constituents of propositions and facts are (see Oliver 1992, Mellor 1992). But even if Ramsey's argument fails, we have seen already that we need his conclusion, that not all predicates correspond to properties, to sustain a general distinction between differing and being alike.

Suppose then we agree with Ramsey that only some predicates, in some *atomic* sentences (those containing no other sentences), correspond to universals. Can we infer an intrinsic difference between universals and particulars from the subject-predicate distinction in *these* sentences? Only, Ramsey says, if such a difference can explain the idea that 'Socrates is a real independent entity, wisdom . . . a quality of something else' (p. 64)— the idea Frege expresses by calling concepts like wisdom 'incomplete'. But Ramsey argues that no difference between universals and particulars can explain this idea, which arises from associating 'wise' only with propositions of the atomic form '*x* is wise' while associating 'Socrates' with *all* propositions containing 'wise', including 'Socrates is neither wise nor just'. Yet we can just as well associate 'wise' with this and all other propositions containing it, while associating 'Socrates' only with the atomic form 'Socrates is *q*', where *q* is a universal—which, if there are no complex universals, can no more include 'Socrates is neither wise nor just' than '*x* is wise' can include 'Neither Socrates nor Plato is wise' (pp. 65–6). So no intrinsic difference between universals and particulars can be inferred from—since none can explain—our association of atomic forms with predicates but not with subjects.

But why then do we treat predicates and subjects differently in this way, thus making universals seem less 'real and independent' than particulars? Ramsey's explanation is this. A predicate symbol 'φ' can stand alone only if it corresponds to a real universal, not if it abbreviates a complex predicate like 'has *R* to *a* or *S* to *b*'. This we *must* abbreviate to 'φx', to distinguish it from the two-place '. . . has *R* to *a* or . . . has *S* to *b*', which we should write '$\varphi(x,y)$'. But since it rarely matters whether 'φ' corresponds to a universal, logicians like Frege always write 'φ' as 'φx', '$\varphi(x,y)$' etc., thus associating all predicates with atomic forms (pp. 69–71). We cannot therefore infer from this practice that particulars differ intrinsically from universals. A logician, says Ramsey, can take

any type of objects whatever as the subject of his reasoning, and call them individuals, meaning by that simply that he has chosen this type to reason about (pp. 71-2).

In short, as Frege's definition of an object ('anything that is not a function, so that an expression for it does not contain any empty place') can apply as easily to universals as to particulars, it tells us nothing about the difference between them.

5. ONTOLOGICAL COMMITMENT TO PROPERTIES

Despite their differences, Frege, Russell and Ramsey all think there are properties. Quine (who calls properties 'attributes') denies this, thus making him, in our sense, a nominalist. Terminology is a mess here, since 'nominalism' means different things in different mouths. In Quine's it means the denial of abstract entities, i.e. those that lack causes, effects, and spatio-temporal location. But since Quine (1960, chapter 7, §55) believes in sets, which, like properties, he takes to be abstract, he is not a nominalist in *his* sense—especially as, to add to the confusion, he uses 'universal' as a synonym for 'abstract entity', whereas universals for us are one candidate for being properties.

One other confusion needs allaying before we can discuss Quine's views. As we shall see in §10, Lewis identifies properties with sets of actual and possible particulars. Why then does Quine say that sets exist but properties (his 'attributes') do not? The reason is that his sets contain only actual particulars, and properties cannot be sets of them. For sets are the same if they have the same members, and we have noted already that different properties, like having a heart and having kidneys, can have the same actual instances.

With this preamble, we turn to chapter V, 'On What There Is', in which Quine exposes some bad arguments for the existence of certain kinds of entity. Take the fictional flying horse Pegasus. Common sense declares 'Pegasus' to be an empty name, i.e. not to name anything. But Quine's fictional philosopher McX says it must name something, or 'we should not be talking about anything when we use the word; therefore it would be nonsense to say even that Pegasus is not' (p. 75). McX concludes that, as Pegasus cannot be found in reality outside our minds, it is an idea in our minds. But this for Quine is a confusion: we should no more conflate Pegasus with our idea of Pegasus than we conflate the Parthenon with our idea of the Parthenon.

Quine's other and more sophisticated philosopher, Wyman, then claims that Pegasus exists as a possible but non-actual entity. But Quine complains that Wyman's ontology of possible entities 'offends the aesthetic sense of us who have a taste for desert landscapes' (p. 76). He adds moreover that, as we cannot say when merely possible entities are the same or different, talk of them is senseless.

Quine accuses both McX and Wyman of assuming that a name must name something for a sentence containing it to have any sense, an assumption he uses Russell's (1919, chapter 16) theory of definite descriptions to undermine. Take the sentence 'The author of *Waverley* was a poet', featuring the definite description 'the author of *Waverley*'. Russell said this means that something wrote *Waverley* and was a poet, and nothing else wrote *Waverley*. Similarly, 'The author of *Waverley* does not exist' means it is not the case both that something wrote *Waverley* and nothing else wrote *Waverley*: i.e. either nothing, or two or more things, wrote *Waverley*. The key point is, as Quine puts it, that

> when a statement of being or nonbeing is analysed by Russell's theory of descriptions, it ceases to contain any expression which even purports to name the alleged entity whose being is in question, so that the meaningfulness of the statement no longer can be thought to presuppose that there be such an entity (p. 79).

Quine then extends Russell's theory to cover names like 'Pegasus', by replacing them with definite descriptions like 'the thing that pegasizes'.

But what, if not our use of names or descriptions, tells us what (we think) exists? Quine proposes a two-step answer to that question. First, we work out which of our theories are true, and then we work out their ontological commitments, which are those of the sentences we use to state them. And a sentence is ontologically committed to an entity (or kind of entity) if and only if that entity (or kind) must exist for the sentence to be true, a commitment determined by the criterion Quine expresses in his slogan that

> to be assumed as an entity is, purely and simply, to be reckoned as a value of a variable (p. 83).

The idea here is that ontological commitment is expressed by the general word 'something', represented in first-order logic by the *existential quantifier*, '∃', as in 'Something is mortal', represented by '$(\exists x)Mx$', where 'Mx' means 'x is mortal'. Now when we say 'Something is mortal' we have in mind some set of entities, one or more of which, we are saying, is mortal. If the set is the set of human beings, what we say is true; if the set only contains immortal gods, what we say is false. Such a set is what logicians call a *domain of quantification*, to which the truth of a quantified sentence is relative: '$(\exists x)Mx$' is true if and only if some entity in the domain is mortal. The domain's entities are the *values* of the *bound variables* of quantification, such as the variable 'x' following 'M' in '$(\exists x)Mx$', and these variables are said to *range over* their values. Thus for our sentence to be true some entity in our quantifier's domain must be mortal—this mortal entity must be a value of the variable of quantification—and this is what commits our sentence to some mortal entity. In Quine's words,

> we are convicted of a particular ontological presupposition if, and only if, the alleged presuppositum has to be reckoned among the entities over which our variables range in order to render one of our affirmations true (p. 83).

It follows that, for Quine, names and descriptions are not basic bearers of ontological commitment. For, by his extension of Russell's theory of descriptions, any name or description can be eliminated from a sentence by translating it into another one containing only general expressions: as in 'Something wrote *Waverley* and was a poet, and nothing else wrote *Waverley*', Russell's translation of 'The author of *Waverley* was a poet'.

What does all this tell us about properties? Because Quine's criterion of ontological commitment does not apply to predicates, such as 'is red' and 'is taller than', he denies that they harbour any such commitment even though, as we have seen, such predicates—if not 'is grue'—are often taken to correspond to properties. Is he right?

The relationship of properties to linguistic expressions can be put in various ways. Frege thought, as we have seen, that the linguistic distinction between singular terms (names and definite descriptions) and predicates corresponds to an ontological distinction between complete entities (his 'objects') and incomplete entities (his 'concepts', our properties). He claimed therefore that abstract singular terms corresponding to predicates, like 'red' in 'Red is a colour', could not refer to properties; whereas, for Russell, properties can be the referents both of abstract singular terms, like 'justice', and of their associated predicates, like 'is just'.

But Frege and Russell both agree that predicates refer, and so harbour ontological commitment: 'Socrates is mortal' is committed both to Socrates *and* to the property of being mortal which he is thereby said to have. And Frege and Russell can happily agree with Quine's McX when he says:

There are red houses, red roses, red sunsets; this much is prephilosophical common sense in which we must all agree. These houses, roses, and sunsets have something in common; and this which they have in common is all I mean by the attribute of redness (p. 81).

For Quine, however, it is only 'a popular and misleading manner of speaking' (p. 81) to say that red houses, roses, and sunsets have something in common. Quine thinks the predicate 'is red' is simply 'true of' the particulars to which it applies, and rejects the rhetorical question we asked in §3: what makes such predicates apply to some particulars and not others, if not that particulars have or lack corresponding properties? He thinks this property-explanation of the extensions of predicates is bogus: he thinks it suffices to say that some objects are red and some not, and the fact 'that the houses and roses and sunsets are all of them red may be taken as ultimate and irreducible' (p. 81).

Quine also dismisses two other arguments for properties. First, since his discussion of 'Pegasus' shows how sentences can be meaningful without their constituents naming anything, so in particular predicates need not name something for sentences featuring them to be meaningful. The second argument he rejects takes properties to be not referents but meanings of predicates—what Frege would have called their 'senses'. To this Quine objects that 'the explanatory value of special and irreducible intermediary entities called meanings is surely illusory' (p. 82). Our talk of 'having a meaning' (or 'significance'), 'having the same meaning' (or 'synonymy') and 'giving the meaning', can, if at all, be explained without supposing there to be meanings to be had, shared, or given.

Quine admits however that dismissing these arguments is not enough to rule out properties. For two types of linguistic expressions besides predicates may still harbour ontological commitment to properties. First, as we have seen, there are abstract singular terms, like 'humility' in 'Humility is a virtue'. Second, there are what we shall call *property quantifiers*, general expressions occurring in such sentences as 'There are undiscovered fundamental physical properties'. Now for Quine, since we can use Russell's theory of descriptions to turn the former into the latter, the latter are what matter. Hence his worry about the commitments of 'Some zoological species are cross-fertile', which contains a property quantifier that appears to range over a domain of species, to which it therefore seems to commit us unless and until, as he says,

we devise some way of so paraphrasing the statement as to show that the seeming reference to species on the part of our bound variable was an avoidable manner of speaking (p. [13]).

Quine thinks we can show a sentence's apparent ontological commitment to be unreal by producing a paraphrase that lacks it. Thus we can show that 'the average man has 2.4 children' is not really committed to that queer entity, the average man, by paraphrasing it as 'The number of men divided by the number of children is 2.4', which is not so committed. Similarly with properties: Quine's claim that nothing we truly say is committed to them will be warranted if—but only if—nominalist paraphrases are available in all cases.

In chapter VI, 'Statements about Universals', Jackson shows how difficult this paraphrasing project is. He concentrates on abstract singular terms, rather than property quantifiers—or predicates, which he accepts harbour no commitment to properties (which he calls 'universals'). He accepts, for example, that 'Wisdom was a characteristic of Plato' is only apparently committed to a property, wisdom, since it can be paraphrased as 'Plato was wise'. In short, Jackson challenges Quine on his own terms, agreeing that predicates do not harbour ontological commitment, but questioning Quine's ability to provide nominalist paraphrases of sentences featuring abstract singular terms.

6. TROUBLES WITH ONTOLOGICAL COMMITMENT

These arguments about the availability of paraphrases, and their relevance to ontological commitment, seem to us inconclusive. First, those who think relevant paraphrases always exist think it sufficient to produce one or two; those who think some sentences resist paraphrase think it sufficient to criticize a candidate paraphrase. That proves nothing either way.

Second, ontological commitment arguments for properties tell us very little about them. Compare the analogous arguments for particulars. Suppose we follow Quine in seeing commitment to particulars in the first-order quantifiers of our best theories. This does not tell us what such particulars are like. Do they, for example, persist through intervals of time by existing at each time within those intervals, or by having a different temporal part existing at each such time? That question will not be answered by scientific theories committed to particulars such as electrons, protons, and the like. Similarly for properties: the ontological commitments of our theories shed little metaphysical light on the nature of the properties to which they commit us.

A related objection to this approach is that it breaks the links we made at the start between sharing a property and being similar. For if only some shared predicates express genuine similarity, then many predicates, and their associated singular terms, will not pick out properties at all. Armstrong agrees:

I suggest that we reject the notion that just because the predicate 'red' applies to an open class of particulars, therefore there must be a property, redness (1978b, p. 8).

So to preserve the link with similarity, advocates of properties need paraphrases as much as the nominalist does. For if sentences containing the predicate 'is red' or the singular term 'red' are not to be committed to the property of being red, we need some paraphrase to show that this apparent commitment is illusory. This suggests that those who want to use properties to define similarity (or *vice versa*) had better not rest their case on the ontological commitments of sentences, and will have to accept a much looser relationship between properties, predicates, and abstract singular terms, as Mellor does in chapter XVI.

7. DO PREDICATES HARBOUR ONTOLOGICAL
COMMITMENT TO PROPERTIES?

But however tight or loose the link between individual properties and predicates, the question remains: do predicates harbour any ontological commitment to properties? In chapter VII, '"Ostrich Nominalism" or "Mirage Realism"?', Devitt argues that they do not, defending Quine against Armstrong's charge of being an ostrich nominalist, i.e. one who holds that

> there are no universals but the proposition that *a* is *F* is perfectly all right as it is. Quine's refusal to take predicates with any ontological seriousness seems to make him a Nominalist of this kind (Armstrong 1978a, p. 16).

Devitt begins with the following passage from Armstrong:

> The problem of universals is the problem of how numerically different particulars can nevertheless be identical in nature, all be of the same 'type' (1978a, p. 41).

This he takes to be asking for the ontological commitments of sentences expressing sameness of type; which is not of course the only interpretation of Armstrong's 'problems of universals'. (See chapter XIV, pp. 197–201 for Lewis's interpretation, and Oliver 1996, §§16–25, for a detailed discussion of the problem of universals.)

Devitt's schematic example is:

(i) *a* and *b* have the same property (are of the same type), *F*-ness.

Following Quine, Devitt argues that (i) is not committed to *F*-ness, its apparent commitment being revealed as merely apparent by paraphrasing it into

(ii) *a* and *b* are both *F*,

which is paraphrased in turn into the two sentences:

(iii) *a* is *F*;
(iv) *b* is *F*.

Then the ontological commitment of (iii)—and of (iv), with appropriate changes—is given by Quine's semantic theory as follows: (iii) is true if and only if there exists an *x* such that '*a*' designates *x* and '*F*' applies to *x*. In other words, '*a* is *F*' is only committed to *a*, not to *F*-ness. So Quine is not an ostrich nominalist: he does not ignore the problem of universals, as Devitt understands it, since the sentences he uses to express sameness of type are not committed to properties.

How convincing is Devitt's argument? Since he and Quine link ontological commitment to a semantic theory, we need some way of telling when such a theory is correct, and an argument for its supposed link with ontological commitment. To illustrate the problems here, suppose the following clause appears in the correct semantic theory:

'*a* is *F*' is true iff there is a φ such that 'is *F*' designates φ and '*a*' falls under φ.

This suggests that '*a* is *F*' is only committed to *F*-ness, not to an entity designated by '*a*'. And why not? If we can have a primitive semantic relation, *applies to*, relating predicates to entities designated by singular terms, why not another primitive relation, *falls under*, relating singular terms to entities designated by predicates? And parodying Quine, we might add that it is only 'a popular and misleading manner of speaking' to say that there is some one thing which *F*-ness, *G*-ness, and *H*-ness all have in common when *a* is *F* and *G* and *H*.

But do we not need a referent for '*a*' in '*a* is *F*' to infer 'There is some *x* such that *x* is *F*' from '*a* is *F*', since a satisfactory semantics for this requires '*x*' to range over some entities, one of them designated by '*a*'? Perhaps. But may we not equally infer 'There is some φ such that *a* is φ' from '*a* is *F*'? To resist this inference on the grounds that there are no entities for 'φ' to range over both begs the question and goes against natural language, which is replete with such inferences: e.g. from 'John is tall' to 'There is some property which John has', or from 'John is a man and Jane is not' to 'There is something John is and Jane isn't'. If Quine and Devitt are to convince, they need support for their semantic theory which explains away these inferences. Selective deprecation of 'popular ways of speaking' is not enough.

There is another objection to reducing ontological commitment by paraphrase, which threatens Quine's and Devitt's whole way of arguing. Suppose we have a sentence S, apparently committed to some entity *e*, and an equivalent sentence S' which is said to be uncommitted to *e*. This, it is said, shows that S is only apparently committed to *e*. But, as Alston (1958) says, why should we think it is S and not S' that deceives us? Why not say that S' is really committed to *e* because its equivalent S is? What we need here is what we do not have, namely a test for when a sentence is only apparently, and when really, committed or uncommitted to some entity.

Armstrong, however, does not pursue this line in his reply to Devitt in chapter VIII, 'Against "Ostrich Nominalism"'. He argues instead that Devitt and Quine have not shown that all sentences with abstract singular terms, like 'Humility is a virtue', have nominalist paraphrases. Like Jackson, he claims that such paraphrases are hard to come by; so that even by their own rules, which say that predicates do not harbour ontological commitment, Devitt and Quine fail to show that our best theories are uncommitted to properties. He also disputes the rules:

> Quine gives the predicate what has been said to be the privilege of the harlot: power without responsibility. The predicate is informative, it makes a vital contribution to telling us what is the case, the world is different if it is different, yet ontologically it is supposed not to commit us. Nice work: if you can get it (p. 105).

In §3 of chapter VIII, Armstrong defends his theory of properties against Devitt's claim that it 'clutters the landscape without adding to our understanding' (p. 98). For Devitt agrees with Quine that what underpins the linguistic fact that the predicate '*F*' applies to *a* is a 'basic and inexplicable fact about the universe' (p. 97), namely, that *a* is *F*. Devitt then imagines the advocate of properties asking for, and giving, an explanation of this fact. The first answer is: '*a* is *F* in virtue of having the property *F*-ness' (p. 97), where the new fact that *a* has *F*-ness is taken to report a relation between two entities, *a* and *F*-ness. But what, Devitt asks, explains this fact? If we must explain the fact that *a* is *F*, surely we must explain the fact that *a* has *F*-ness? But since we cannot do this without starting an infinite regress we should stop at the beginning with the fact that *a* is *F*.

However, as Devitt acknowledges, this answer is not Armstrong's. Armstrong distinguishes two theories of properties *in re* (which he also calls 'immanent realism', as opposed to the 'transcendent realism' of Frege and Russell, whose properties exist in a platonic heaven, detached from the particulars that have them). Both of these theories claim that 'particulars are a sort of layer-cake. The *one* particular somehow unites within itself *many* different properties' (pp. 108–9), and say that this particular (the thick particular) is composed of its properties together with a factor of particularity (the thin particular).

Then the first of Armstrong's two theories takes the thin particular to be *related* to each of these properties. This, the theory that Devitt criticizes, Armstrong also rejects because it generates an infinite regress. For it needs a relation, call it 'instantiation', linking the thin particular to its properties, which will itself need a further relation to link it to these properties and to the thin particular, and so on. The regress appears vicious, for it never seems to yield a real unity (see Bradley 1897, book 1, chapter 2). So Armstrong opts for a second theory, on which 'the two "factors" are too intimately together to speak of a *relation* between them' (p. 109)—while conceding some force to Devitt's complaint that he has no idea what Armstrong could mean by denying that '*a* has *F*-ness' reports a relation between *a* and *F*-ness.

8. TROPES

From this apparent stalemate between Armstrong and Devitt, we turn to a quite different account of properties. So far, we have contrasted with properties particulars of many kinds, including people, numbers, cities, and sense data. These particulars, diverse as they are, are alike in corresponding not to whole sentences but only to names or other singular terms, like 'Don', 'Bill', '2', 'the capital of Germany', or 'this patch'. Barring abbreviations (e.g. 'Don' said in reply to 'Who's that?') none of these terms is used as a sentence to say, on its own, something true or false. To make true or false sentences, we must combine these terms with others: as in 'Berlin is the capital of Germany', 'Don is taller than Bill', '2 is even', 'This patch is white', and so on.

In this respect, terms for particulars resemble predicates, like 'is taller than', 'is even', and 'is white', which also need combining with other terms to make true or false sentences, as in 'Don is taller than Bill', '2 is even', etc. We saw in §4 how this similarity led Ramsey to question the widely assumed difference of kind between particulars and universals, which also resemble each other in this respect. For neither particulars nor universals are *facts* (i.e. correspond to whole true sentences), merely constituents of facts, like the facts that Berlin is the capital of Germany, Don is taller than Bill, 2 is even, etc.

Not so the entities postulated by Williams in chapter IX, the first part of a two-part article 'On the Elements of Being', and Campbell in chapter X, 'The Metaphysic of Abstract Particulars'. Their views are at once more and less orthodox than Ramsey's. If their acceptance that particulars and universals differ in kind is more orthodox, their denial that the world is constituted by either is less so. For them the world's elements are neither particulars nor universals but *tropes*.

Tropes are instances of properties, like the whiteness of a certain white patch, or Don's humanity: an entity as distinct from Bill's humanity as it is from the particular Don and the universal humanity. And for trope theorists these tropes are not complexes, of a particular patch or person with a universal, whiteness or humanity. On the contrary: tropes are the simples, of which particulars and universals are complexes. Don is just a complex of what Williams calls 'concurrent' tropes (Don's humanity, his shape, his size, etc.), while humanity is just a complex of all tropes exactly similar to the trope that is Don's humanity.

What are these complexes? Williams says they may be *sets* or *sums*, where a set is a *class* of which the terms are members; a sum is a whole of which the terms are parts ... [the difference being that while] a sum is of the same type with its terms ... there is some excuse for considering [a class] of a different 'type' from its members (p. 117).

This for Williams makes particulars, such as people, sums of their tropes, and humanity

the class whose members are not Socrates, Napoleon, and so forth, but the human trope in Socrates, the one in Napoleon, and so forth (p. 118);

so that

'Socrates is wise', or generically '*a* is φ', means that the concurrence sum (Socrates) includes a trope which is a member of the similarity set (Wisdom) (p. 119).

Williams and Campbell follow Stout (1922–3, 1923) in calling tropes 'abstract particulars', as opposed to 'concrete' particulars like Socrates or 'abstract' universals like wisdom. And Socrates's wisdom certainly passes one common test for being a particular as well, if not better, than Socrates himself. Campbell puts it like this:

Particular being's distinguishing mark is that it is exhausted in the one embodiment, or occasion, or example. For the realm of space, this restricts particulars to a single location at any one time. Particulars thus seem to enjoy a relatively unproblematical mode of being (p. 125).

This, however, conflates two different things. Having a single 'embodiment' is one thing, having a single location is another. We must not mistake unrepeatability in space or time for the logical or metaphysical unrepeatability that Campbell, like most philosophers, takes to mark off particulars. But then it is not clear that the latter *does* mark off particulars like Socrates from universals like wisdom. For in whatever sense wisdom occurs repeatedly in the atomic facts that Socrates is wise, Plato is wise, etc., Socrates also occurs repeatedly in the atomic facts that Socrates is wise, Socrates is human, etc.

The trope that is Socrates's wisdom, by contrast, really is unrepeatable in the relevant sense—which is why we, unlike Armstrong (in §2 of chapter XII), decline to call it a 'particularized property': properties for us are essentially repeatable. For this trope is not just a constituent, of the fact that Socrates is wise, that may also occur in other atomic facts. Arguably it *is* an atomic fact, since Socrates's wisdom corresponds neither to 'Socrates' nor to 'is wise' but to the whole atomic sentence 'Socrates is wise'. Moreover, given enough other concurrent tropes to constitute Socrates, what this trope does is make that proposition true. In short, tropes are facts not only in the weak sense of corresponding to (or being) true propositions but in the strong sense of *making* propositions true. For this reason, and to avoid confusion, we shall not, despite their unrepeatability, call tropes 'particulars', but reserve that term for entities traditionally so-called, such as Socrates, which do not correspond to whole truths.

In these terms the question about trope theory is this: are atomic truths made true by simples (tropes) or by complexes (of particulars and universals)? Williams and Campbell advance various arguments for tropes. First, tropes are what we mainly perceive and evaluate:

What we primarily *see* of the moon, for example, is its shape and colour . . . What most men value the moon for is its brightness; what a child wants of a lollipop is a certain flavour and endurance (Williams p. 125).

Mental entities too, mysterious to Williams as particulars, seem to him unproblematic as tropes:

A pain is a trope *par excellence* . . . the ideas and impressions of Hume, the sense data of recent epistemology . . . understood as tropes, and as neither things nor essences, a hundred riddles about them dissolve (pp. 123–4).

To these considerations Campbell adds the claim that many causes must be tropes, as in 'The weakness of the cable caused the collapse of the bridge' (p. 129), where the cable *'qua* weak' cannot cause the collapse without the cable *'qua* steel' doing so unless these entities differ. What then, he asks, can they be, if not the tropes that are the weakness and the steeliness of the cable? And if, as he says, 'the philosophy of cause calls for tropes, that on its own is virtually sufficient recommendation for a place in the ontological sun' (p. 130).

Campbell argues moreover that trope theory offers the best account of both particulars and universals. He thinks it explains particulars better than theories that must, besides universals, either postulate

some additional, particularizing reality . . . which, because it lies beyond qualities, lies by its very nature beyond our explorations, describings and imaginings, all of which are of necessity restricted to the qualities things have (p. 131)

or, by taking particulars to be bundles of universals, make the Identity of Indiscernibles a necessary truth: a thesis he thinks refuted by the possibility of, for example, a world with two uniform spheres in a non-absolute space (p. 132).

Campbell also thinks his theory explains universals better than a resemblance nominalism that must postulate either *kinds* of resemblance—as in colour or shape—or a primitive concept of overall resemblance. For as we noted in §3, the former are no better than the universals of colour and shape they replace; while the latter, like Frege's functions, will identify coextensive properties, like being cordate (having a heart) and being renate (having a kidney). Trope theory faces no such objections: for even if the class of cordate and renate *particulars* is the same, the class of cordate and renate *tropes* is not. Trope theorists, unlike nominalists, can easily distinguish coextensive properties without invoking different kinds of resemblance.

So far so good; but not far enough. Let us grant that, as Williams says, what we see and value are not just particulars but facts, like the fact that the moon is bright; and that when we are in pain, or in other mental states, these are not particulars we are somehow related to but monadic facts about us. Let us grant too that, as Campbell says, causation also relates facts, like the facts that a cable is weak and that a bridge collapses. Even then, as Daly argues in chapter XI, 'Tropes', it does not follow that these perceived, evaluated, mental, and causally related facts are *tropes*, the simple entities of trope theory, as opposed to complexes of particulars and universals.

Daly also argues that what we may call the 'P+U'—particular(s) plus universal—theory of (atomic) facts can easily explain the features of properties that Campbell thinks favour tropes. It can say for example that a's redness (the fact that a is red) is an abstract particular because it contains the particular a and the abstract *redness*, and that redness recurs in the atomic facts that a is red, b is red, etc. Daly adds moreover that if trope theory is not to start a vicious regress of resemblance tropes—resemblance between red tropes, which must resemble each other, and so on—it must take resemblance to be a universal. And even if, with just one resemblance relation, trope theory needs fewer universals than P+U theory, it needs just as many corresponding kinds of tropes; so it does not in fact economize in kinds of entities.

Similarly for particulars. We saw in §7 how hard it is for P+U theorists to explain their '+', the instantiation relation that red particulars seem to have to the universal redness, without starting a vicious regress. Trope theory seems to dodge this problem by making particulars bundles of concurrent tropes. But then, Daly argues, concurrence itself must also be a universal, instantiated by the tropes it relates, thereby setting up a similar regress. In short, whatever instantiation problem P+U theory has, trope theory has it too.

9. ARMSTRONG ON UNIVERSALS VERSUS TROPES

In chapter XII, 'Properties', Armstrong sketches his reasons for believing in properties and compares and contrasts two theories of properties: his own, of properties as universals, and the trope theory of Williams and Campbell. But first he attacks those who dispense with properties in favour of predicates by asking what account they can give of change:

A cold thing becomes hot. For one who puts his or her faith in predicates this is a matter first of the predicate 'cold', or its semantic equivalent, *applying to* or *being true of* the object, and, second, the predicate 'hot' becoming applicable after 'cold' loses applicability (p. 161).

To this Armstrong objects that a particular could change even when there are no predicates and, moreover, that 'the change is something intrinsic to the object' (p. 161) and nothing to do with its relationship to linguistic expressions. All this must be granted. But no one will deny it. Certainly Quine can explain the application of a predicate to a particular, as follows: 'is F' applies to a because a is F. It is the fact that a is F (in the weakest sense of 'fact') which he takes to be 'ultimate and irreducible', not the fact that 'is F' applies to a.

Armstrong places a good deal of weight on this demand for an explanation of the application of predicates to particulars:

But when we have said that these predicates apply, we have surely not said enough. The situation cries out for explanation. ... Must there not be something quite specific about the things which allows, indeed ensures, that these predicates apply? The predicates require *ontological correlates*. The predicate theory does have correlates indeed, but they are no more than the objects themselves, and so are far too coarse (p. 164).

But Quine has not only the objects but also facts about them: he need not accept Armstrong's reading of 'something quite specific about the things which . . . ensures that these predicates apply' as something *in* those things. We may of course take Quine's facts to need explaining in terms of particulars having properties. But that is another issue, returning us to the debate between Devitt and Armstrong discussed in §7.

Armstrong's invoking properties to explain the application of predicates may motivate his claim that properties must have instances. But it does not make him admit as many properties as there are applicable predicates. Instead he invokes Plato's metaphor of 'carving the beast (the great beast of reality) at the joints' (p. 166) to argue for grounding genuine similarities in shared properties. What these properties are he thinks it is the job of science, indeed of physics, to tell us. So since his is 'an *a posteriori*, a scientific, realism' (p. 167) about properties, he cannot and does not assume that to any old predicate there corresponds a property. For, as we have already noted, many predicates besides 'grue' may fail to entail a genuine similarity between the particulars they apply to (as in Wittgenstein's example of 'is a game').

Armstrong's *a posteriori* realism about properties seems ontologically economical, as it reduces the number of properties to those that figure in the laws of physics. But, as he notes, Campbell has argued that it is not really so, since physics deals in quantities like lengths and masses. If these are continuous, there will be continuum many properties corresponding, for example, to all the different lengths particulars have. To this Armstrong replies by distinguishing, as Bacon (1995, p. 87), Lewis (1973, p. 87) and others do, between *quantitative* and *qualitative economy*, and arguing that what matters is not how few *entities* we postulate (quantitative economy) but how few *kinds* of entity (qualitative economy).

This distinction seems to us misconceived, since our concept of a kind seems flexible enough for us to reduce the number of kinds by subsuming all entities under fewer kinds. Why, for example, can Armstrong not say that our myriad lengths, masses, etc., are all instances of a single kind, namely *property*? Nor does the distinction satisfy Ockham's razor, the principle that we need reasons to believe in entities. So if there can be just one entity of a given kind, the ontological economy of a theory may well depend on how many entities of a kind it postulates. Yet it is hard to count more than a finite number of entities, since adding one to a denumerable infinity of them does not increase their number. In short, we think the whole idea of ontological economy needs urgent attention.

In §2 of 'Properties', Armstrong admits that trope theory can do better than he once allowed. In particular, he admits that it can mirror his own theory of properties as universals, with two exceptions. One is that while he can explain features of the resemblances of F particulars (e.g. its transitivity) as a consequence of the identity of the universal they share, for trope theory this and other features of the resemblance of F-tropes remain unexplained.

The other exception concerns Armstrong's (1983) account of laws, on which the law that all Fs are G is a 'nomic necessitation' relation N holding between the universals F and G: $N(F,G)$. Armstrong claims that trope theory cannot mirror this account, but does not say why. We think the reason may be this. A trope theorist can only mimic Armstrong's $N(F,G)$ by having lots of F-tropes related by lots of N-tropes to lots of G-tropes. But for it to be a law that all Fs are G no F-trope can fail to be related by an N-trope to a G-trope. But why not? Why must all F-tropes be related by N-tropes to G-tropes just because some are?

10. PROPERTIES AS SETS OF POSSIBLE PARTICULARS

Chapter XIII, 'Modal Realism at Work: Properties', returns us to the idea of properties as sets, not of similar tropes but of particulars. Lewis here uses properties to illustrate the advantages of his ontology of possible worlds. In §5 we remarked that properties cannot be the sets of their actual instances, and Lewis agrees. But he argues that they can be the sets of their *possible* instances (which of course include their actual instances). This allows properties, like being a unicorn, to exist without being instantiated, since the set of possible unicorns can exist even if none of them is actual. It can also distinguish coextensive properties like having a heart and having kidneys, since even if all actual animals have both, not all possible ones do: the sets of all possible cordate and renate animals are not identical.

On this theory of properties, different particulars can have the very same property, by belonging to the same set; and one particular can have different properties by belonging to different sets. As in our §1, relations are taken to be properties of n-tuples of particulars, and then identified with sets of n-tuples of possible particulars. Thus a is related to R to b iff the ordered pair $\langle a,b \rangle$ is a member of the set of such pairs identified with R.

The nature of properties is determined on this account by that of sets. Sets are usually taken to be abstract entities; by which, as we noted in §5, is usually meant that they lack causes, effects and spatio-temporal location. Those sceptical of such entities will naturally worry about properties so construed. But even those who accept abstract entities may still worry about the sets which Lewis identifies with properties. For anyone who denies the existence of non-actual particulars must either reject Lewis's identification of properties with sets containing them or find an adequate substitute for those sets. We cannot discuss these options here, except to note that no one who constructs possible worlds and their particulars from properties can then identify properties with sets of possible particulars; just as no one who constructs possible worlds from propositions can then identify propositions with sets of possible worlds. (See the items listed under 'Properties and the Metaphysics of Modality' in our Select Bibliography.)

But even granting Lewis his non-actual particulars, one may still object that his theory, like that of Frege discussed in §2, yields both too few properties and too many. Too few, since while it can distinguish *contingently* coextensive properties like having a heart and having kidneys, it cannot distinguish *necessarily* coextensive ones, like having three sides and having three angles, the sets of whose possible instances are identical. Yet if properties differ when the meanings of their names or the corresponding predicates differ, triangularity and trilaterality are different properties.

But are they? Well, yes and no. Lewis thinks we have different ideas of properties, with different identity conditions, any of which he can identify with some suitable system of set-theoretical entities, in this case perhaps with structured sets. It is however less easy to meet in this way the objection that Lewis gives us too many properties. It does this because, if properties are just sets of possible particulars, then there are as many properties as there are such sets. And although set theory will rule out some (e.g. the set of all sets) to cope with Russell's paradox, it will still, on any plausible assumptions about how many possible particulars there are, leave far more sets, and hence properties, than we could name in any language fit for communication. Is that really a useful conception of properties? Before seeing in §13 why Lewis thinks it is, we must consider a useful distinction he uses to support his tolerance of different ideas of properties: that between roles and their occupants.

11. ONTOLOGICAL CATEGORIES: ROLES AND OCCUPANTS

We may associate names for kinds of entity with roles we want entities of those kinds—the occupants of the roles—to fill. We, for example, have associated with 'property' the role of accounting for similarity, difference, and genuine change; while others, as we have seen, associate 'property' with other roles. This has led to much debate about properties being conducted at cross-purposes. It has also led to much terminological confusion, with some theorists calling 'property' whatever fills certain roles, while others reserve the term for specific occupants of them; and similarly, as Lewis notes (pp. 185–6), for 'universal'.

We should therefore distinguish two questions: what roles do we want properties to fill, and what occupants (if any) can we find for these roles, perhaps finding different occupants for different roles. When this distinction is drawn, some of our seemingly rival candidates for being properties—sets of possible particulars (Lewis), transcendent universals (Russell) or immanent universals (Armstrong), or classes of exactly similar tropes (Williams and Campbell)—look more like candidates for different roles than competitors for the same one.

This is how Lewis can accommodate those who, associating 'property' with the meanings of predicates or abstract singular terms, complain that his sets fail to distinguish triangularity from trilaterality, by offering them structured sets to fill that role. Similarly, to those of us who associate 'property' with similarity, and complain that his sets give us too many properties to fill that role, he offers a choice between *abundant* properties and *sparse* ones:

The abundant properties may be as extrinsic, as gruesomely gerrymandered, as miscellaneously disjunctive, as you please. They pay no heed to the qualitative joints, but carve things up every which way. Sharing of them has nothing to do with similarity. ... The sparse properties are another story. Sharing of them makes for similarity, they carve at the joints, they are intrinsic, they are highly specific, the sets of their instances are *ipso facto* not entirely miscellaneous, there are only just enough of them to characterise things completely and without redundancy (p. 178).

But if these are the roles of sparse properties, what occupants can Lewis offer for them? In the second half of chapter XIII, and in chapter XIV, 'New Work for a Theory of Universals', he gives complementary answers to that question (together, in the former, with an important supplement on tropes).

12. NATURAL PROPERTIES

Lewis calls his sparse properties 'natural' and considers two ways of saying what they are. One is to identify them with an elite minority of his abundant properties, his sets of possible particulars. The other is to identify them with a different kind of entity, such as Armstrong's universals or equivalence classes of similar tropes.

But one way or the other, Lewis argues, we must admit natural properties, since they are invoked in so many conceptual analyses—of duplication, determinism, materialism, laws of nature, causation, events, and the contents of thought and language. And one need not accept all these analyses to be impressed with the ideological economy—the reduction in the number of primitive predicates—that invoking natural properties brings.

What must occupants of these natural property roles be like? First, natural properties must be so linked to similarity that we can define 'x is a duplicate of y' as 'x and y have the same perfectly natural properties', where 'is a duplicate of' expresses resemblance in every intrinsic, qualitative respect. Then there is the idea of naturalness as a matter of degree, with perfectly natural properties as a limiting case. Thus Lewis suggests that the charge and mass of subatomic particles are perfectly natural, with colours less natural than that, and grue and bleen less natural still.

Next, since there are objective similarities in nature, the natural properties which make for them must be objective. Properties are not made natural by us, either by our innate quality spacing (*contra* Quine 1969) or by our agreement and unhesitating classification of new instances given old ones (*contra* Quinton 1973, pp. 263–5). Finally, naturalness for Lewis is absolute: a given property is equally natural in all possible worlds. Lewis's natural properties, unlike those of Fodor (1976, p. 14), Armstrong (chapter XII), Shoemaker (chapter XV), and Mellor (chapter XVI), cannot therefore be defined as those that figure in causation or laws of nature, which if contingent will make the naturalness of properties vary from world to world.

Lewis makes a property's naturalness depend on how simply it can be defined in terms of perfectly natural ones: 'is a somewhat natural property' is one that 'can be reached by not-too-complicated chains of definability from the perfectly natural properties' (p. 179). There is however a serious objection to this, pointed out by Hirsch (1993, p. 75). Sharing of natural properties is meant to entail qualitative, intrinsic similarity; and the more natural the properties shared, the greater the similarity. But now consider two particulars, a with one perfectly natural property F, b with a quite different one G. Does the mere fact that a and b share the very simply definable disjunctive property F-or-G really make them similar? Armstrong (1978b, p. 20) thinks the idea 'laughable'; yet Lewis's definition entails it.

We doubt that similarity can be measured in this or any other way (e.g. by the proportion of their perfectly natural properties that two particulars share). But whether it can or not, we still need to say what the perfectly natural properties are. Lewis's own penchant for ontological economy makes him identify them with some of his abundant properties, his sets of possible particulars, picking them out with a predicate 'is perfectly natural', which must be either primitive or defined.

Lewis then canvases three possible definitions of 'is a perfectly natural property', the first in terms of a complex resemblance predicate which is multigrade and contrastive and applies to the relevant particulars: 'Something like: $x_1, x_2 \ldots$ resemble one another and do not likewise resemble any of $y_1, y_2 \ldots$'. Although Lewis questions whether so complex a primitive predicate is better than a primitive 'is perfectly natural', he says he cannot decide the question. But as this predicate may contain a—perhaps nondenumerable—infinity of variables, we would rule it out as incapable of occurring in any language we could understand.

Lewis's other definitions invoke entities corresponding to his perfectly natural properties, thus giving an ontological basis to his distinction between these and other properties. The first invokes something like Armstrong's universals, defining 'is a perfectly natural property' as 'is such that all and only its members instantiate some one universal'. The second invokes a one–one correspondence between perfectly natural properties and maximal sets of duplicate tropes, like the mass tropes of all actual and possible particulars of mass m. As all these tropes are perfect duplicates, we can form a maximal set of them under the equivalence relation of duplication, and define 'is a perfectly natural property' as 'is such that all and only its members instantiate one or other of the tropes in some maximal set of duplicate tropes'.

Both these definitions invoke new kinds of entities, universals, or tropes. And if the utility of invoking natural properties in other analyses gives us some reason to believe in them, presumably that of invoking universals or tropes in analysing 'is a perfectly natural property' gives some reason to believe in them too—at least to those who can accept the existence of non-actual particulars that both these definitions presuppose.

But what of those who reject non-actual entities? Can they not identify (perfectly) natural properties directly with actual universals or sets of actual tropes? Hardly the latter, since a given property could not then have more or fewer instances than it actually has. Nor is the former entirely uncontentious, since some conceptual analyses that invoke natural properties may require some of them to be uninstantiated. That would mean letting some actual universals lack actual instances, and whether that is possible may depend on what determines what actual universals there are, the question tackled by Shoemaker and Mellor in chapters XV and XVI.

13. A ROLE FOR ABUNDANT PROPERTIES: SEMANTIC VALUES

So much for Lewis's natural properties. We return now to his abundant properties, and make some more points about ontological commitment, a notion we have seen to involve two other ideas. First, a sentence's commitment can be revealed by a paraphrase of it: hence the distinction between apparent and real commitment. Second, a sentence's real commitment is given by the correct semantic theory for it and the language that contains it.

Lewis however thinks the existence of paraphrases is irrelevant:

> Perhaps sometimes we might find paraphrases that will absolve us from the need to subject the original sentence to semantic analysis. ... But even if such paraphrases sometimes exist—even if they always exist, which seems unlikely—they work piecemeal and frustrate any systematic approach to semantics (pp. 194–5).

Hence, in applying compositional semantics to sentences like 'Humility is a virtue' and 'He has the same virtues as his father', we should assign semantic values to abstract singular terms and let such entities be the values of the variables of the property-quantifiers. And these entities will have to be his abundant properties. Armstrong's universals will not do because there are too few of them: there is, for example, no universal of humility.

But this is too quick. Take the model-theoretic semantics of Lewis's 'General Semantics' (1983, §VII), which makes the extensions of proper names and quantified noun phrases sets of properties ('characters'). Does this imply—assuming David Lewis is not a set—that 'David Lewis is mortal' is committed not to David Lewis but to the set of his properties?

Here is how Lewis conceives of a systematic semantics:

> First list a finite vocabulary of basic expressions—words, near enough—and assign each of them some sort of syntactic category and semantic value. Then list rules for building expressions from other expressions; and within each rule, specify the syntactic category and the semantic values of the new expressions as a function of the categories and values of the old expressions whence it was built. One syntactic category will be the sentences. Then specify truth conditions for sentences in terms of their semantic values. ... The semantic values have two jobs. They are there to generate other semantic values; and they are there to generate truth conditions of sentences (1986, p. 14).

On this kind of theory, while semantic values are meant to generate truth-conditions, that fact does not determine what semantic values are: anything that does the job will do. Such a theory is unconcerned with the ontological commitments of sentences, which is presumably why Lewis does not talk in such terms. For him, semantic values simply fill a theoretical role that requires abstract singular terms to have such values. But then such terms can hardly harbour ontological commitment to those values. For if we can assign to 'David Lewis' either the man himself or the set of his properties (with compensating changes in the values of other types of expression), we can play the same trick with 'humility', and assign to it either Lewis's abundant property (the set of possible humble particulars) or the set of this property's properties. With no way of deciding which assignment reveals the ontological commitments of sentences containing 'humility', we should surely admit that this sort of semantic theory tells us little about ontological commitment.

Yet semantic theory may still give us some reason to believe in properties. For one good role for properties is indeed to be the semantic values of abstract singular terms. So any reason to think that such terms should be assigned semantic values is a reason to think that there are properties. But that will not tell us what they are, nor how to determine the ontological commitments of sentences.

14. PROPERTIES: CAUSATION AND LAWS

In chapter XV, 'Causality and Properties', Shoemaker presents a causal theory of what properties are. By 'properties' he means what we mean, and what Lewis means by 'natural properties'. His motivation is largely epistemological: he wants to show how we can know what properties particulars have. (This is why he does not mind his theory not applying to properties that particulars like numbers can be known *a priori* to have, like being even or prime.)

Shoemaker's theory invokes the concept of a *causal power*, which he says to start with is a 'function from circumstances to effects' (p. 233). That is, particulars share a power if and only if they have the same (kind of) effects in the same (kind of) circumstances. Later he lets powers be 'statistical tendencies or propensities' (p. 253), which would make them functions from circumstances to *chances* of effects; but here we may stick to the simpler deterministic cases. He then takes a particular's powers to be fixed by its properties, so that

the properties on which powers depend can be thought of as functions from [sets of] properties to [sets of] powers (pp. 233–4).

Finally, defining a *conditional power* as one which a particular will have *if* it has certain properties, as when a

knife-shaped object has the conditional power of being able to cut wood if knife-sized and made of steel (p. 235),

he identifies properties with clusters of conditional powers.

Shoemaker bases his theory on the fact that to observe anything is to be affected by it. So if properties were independent of causal powers, no observation could tell us what properties particulars have nor, therefore, when or in what ways they resemble each other, stay the same, or change. But as observation can and does give us such knowledge, he concludes that some causal theory of properties must be true. Sceptics may of course object that assuming we *do* know whether and how particulars resemble one another begs the question. But we think not: an inference to the only available explanation of knowledge that we all think we have may not be conclusive, but it is not unreasonable.

Another argument for Shoemaker's theory is that we need properties to explain causation. For even those who say that causation only relates particulars still need the particulars it relates to have properties, say F and G, to make them instantiate laws of nature, say that all F-particulars are followed by G-particulars. But then is it not circular to use causation to explain properties and properties to explain causation? Indeed it is, as Shoemaker admits. For his theory

says, in brief, that properties are identical . . . just in case their coinstantiation with the same properties gives rise to the same powers . . . and [sameness of powers] will have to be explained in terms of sameness of circumstances and sameness of effects, the notions of which both involve the notion of sameness of property (pp. 242–3).

But we agree with Shoemaker that this circularity is neither avoidable nor vicious, showing merely that

the notion of a property and the notion of a causal power belong to a system of internally related concepts, no one of which can be explicated without the use of the others (p. 243).

Where we do disagree is with Shoemaker's claim that no property could lack any of its conditional powers, and hence that all the laws they depend on must hold in all possible worlds. His argument for this starts from the fact that, as a property's powers are independent of what particulars have the property and when, they cannot change over time. Even though he grants that this does not obviously make all a property's powers essential to it, he maintains that his theory does entail this. For the identity of any property, like being knife-shaped, depends for him on that of other properties, such as being steel, which are linked to it by the causal laws on which its conditional powers depend. And from this he thinks it follows that 'if the laws are different then the properties will have to be different as well' (p. 248).

But this does not follow. A property like mass may well be identified, i.e. distinguished from all others, by the laws (of motion, gravity, etc.) that link it to other properties and thereby fix its powers. Similarly, a particular like Socrates can be distinguished from all others by facts about when, where, and how he lived and died. But just as Socrates could still have lived and died in slightly, if not entirely, different ways, so mass could still figure in slightly, if not entirely, different laws: e.g. in a Newtonian world where accelerating things does not automatically increase their mass, as

Einstein's special theory of relativity says it does in our world. So we think, *pace* Shoemaker, that a causal theory of properties need not deny the apparent contingency of laws of nature and of the causation they entail.

15. NATURAL PROPERTIES IN SEMANTICS

With this amendment Shoemaker's theory of property comes close to Mellor's in chapter XVI, 'Properties and Predicates'. The main difference is that Mellor invokes laws rather than causation, claiming that all empirical properties are

identified *a posteriori* by scientific theories, construed as Ramsey sentences: i.e., as saying for example that *there are* properties C, F and G such that in C-circumstances all F-events have such-and-such a chance of being followed by G-events. . . . [So] if we stated all the laws there are in a single Ramsey sentence Σ, the properties Σ would quantify over are all the properties there are (p. 260).

Mellor then asks, using the singular term 'Red' and the predicate 'is red' as his exemplars, how properties so identified relate to the meanings of our predicates. First he says that for the property of being red to exist, there must be a property P such that

anything which anyone sees to be rightly called red always has . . . P and its being P is what causes them to see that (p. 261).

If there is such a property, what and how does it contribute to the meaning of the singular term 'Red'? Suppose 'Red' *refers* to P. What gives it this reference: what, in other words, is its *sense*? Obviously the fact that we have learned to let P-particulars cause us to call them red. But this makes P the reference of 'Red' by making it the sense of 'is red', i.e. that which makes P-particulars the extension of that predicate.

But even if P is the sense of 'is red', in this minimal reference-fixing sense of 'sense', that fact does not make P what 'is red' means in any stronger sense: it does not tell us what to infer from a particular's being red. For even if the laws P occurs in discourage some inferences and encourage others—for example that red fires are hot—they do not force us to draw these, or indeed any, inferences.

That P is not what 'is red' means is also shown by the fact that our use of 'is red' does not even entail that P exists, i.e. that all red particulars do share a single property. Nor do they, in Mellor's view: very different properties of red light, and of the things that reflect, transmit, and emit it, cause us to call them red. The most that all these very diverse red particulars—ranging from photons through tomatoes and stained glass to fires—share is a disjunction of the diverse properties that make us call them red. But if, as Mellor follows Ramsey in holding, there are no complex properties, then since this disjunction is not itself a property, there is *no* property they all share, i.e. there is no such property as being red.

And even if there is such a property, we have seen that it can neither be nor tell us what the predicate 'is red' means. The most it can do, *via* the laws that contain it, is constrain this predicate's meaning by limiting inferences we could safely use it to draw. This is why properties of this kind seem to be, as we have noted, so useless in semantics—a fact that may well explain their widespread neglect or rejection by philosophers for whom the philosophy of language has become the be-all and end-all of metaphysics.

Properties defined by the laws or causation they figure in may however contribute more to semantics than at first appears. In particular, they may answer some of the questions raised by Wittgenstein (1956, §§ 138–242), Kripke (1982) and others about how we follow linguistic rules, like those governing our use of predicates like 'is red' or 'is green'. Take our variant of Goodman's 'grue' ('green and $t < t_1$ or blue and $t \geq t_1$') and imagine a body of 'grue-speakers' who spell 'grue' 'green'. How do our present pre-t_1 rules for using 'green' stop us being such a body, i.e. stop our predicate 'is green' applying after t_1 to blue and not to green particulars?

Well, suppose we apply 'is green' as Mellor says we apply 'is red', by letting a particular's having one or more properties G cause us to call it 'green'. Suppose also that, as Mellor follows Churchland (1988, chapter 7.5) in urging, we can learn to do this by example, being corrected by existing users of 'green', without having any prior concepts of green or of G. Then as the laws that make G-particulars have this effect on us hold, like all laws, at all times, they will hold both before and after t_1. This means that, then as now, anything we call 'green' will be G, and hence green and not blue, thus distinguishing the rule that governs our use of 'is green' from that of grue-speakers who spell 'grue' 'green'.

There is of course much more to be said, both about rule-following and about the role, large or small, of properties in semantics, where the chief question is whether it needs more than the natural properties with which we began. We cannot say, since we confess we do not know what semantics is, or should be. So we do not know what it demands. But whatever it demands, we think there will still be a strong non-semantic case for natural properties.

REFERENCES

Alston, W. (1958), 'Ontological Commitments', *Philosophical Studies*, 9, 8–17.

Armstrong, D. M. (1978a), *Nominalism and Realism: Universals and Scientific Realism Volume I* (Cambridge: Cambridge University Press).

—— (1978b) *A Theory of Universals: Universals and Scientific Realism Volume II* (Cambridge: Cambridge University Press).

—— (1983), *What is a Law of Nature?* (Cambridge: Cambridge University Press).

Bacon, J. (1995), *Universals and Property-Instances: The Alphabet of Being* (Oxford: Basil Blackwell).

Bradley, F. H. (1897), *Appearance and Reality*, 2nd edition (Oxford: Clarendon Press).

Churchland, P. M. (1988), *Matter and Consciousness*, revised edition (Cambridge, Mass.: MIT Press).

Fodor, J. A. (1976), *The Language of Thought* (Hassocks: Harvester Press).

Frege, G. (1892–5), '[Comments on Sense and Meaning]' in his *Posthumous Writings*, edited by H. Hermes, F. Kambartel and F. Kaulbach (Oxford: Basil Blackwell, 1979), 118–25.

Geach, P. T. (1969), *God and the Soul* (London: Routledge & Kegan Paul).

Goodman, N. (1965), *Fact, Fiction, and Forecast*, 2nd edition (New York: Bobbs-Merrill).

Hirsch, E. (1993), *Dividing Reality* (New York: Oxford University Press).

Kripke, S. A. (1982), *Wittgenstein on Rules and Private Language* (Cambridge, Mass.: Harvard University Press).

Lewis, D. K. (1973), *Counterfactuals* (Cambridge, Mass.: Harvard University Press).

—— (1983), 'General Semantics' in his *Philosophical Papers* Volume 1 (Oxford: Oxford University Press), 189–232.

—— (1986), *On the Plurality of Worlds* (Oxford: Basil Blackwell).

Loux, M. J., editor (1970), *Universals and Particulars: Readings in Ontology* (Garden City, New York: Doubleday).

Mellor, D. H. (1992), 'There are no Conjunctive Universals', *Analysis*, 52, 97–103.

Oliver, A. (1992), 'Could There be Conjunctive Universals?' *Analysis*, 52, 88–97.

—— (1996), 'The Metaphysics of Properties', *Mind*, 105, 1–80.

Quine, W. V. O. (1960), *Word and Object* (Cambridge, Mass.: MIT Press).

—— (1969), 'Natural Kinds', in his *Ontological Relativity and Other Essays* (New York: Columbia University Press), 114–38.

Quinton, A. (1973), *The Nature of Things* (London: Routledge & Kegan Paul).

Russell, B. (1919), *Introduction to Mathematical Philosophy* (London: Allen & Unwin).

Schoedinger, A. B., editor (1992), *The Problem of Universals* (Atlantic Highlands, New Jersey: Humanities Press).

Stout, G. F. (1922–3), 'The Nature of Universals and Propositions', *Proceedings of the British Academy*, 10, 157–72.

—— (1923), 'Are the Characteristics of Particular Things Universal or Particular? II', *Aristotelian Society Supplementary Volume*, 3, 114–27.

Wittgenstein, L. (1956), *Philosophical Investigations*, edited by G. E. M. Anscombe (Oxford: Blackwell).

I

FUNCTION AND CONCEPT

GOTTLOB FREGE

My starting-point is what is called a function in mathematics. The original meaning of this word was not so wide as that which it has since obtained; it will be well to begin by dealing with this first usage, and only then consider the later extensions. I shall for the moment be speaking only of functions of a single argument. The first place where a scientific expression appears with a clear-cut meaning is where it is required for the statement of a law. This case arose as regards functions upon the discovery of higher Analysis. Here for the first time it was a matter of setting forth laws holding for functions in general. So we must go back to the time when higher Analysis was discovered, if we want to know what the word 'function' was originally taken to mean. The answer that we are likely to get to this question is: 'A function of x was taken to be a mathematical expression containing x, a formula containing the letter x.'

Thus, e.g., the expression

$$2x^3+x$$

would be a function of x, and

$$2.2^3+2$$

would be a function of 2. This answer cannot satisfy us, for here no distinction is made between form and content, sign and thing signified; a mistake, admittedly, that is very often met with in mathematical works, even those of celebrated authors. I have already pointed out on a previous occasion the defects of the current formal theories in arithmetic. We there have talk about signs that neither have nor are meant to have any content, but nevertheless properties are ascribed to them which are unintelligible except as belonging to the content of a sign. So also here; a mere expression, the form for a content, cannot be the heart of the matter; only the content itself can be that. Now what is the content of '2.2^3+2'? What does it mean? The same thing as '18' or '3.6'. What is expressed in the equation '$2.2^3+2=18$' is that the right-hand complex of signs has the same

This is an edited version of pp. 21–41 of *Translations from the Philosophical Writings of Gottlob Frege*, 3rd edition, edited by P. Geach and M. Black (Oxford: Basil Blackwell, 1980). Reprinted by permission of Blackwell Publishers.

meaning as the left-hand one. I must here combat the view that, e.g., $2+5$ and $3+4$ are equal but not the same. This view is grounded in the same confusion of form and content, sign and thing signified. It is as though one wanted to regard the sweet-smelling violet as differing from *Viola odorata* because the names sound different. Difference of sign cannot by itself be a sufficient ground for difference of the thing signified. The only reason why in our case the matter is less obvious is that what the numeral 7 means is not anything perceptible to the senses. There is at present a very wide-spread tendency not to recognize as an object anything that cannot be perceived by means of the senses; this leads here to numerals' being taken to be numbers, the proper objects of our discussion; and then, I admit, 7 and $2+5$ would indeed be different. But such a conception is untenable, for we cannot speak of any arithmetical properties of numbers whatsoever without going back to what the signs mean. For example, the property belonging to 1, of being the result of multiplying itself by itself, would be a mere myth; for no microscopical or chemical investigation, however far it was carried, could ever detect this property in the possession of the innocent character that we call a figure one. Perhaps there is talk of a definition; but no definition is creative in the sense of being able to endow a thing with properties that it has not already got—apart from the one property of expressing and signifying something in virtue of the definition.[1] The characters we call numerals have, on the other hand, physical and chemical properties depending on the writing material. One could imagine the introduction some day of quite new numerals, just as, e.g., the Arabic numerals superseded the Roman. Nobody is seriously going to suppose that in this way we should get quite new numbers, quite new arithmetical objects, with properties still to be investigated. Thus we must distinguish between numerals and what they mean; and if so, we shall have to recognize that the expressions '2', '$1+1$', '$3-1$', '6:3' all mean the same thing, for it is quite inconceivable where the difference between them could lie. Perhaps you say: $1+1$ is a sum, but 6:3 is a quotient. But what is 6:3? The number that when multiplied by 3 gives the result 6. We say '*the* number,' not 'a number'; by using the definite article, we indicate that there is only a single number. Now we have:

$$(1+1)+(1+1)+(1+1) = 6,$$

and thus $(1+1)$ is the very number that was designated as (6:3). The different expressions correspond to different conceptions and aspects, but nevertheless always to the same thing. Otherwise the equation $x^2=4$ would

[1] In definition it is always a matter of associating with a sign a sense or a meaning. Where sense and meaning are missing, we cannot properly speak either of a sign or of a definition.

not just have the roots 2 and -2, but also the root $(1+1)$ and countless others, all of them different, even if they resembled one another in a certain respect. By recognizing only two real roots, we are rejecting the view that the sign of equality does not mean a complete coincidence but only a partial agreement. If we adhere to this truth, we see that what the expressions:

'2.1^3+1',
'2.2^3+2',
'2.4^3+4',

mean are numbers, viz. 3, 18, 132. So if a function were really the meaning of a mathematical expression, it would just be a number; and nothing new would have been gained for arithmetic [by speaking of functions]. Admittedly, people who use the word 'function' ordinarily have in mind expressions in which a number is just indicated indefinitely by the letter x, e.g.

'$2.x^3+x$';

but that makes no difference; for this expression likewise just indefinitely indicates a *number*, and it makes no essential difference whether I write it down or just write down 'x'.

All the same, it is precisely by the notation that uses 'x' to indicate [a number] indefinitely that we are led to the right conception. People call x the argument, and recognize the same function again in

'2.1^3+1',
'2.4^3+4',
'2.5^3+5',

only with different arguments, viz. 1, 4, and 5. From this we may discern that it is the common element of these expressions that contains the essential peculiarity of a function; i.e. what is present in

'$2.x^3+x$'

over and above the letter 'x'. We could write this somewhat as follows:

'$2.(\ )^3+(\ )$'.

I am concerned to show that the argument does not belong with a function, but goes together with the function to make up a complete whole; for a function by itself must be called incomplete, in need of supplementation, or 'unsaturated'. And in this respect functions differ fundamentally from numbers. Since such is the essence of functions, we can explain why, on the one hand, we recognize the same function in '2.1^3+1' and '2.2^3+2', even though the numbers these expressions mean are different, whereas on the other hand, we do not find one and the same function in '2.1³+1' and '4−1' in spite of their equal numerical values. Moreover, we now see how people are easily led to regard the form of an expression as what is essential to a function. We recognize the function in the expression by imagining the latter as split up, and the possibility of thus splitting it up is suggested by its structure.

The two parts into which a mathematical expression is thus split up, the sign of the argument and the expression of the function, are dissimilar; for the argument is a number, a whole complete in itself, as the function is not. (We may compare this with the division of a line by a point. One is inclined in that case to count the dividing-point along with both segments; but if we want to make a clean division, i.e. so as not to count anything twice over or leave anything out, then we may only count the dividing-point along with one segment. This segment thus becomes fully complete in itself, and may be compared to the argument; whereas the other is lacking in something—viz. the dividing-point, which one may call its endpoint, does not belong to it. Only by completing it with this endpoint, or with a line that has two endpoints, do we get from it something entire.) For instance, if I say 'the function $2.x^3+x$', x must not be considered as belonging to the function; this letter only serves to indicate the kind of supplementation that is needed; it enables one to recognize the places where the sign for the argument must go in.

We give the name 'the value of a function for an argument' to the result of completing the function with the argument. Thus, e.g., 3 is the value of the function $2x^3+x$ for the argument 1, since we have: $2.1^3+1=3$.

There are functions, such as $2+x−x$ or $2+0.x$, whose value is always the same, whatever the argument; we have $2=2+x−x$ and $2=2+0.x$. Now if we counted the argument as belonging with the function, we should hold that the number 2 is this function. But this is wrong. Even though here the value of the function is always 2, the function itself must nevertheless be distinguished from 2; for the expression for a function must always show one or more places that are intended to be filled up with the sign of the argument.

The method of analytic geometry supplies us with a means of intuitively representing the values of a function for different arguments. If we regard the argument as the numerical value of an abscissa, and the corresponding value of the function as the numerical value of the ordinate of a point, we obtain a set of points that presents itself to intuition (in ordinary cases) as a curve. Any point on the curve corresponds to an argument together with the associated value of the function.

Thus, e.g.

$$y = x^2 - 4x$$

yields a parabola; here 'y' indicates the value of the function and the numerical value of the ordinate, and 'x' similarly indicates the argument and the numerical value of the abscissa. If we compare with this the function

$$x(x-4),$$

we find that they have always the same value for the same argument. We have generally:

$$x^2 - 4x = x(x-4),$$

whatever number we take for x. Thus the curve we get from

$$y = x^2 - 4x$$

is the same as the one that arises out of

$$y = x(x-4).$$

I express this as follows: the function $x(x-4)$ has the same graph as the function $x^2 - 4x$.

If we write

$$x^2 - 4x = x(x-4),$$

we have not put one function equal to the other, but only the values of one equal to those of the other. And if we so understand this equation that it is to hold whatever argument may be substituted for x, then we have thus expressed that an equality holds generally. But we can also say: 'the graph of the function $x(x-4)$ is equal to that of the function $x^2 - 4x$', and here we have an equality between graphs. The possibility of regarding the equality holding generally between values of functions as a [particular] equality, viz. an equality between graphs is, I think, indemonstrable; it must be taken to be a fundamental law of logic.[2]

We may further introduce a brief notation for the graph of a function. To this end I replace the sign of the argument in the expression for the function by a Greek vowel, enclose the whole in brackets, and prefix to it the same Greek letter with a smooth breathing. Accordingly, e.g.,

$$\acute{\varepsilon}\,(\varepsilon^2 - 4\,\varepsilon)$$

is the graph of the function $x^2 - 4x$ and

---

[2] In many phrases of ordinary mathematical terminology, the word 'function' certainly corresponds to what I have here called the graph of a function. But function, in the sense of the word employed here, is the logically prior [notion].

$$\grave{\alpha}\,(\alpha.(\alpha-4))$$

is the graph of the function $x(x-4)$, so that in

'$\grave{\varepsilon}(\varepsilon^2-4\varepsilon)=\grave{\alpha}(\alpha.(\alpha-4))$'

we have the expression for: the first graph is the same graph as the second. A different choice of Greek letters is made on purpose, in order to indicate that there is nothing that obliges us to take the same one.

If we understand

'$x^2-4\mathrm{x}=x(x-4)$'

in the same sense as before, this expresses the same sense, but in a different way. It presents the sense as an equality holding generally; whereas the newly-introduced expression is simply an equation, and its right side, and equally its left side, will mean something complete in itself. In

'$x^2-4x=x(x-4)$'

the left side considered in isolation indicates a number only indefinitely, and the same is true of the right side. If we just had 'x^2-4x' we could write instead 'y^2-4y' without altering the sense; for 'y' like 'x' indicates a number only indefinitely. But if we combine the two sides to form an equation, we must choose the same letter for both sides, and we thus express something that is not contained in the left side by itself, nor in the right side, nor in the 'equals' sign; viz. generality. Admittedly what we express is the generality of an equality; but primarily it is a generality.

Just as we indicate a number indefinitely by a letter, in order to express generality, we also need letters to indicate a function indefinitely. To this end people ordinarily use the letters f and F, thus: '$f(x)$', '$F(x)$', where 'x' replaces the argument. Here the need of a function for supplementation is expressed by the fact that the letter f or F carries along with it a pair of brackets; the space between these is meant to receive the sign for the argument. Thus

$$\grave{\varepsilon}f(\varepsilon)$$

indicates the graph of a function that is left undetermined.

Now how has the meaning of the word 'function' been stretched by the progress of science? We can distinguish two directions in which this has happened.

In the first place, the field of mathematical operations that serve for constructing functions has been extended. Besides addition, multiplication, exponentiation, and their converses, the various means of transition to the limit have been introduced—to be sure, people have not always been clearly aware that they were thus adopting something essentially new. People have gone further still, and have actually been obliged to resort to ordinary language, because the symbolic language of Analysis failed: e.g. when they were speaking of a function whose value is 1 for rational and 0 for irrational arguments.

Secondly, the field of possible arguments and values for functions has been extended by the admission of complex numbers. In conjunction with this, the sense of the expressions 'sum', 'product', etc., had to be defined more widely.

In both directions I go still further. I begin by adding to the signs $+$, $-$, etc., which serve for constructing a functional expression, also signs such as $=$, $>$, $<$, so that I can speak, e.g., of the function $x^2=1$, where x takes the place of the argument as before. The first question that arises here is what the values of this function are for different arguments. Now if we replace x successively by -1, 0, 1, 2, we get:

$$(-1)^2=1,$$
$$0^2=1,$$
$$1^2=1,$$
$$2^2=1.$$

Of these equations the first and third are true, the others false. I now say: 'the value of our function is a truth-value', and distinguish between the truth-values of what is true and what is false. I call the first, for short, the True; and the second, the False. Consequently, e.g., what '$2^2=4$' means is the True as, say, '2^2' means 4. And '$2^2=1$' means the False. Accordingly

'$2^2=4$', '$2>1$', '$2^4=4^2$',

all mean the same thing, viz. the True, so that in

$$(2^2=4)=(2>1)$$

we have a correct equation.

The objection here suggests itself that '$2^2=4$' and '$2>1$' nevertheless tell us quite different things, express quite different thoughts; but likewise '$2^4=4^2$' and '$4.4=4^2$' express different thoughts; and yet we can replace '2^4' by '4.4', since both signs have the same meaning. Consequently, '$2^4=4^2$' and '$4.4=4^2$' likewise have the same meaning. We see from this that from sameness of meaning there does not follow sameness of the thought [expressed]. If we say 'the Evening Star is a planet with a shorter period of revolution than the Earth', the thought we express is other than in the sentence 'the Morning Star is a planet with a shorter period of revolution than the Earth'; for one who does not know that the Morning Star is the Evening Star might regard one as true and the other as false. And yet both sentences must mean the same thing; for it is just a matter of interchange of the words 'Evening Star' and 'Morning Star', which mean the same thing, i.e. are proper names of the same heavenly body. We must distinguish between sense and meaning. '2^4' and '4^2' certainly have the same meaning, i.e. are proper names of the same number; but they have not the same sense; consequently, '$2^4 = 4^2$' and '$4.4 = 4^2$' mean the same thing, but have not the same sense (i.e., in this case: they do not contain the same thought).[3]

Thus, just as we write:

'$2^4 = 4.4$'

we may also write with equal justification

'$(2^4 = 4^2) = (4.4 = 4^2)$'

and

'$(2^2 = 4) = (2 > 1)$'.

It might further be asked: What, then, is the point of admitting the signs =, >, <, into the field of those that help to build up a functional expression? Nowadays, it seems, more and more supporters are being won by the view that arithmetic is a further development of logic; that a more rigorous establishment of arithmetical laws reduces them to purely logical laws and to such laws alone. I too am of this opinion, and I base upon it the requirement that the symbolic language of arithmetic must be expanded into a logical symbolism. I shall now have to indicate how this is done in our present case.

We saw that the value of our function $x^2 = 1$ is always one of the two truth-values. Now if for a definite argument, e.g. -1, the value of the function is the True, we can express this as follows: 'the number -1 has the property that its square is 1'; or, more briefly, '-1 is a square root of 1'; or, '-1 falls under the concept: square root of 1'. If the value of the function $x^2 = 1$ for an argument, e.g. for 2, is the False, we can express this as follows: '2 is not a square root of 1' or '2 does not fall under the concept: square root of 1'. We thus see how closely that which is called a concept in logic is connected with what we call a function. Indeed, we may say at once: a concept is a function whose value is always a truth-value. Again, the value of the function

$(x+1)^2 = 2(x+1)$

___

[3] I do not fail to see that this way of putting it may at first seem arbitrary and artificial, and that it would be desirable to establish my view by going further into the matter. Cf. my forthcoming essay 'Ueber Sinn und Bedeutung' ['Sense and Meaning'] in the *Zeitschrift für Philosophie und Philosophische Kritik*.

is always a truth-value. We get the True as its value, e.g., for the argument −1, and this can also be expressed thus: −1 is a number less by 1 than a number whose square is equal to its double. This expresses the fact that −1 falls under a concept. Now the functions

$$x^2 = 1 \quad \text{and} \quad (x+1)^2 = 2(x+1)$$

always have the same value for the same argument, viz. the True for the arguments −1 and +1, and the False for all other arguments. According to our previous conventions we shall also say that these functions have the same graph, and express this in symbols as follows:

$$\grave{\varepsilon}(\varepsilon^2 = 1) = \grave{\alpha}((\alpha+1)^2 = 2(\alpha+1)).$$

In logic this is called identity of the extension of concepts. Hence we can designate as an extension the graph of a function whose value for every argument is a truth-value.

We shall not stop at equations and inequalities. The linguistic form of equations is a statement. A statement contains (or at least purports to contain) a thought as its sense; and this thought is in general true or false; i.e. it has in general a truth-value, which must be regarded as what the sentence means, just as (say) the number 4 is what the expression '2+2' means or London what the expression 'the capital of England' means.

Statements in general, just like equations or inequalities or expressions in Analysis, can be imagined to be split up into two parts; one complete in itself, and the other in need of supplementation, or 'unsaturated'. Thus, e.g., we split up the sentence

'Caesar conquered Gaul'

into 'Caesar' and 'conquered Gaul'. The second part is 'unsaturated'—it contains an empty place; only when this place is filled up with a proper name, or with an expression that replaces a proper name, does a complete sense appear. Here too I give the name 'function' to what is meant by this 'unsaturated' part. In this case the argument is Caesar.

We see that here we have undertaken to extend [the application of the term] in the other direction, viz. as regards what can occur as an argument. Not merely numbers, but objects in general, are now admissible; and here persons must assuredly be counted as objects. The two truth-values have already been introduced as possible values of a function; we must go further and admit objects without restriction as values of functions. To get an example of this, let us start, e.g., with the expression

'the capital of the German Empire'.

This obviously takes the place of a proper name, and stands for an object. If we now split it up into the parts

'the capital of' and 'the German Empire'

where I count the [German] genitive form as going with the first part, then this part is 'unsaturated', whereas the other is complete in itself. So in accordance with what I said before, I call

'the capital of x'

the expression of a function. If we take the German Empire as the argument, we get Berlin as the value of the function.

When we have thus admitted objects without restriction as arguments and values of functions, the question arises what it is that we are here calling an object. I regard a regular definition as impossible, since we have here something too simple to admit of logical analysis. It is only possible to indicate what is meant. Here I can only say briefly: An object is anything that is not a function, so that an expression for it does not contain any empty place.

A statement contains no empty place, and therefore we must take what it means to be an object. But what a statement means is a truth-value. Thus the two truth-values are objects.

Earlier on we presented equations between graphs, e.g.:

$$`\acute\varepsilon(\varepsilon^2-4\varepsilon)=\acute\alpha(\alpha(\alpha-4))'.$$

We can split this up into '$\acute\varepsilon(\varepsilon^2-4\varepsilon)$' and '$(\ )=\acute\alpha(\alpha(\alpha-4))$'. This latter part needs supplementation, since on the left of the 'equals' sign it contains an empty place. The first part, '$\acute\varepsilon(\varepsilon^2-4\varepsilon)$', is fully complete in itself and thus stands for an object. Graphs of functions are objects, whereas functions themselves are not. We gave the name 'graph' also to $\acute\varepsilon(\varepsilon^2=1)$, but we could also have termed it the extension of the concept: square root of 1. Extensions of concepts likewise are objects, although concepts themselves are not. . . .

I will now add something about functions with two arguments. We get the expression for a function by splitting up the complex sign for an object into a 'saturated' and an 'unsaturated' part. Thus, we split up this sign for the True,

3>2,

into '3' and '$x>2$'. We can further split up the 'unsaturated' part '$x>2$' in the same way, into '2' and

$x>y$,

where 'y' enables us to recognize the empty place previously filled up by '2'. In

$$x>y$$

we have a function with two arguments, one indicated by 'x' and the other by 'y'; and in

$$3>2$$

we have the value of this function for the arguments 3 and 2. We have here a function whose value is always a truth-value. We called such functions of one argument concepts; we call such functions of two arguments relations. Thus we have relations also, e.g., in

$$x^2+y^2 = 9$$

and in

$$x^2+y^2 > 9,$$

whereas the function

$$x^2+y^2$$

has numbers as values. We shall therefore not call this a relation.

II

THE WORLD OF UNIVERSALS

BERTRAND RUSSELL

At the end of the preceding chapter we saw that such entities as relations appear to have a being which is in some way different from that of physical objects, and also different from that of minds and from that of sense-data. In the present chapter we have to consider what is the nature of this kind of being, and also what objects there are that have this kind of being. We will begin with the latter question.

The problem with which we are now concerned is a very old one, since it was brought into philosophy by Plato. Plato's 'theory of ideas' is an attempt to solve this very problem, and in my opinion it is one of the most successful attempts hitherto made. The theory to be advocated in what follows is largely Plato's, with merely such modifications as time has shown to be necessary.

The way the problem arose for Plato was more or less as follows. Let us consider, say, such a notion as *justice*. If we ask ourselves what justice is, it is natural to proceed by considering this, that, and the other just act, with a view to discovering what they have in common. They must all, in some sense, partake of a common nature, which will be found in whatever is just and in nothing else. This common nature, in virtue of which they are all just, will be justice itself, the pure essence the admixture of which with facts of ordinary life produces the multiplicity of just acts. Similarly with any other word which may be applicable to common facts, such as 'whiteness' for example. The word will be applicable to a number of particular things because they all participate in a common nature or essence. This pure essence is what Plato calls an 'idea' or 'form'. (It must not be supposed that 'ideas', in his sense, exist in minds, though they may be apprehended by minds.) The 'idea' *justice* is not identical with anything that is just: it is something other than particular things, which particular things partake of. Not being particular, it cannot itself exist in the world of sense. Moreover it is not fleeting or changeable like the things of sense: it is eternally itself, immutable and indestructible.

Reprinted from Bertrand Russell, *The Problems of Philosophy* (Oxford: Oxford University Press, 1967) chapter 9. By permission of Oxford University Press.

Thus Plato is led to a supra-sensible world, more real than the common world of sense, the unchangeable world of ideas, which alone gives to the world of sense whatever pale reflection of reality may belong to it. The truly real world, for Plato, is the world of ideas; for whatever we may attempt to say about things in the world of sense, we can only succeed in saying that they participate in such and such ideas, which, therefore, constitute all their character. Hence it is easy to pass on into a mysticism. We may hope, in a mystic illumination, to *see* the ideas as we see objects of sense; and we may imagine that the ideas exist in heaven. These mystical developments are very natural, but the basis of the theory is in logic, and it is as based in logic that we have to consider it.

The word 'idea' has acquired, in the course of time, many associations which are quite misleading when applied to Plato's 'ideas'. We shall therefore use the word 'universal' instead of the word 'idea', to describe what Plato meant. The essence of the sort of entity that Plato meant is that it is opposed to the particular things that are given in sensation. We speak of whatever is given in sensation, or is of the same nature as things given in sensation, as a *particular*; by opposition to this, a *universal* will be anything which may be shared by many particulars, and has those characteristics which, as we saw, distinguish justice and whiteness from just acts and white things.

When we examine common words, we find that, broadly speaking, proper names stand for particulars, while other substantives, adjectives, prepositions, and verbs stand for universals. Pronouns stand for particulars, but are ambiguous: it is only by the context or the circumstances that we know what particulars they stand for. The word 'now' stands for a particular, namely the present moment; but like pronouns, it stands for an ambiguous particular, because the present is always changing.

It will be seen that no sentence can be made up without at least one word which denotes a universal. The nearest approach would be some such statement as 'I like this'. But even here the word 'like' denotes a universal, for I may like other things, and other people may like things. Thus all truths involve universals, and all knowledge of truths involves acquaintance with universals.

Seeing that nearly all the words to be found in the dictionary stand for universals, it is strange that hardly anybody except students of philosophy ever realizes that there are such entities as universals. We do not naturally dwell upon those words in a sentence which do not stand for particulars; and if we are forced to dwell upon a word which stands for a universal, we naturally think of it as standing for some one of the particulars that come under the universal. When, for example, we hear the sentence 'Charles I's head was cut off', we may naturally enough think of Charles I, or Charles I's head, and of the operation of cutting off *his* head, which are all particulars; but we do not naturally dwell upon what is meant by the word 'head' or the word 'cut', which is a universal. We feel such words to be incomplete and insubstantial; they seem to demand a context before anything can be done with them. Hence we succeed in avoiding all notice of universals as such, until the study of philosophy forces them upon our attention.

Even among philosophers, we may say, broadly, that only those universals which are named by adjectives or substantives have been much or often recognized, while those named by verbs and prepositions have been usually overlooked. This omission has had a very great effect upon philosophy; it is hardly too much to say that most metaphysics, since Spinoza, has been largely determined by it. The way this has occurred is, in outline, as follows: Speaking generally, adjectives and common nouns express qualities or properties of single things, whereas prepositions and verbs tend to express relations between two or more things. Thus the neglect of prepositions and verbs led to the belief that every proposition can be regarded as attributing a property to a single thing, rather than as expressing a relation between two or more things. Hence it was supposed that, ultimately, there can be no such entities as relations between things. Hence either there can be only one thing in the universe, or, if there are many things, they cannot possibly interact in any way, since any interaction would be a relation, and relations are impossible.

The first of these views, advocated by Spinoza and held in our own day by Bradley and many other philosophers, is called *monism*; the second, advocated by Leibniz but not very common nowadays, is called *monadism*, because each of the isolated things is called a *monad*. Both these opposing philosophies, interesting as they are, result, in my opinion, from an undue attention to one sort of universals, namely the sort represented by adjectives and substantives rather than by verbs and prepositions.

As a matter of fact, if anyone were anxious to deny altogether that there are such things as universals, we should find that we cannot strictly prove that there are such entities as *qualities*, i.e. the universals represented by adjectives and substantives, whereas we can prove that there must be *relations*, i.e. the sort of universals generally represented by verbs and prepositions. Let us take in illustration the universal *whiteness*. If we believe that there is such a universal, we shall say that things are white because they have the quality of whiteness. This view, however, was strenuously denied by Berkeley and Hume, who have been followed in this by later empiricists. The form which their denial took was to deny that there are such things as 'abstract ideas'. When we want to think of whiteness, they said, we form an image of some particular white thing, and reason concerning this particular, taking care not to deduce anything concerning it which we cannot see to be equally true of any other white thing. As an account of our actual mental processes, this is no doubt largely true. In geometry, for example, when we wish to prove something about all triangles, we draw a particular triangle and reason about it, taking care not to use any characteristic which it does not share with other triangles. The beginner, in order to avoid error, often finds it useful to draw several triangles, as unlike each other as possible, in order to make sure that his reasoning is equally applicable to all of them. But a difficulty emerges as soon as we ask ourselves how we know that a thing is white or a triangle. If we wish to avoid the universals *whiteness* and *triangularity*, we shall choose some particular patch of white or some particular triangle, and say that anything is white or a triangle if it has the right sort of resemblance to our chosen particular. But then the resemblance required will have to be a universal. Since there are many white things, the resemblance must hold between many pairs of particular white things; and this is the characteristic of a universal. It will be useless to say that there is a different resemblance for each pair, for then we shall have to say that these resemblances resemble each other, and thus at last we shall be forced to admit resemblance as a universal. The relation of resemblance, therefore, must be a true universal. And having been forced to admit this universal, we find that it is no longer worth while to invent difficult and implausible theories to avoid the admission of such universals as whiteness and triangularity.

Berkeley and Hume failed to perceive this refutation of their rejection of 'abstract ideas', because, like their adversaries, they only thought of *qualities*, and altogether ignored *relations* as universals. We have therefore here another respect in which the rationalists appear to have been in the right as against the empiricists, although, owing to the neglect or denial of relations, the deductions made by rationalists were, if anything, more apt to be mistaken than those made by empiricists.

Having now seen that there must be such entities as universals, the next point to be proved is that their being is not merely mental. By this is meant that whatever being belongs to them is independent of their being thought of or in any way apprehended by minds. We have already touched on this subject at the end of the preceding chapter, but we must now consider more fully what sort of being it is that belongs to universals.

Consider such a proposition as 'Edinburgh is north of London'. Here we have a relation between two places, and it seems plain that the relation subsists independently of our knowledge of it. When we come to know that Edinburgh is north of London, we come to know something which has to do only with Edinburgh and London: we do not cause the truth of the proposition by coming to know it, on the contrary we merely apprehend a fact which was there before we knew it. The part of the earth's surface where Edinburgh stands would be north of the part where London stands, even if there were no human being to know about north and south, and even if there were no minds at all in the universe. This is, of course, denied by many philosophers, either for Berkeley's reasons or for Kant's. But we have already considered these reasons, and decided that they are inadequate. We may therefore now assume it to be true that nothing mental is presupposed in the fact that Edinburgh is north of London. But this fact involves the relation 'north of', which is a universal; and it would be impossible for the whole fact to involve nothing mental if the relation 'north of', which is a constituent part of the fact, did involve anything mental. Hence we must admit that the relation, like the terms it relates, is not dependent upon thought, but belongs to the independent world which thought apprehends but does not create.

This conclusion, however, is met by the difficulty that the relation 'north of' does not seem to *exist* in the same sense in which Edinburgh and London exist. If we ask 'Where and when does this relation exist?' the answer must be 'Nowhere and nowhen'. There is no place or time where we can find the relation 'north of'. It does not exist in Edinburgh any more than in London, for it relates the two and is neutral as between them. Nor can we say that it exists at any particular time. Now everything that can be apprehended by the senses or by introspection exists at some particular time. Hence the relation 'north of' is radically different from such things. It is neither in space nor in time, neither material nor mental; yet it is something.

It is largely the very peculiar kind of being that belongs to universals which has led many people to suppose that they are really mental. We can think *of* a universal, and our thinking then exists in a perfectly ordinary sense, like any other mental act. Suppose, for example, that we are thinking of whiteness. Then *in one sense* it may be said that whiteness is 'in our mind'. We have here the same ambiguity as we noted in discussing Berkeley in chapter 4. In the strict sense, it is not whiteness that is in our mind, but the act of thinking of whiteness. The connected ambiguity in the word 'idea', which we noted at the same time, also causes confusion here. In one sense of this word, namely the sense in which it denotes the *object* of an act of thought, whiteness is an 'idea'. Hence, if the ambiguity is not guarded against, we may come to think that whiteness is an 'idea' in the other sense, i.e. an act of thought; and thus we come to think that whiteness is mental. But in so thinking, we rob it of its essential quality of universality. One man's act of thought is necessarily a different thing from another man's; one man's act of thought at one time is necessarily a different thing from the same man's act of thought at another time. Hence, if whiteness were the thought as opposed to its object, no two different men could think of it, and no one man could think of it twice. That which many different thoughts of whiteness have in common is their *object*, and this object is different from all of them. Thus universals are not thoughts, though when known they are the objects of thoughts.

We shall find it convenient only to speak of things *existing* when they are in time, that is to say, when we can point to some time *at* which they exist (not excluding the possibility of their existing at all times). Thus thoughts and feelings, minds and physical objects *exist*. But universals do not exist in this sense; we shall say that they *subsist* or *have being*, where 'being' is opposed to 'existence' as being timeless. The world of universals, there-fore, may also be described as the world of being. The world of being is unchangeable, rigid, exact, delightful to the mathematician, the logician, the builder of metaphysical systems, and all who love perfection more than life. The world of existence is fleeting, vague, without sharp bound-aries, without any clear plan or arrangement, but it contains all thoughts and feelings, all the data of sense, and all physical objects, everything that can do either good or harm, everything that makes any difference to the value of life and the world. According to our temperaments, we shall prefer the contemplation of the one or of the other. The one we do not prefer will probably seem to us a pale shadow of the one we prefer, and hardly worthy to be regarded as in any sense real. But the truth is that both have the same claim on our impartial attention, both are real, and both are important to the metaphysician. Indeed no sooner have we distinguished the two worlds than it becomes necessary to consider their relations.

But first of all we must examine our knowledge of universals. This consideration will occupy us in the following chapter, where we shall find that it solves the problem of *a priori* knowledge, from which we were first led to consider universals.

III

ON OUR KNOWLEDGE OF UNIVERSALS

BERTRAND RUSSELL

In regard to one man's knowledge at a given time, universals, like particulars, may be divided into those known by acquaintance, those known only by description, and those not known either by acquaintance or by description.

Let us consider first the knowledge of universals by acquaintance. It is obvious, to begin with, that we are acquainted with such universals as white, red, black, sweet, sour, loud, hard, etc., i.e. with qualities which are exemplified in sense-data. When we see a white patch, we are acquainted, in the first instance, with the particular patch; but by seeing many white patches, we easily learn to abstract the whiteness which they all have in common, and in learning to do this we are learning to be acquainted with whiteness. A similar process will make us acquainted with any other universal of the same sort. Universals of this sort may be called 'sensible qualities'. They can be apprehended with less effort of abstraction than any others, and they seem less removed from particulars than other universals are.

We come next to relations. The easiest relations to apprehend are those which hold between the different parts of a single complex sense-datum. For example, I can see at a glance the whole of the page on which I am writing; thus the whole page is included in one sense-datum. But I perceive that some parts of the page are to the left of other parts, and some parts are above other parts. The process of abstraction in this case seems to proceed somewhat as follows: I see successively a number of sense-data in which one part is to the left of another; I perceive, as in the case of different white patches, that all these sense-data have something in common, and by abstraction I find that what they have in common is a certain relation between their parts, namely the relation which I call 'being to the left of'. In this way I become acquainted with the universal relation.

In like manner I become aware of the relation of before and after in

Reprinted from Bertrand Russell, *The Problems of Philosophy* (Oxford: Oxford University Press, 1967) chapter 10. By permission of Oxford University Press.

time. Suppose I hear a chime of bells: when the last bell of the chime sounds, I can retain the whole chime before my mind, and I can perceive that the earlier bells came before the later ones. Also in memory I perceive that what I am remembering came before the present time. From either of these sources I can abstract the universal relation of before and after, just as I abstracted the universal relation 'being to the left of'. Thus time-relations, like space-relations, are among those with which we are acquainted.

Another relation with which we become acquainted in much the same way is resemblance. If I see simultaneously two shades of green, I can see that they resemble each other; if I also see a shade of red at the same time, I can see that the two greens have more resemblance to each other than either has to the red. In this way I become acquainted with the universal *resemblance* or *similarity*.

Between universals, as between particulars, there are relations of which we may be immediately aware. We have just seen that we can perceive that the resemblance between two shades of green is greater than the resemblance between a shade of red and a shade of green. Here we are dealing with a relation, namely 'greater than', between two relations. Our knowledge of such relations, though it requires more power of abstraction than is required for perceiving the qualities of sense-data, appears to be equally immediate, and (at least in some cases) equally indubitable. Thus there is immediate knowledge concerning universals as well as concerning sense-data.

Returning now to the problem of *a priori* knowledge, which we left unsolved when we began the consideration of universals, we find ourselves in a position to deal with it in a much more satisfactory manner than was possible before. Let us revert to the proposition 'two and two are four'. It is fairly obvious, in view of what has been said, that this proposition states a relation between the universal 'two' and the universal 'four'. This suggests a proposition which we shall now endeavour to establish: namely, *All* a priori *knowledge deals exclusively with the relations of universals.* This proposition is of great importance, and goes a long way towards solving our previous difficulties concerning *a priori* knowledge.

The only case in which it might seem, at first sight, as if our proposition were untrue, is the case in which an *a priori* proposition states that *all* of one class of particulars belong to some other class, or (what comes to the same thing) that *all* particulars having some one property also have some other. In this case it might seem as though we were dealing with the particulars that have the property rather than with the property. The proposition 'two and two are four' is really a case in point, for this may be stated in the form 'any two and any other two are four', or 'any collection formed of two twos is a collection of four'. If we can show that such statements as this really deal only with universals, our proposition may be regarded as proved.

One way of discovering what a proposition deals with is to ask ourselves what words we must understand—in other words, what objects we must be acquainted with—in order to see what the proposition means. As soon as we see what the proposition means, even if we do not yet know whether it is true or false, it is evident that we must have acquaintance with whatever is really dealt with by the proposition. By applying this test, it appears that many propositions which might seem to be concerned with particulars are really concerned only with universals. In the special case of 'two and two are four', even when we interpret it as meaning 'any collection formed of two twos is a collection of four', it is plain that we can *understand* the proposition, i.e. we can see what it is that it asserts, as soon as we know what is meant by 'collection' and 'two' and 'four'. It is quite unnecessary to know all the couples in the world: if it were necessary, obviously we could never understand the proposition, since the couples are infinitely numerous and therefore cannot all be known to us. Thus although our general statement *implies* statements about particular couples, *as soon as we know that there are such particular couples,* yet it does not itself assert or imply that there are such particular couples, and thus fails to make any statement whatever about any actual particular couple. The statement made is about 'couple', the universal, and not about this or that couple.

Thus the statement 'two and two are four' deals exclusively with universals, and therefore may be known by anybody who is acquainted with the universals concerned and can perceive the relation between them which the statement asserts. It must be taken as a fact, discovered by reflecting upon our knowledge, that we have the power of sometimes perceiving such relations between universals, and therefore of sometimes knowing general *a priori* propositions such as those of arithmetic and logic. The thing that seemed mysterious, when we formerly considered such knowledge, was that it seemed to anticipate and control experience. This, however, we can now see to have been an error. *No* fact concerning anything capable of being experienced can be known independently of experience. We know *a priori* that two things and two other things together make four things, but we do *not* know *a priori* that if Brown and Jones are two, and Robinson and Smith are two, then Brown and Jones and Robinson and Smith are four. The reason is that this proposition cannot be understood at all unless we know that there are such people as Brown and Jones and Robinson and Smith, and this we can only know by experience.

Hence, although our general proposition is *a priori*, all its applications to actual particulars involve experience and therefore contain an empirical element. In this way what seemed mysterious in our *a priori* knowledge is seen to have been based upon an error.

It will serve to make the point clearer if we contrast our genuine *a priori* judgement with an empirical generalization, such as 'all men are mortals'. Here as before, we can *understand* what the proposition means as soon as we understand the universals involved, namely *man* and *mortal*. It is obviously unnecessary to have an individual acquaintance with the whole human race in order to understand what our proposition means. Thus the difference between an *a priori* general proposition and an empirical generalization does not come in the *meaning* of the proposition; it comes in the nature of the *evidence* for it. In the empirical case, the evidence consists in the particular instances. We believe that all men are mortal because we know that there are innumerable instances of men dying, and no instances of their living beyond a certain age. We do not believe it because we see a connexion between the universal *man* and the universal *mortal*. It is true that if physiology can prove, assuming the general laws that govern living bodies, that no living organism can last for ever, that gives a connexion between *man* and *mortality* which would enable us to assert our proposition without appealing to the special evidence of *men* dying. But that only means that our generalization has been subsumed under a wider generalization, for which the evidence is still of the same kind, though more extensive. The progress of science is constantly producing such subsumptions, and therefore giving a constantly wider inductive basis for scientific generalizations. But although this gives a greater *degree* of certainty, it does not give a different *kind*: the ultimate ground remains inductive, i.e. derived from instances, and not an *a priori* connexion of universals such as we have in logic and arithmetic.

Two opposite points are to be observed concerning *a priori* general propositions. The first is that, if many particular instances are known, our general proposition may be arrived at in the first instance by induction, and the connexion of universals may be only subsequently perceived. For example, it is known that if we draw perpendiculars to the sides of a triangle from the opposite angles, all three perpendiculars meet in a point. It would be quite possible to be first led to this proposition by actually drawing perpendiculars in many cases, and finding that they always met in a point; this experience might lead us to look for the general proof and find it. Such cases are common in the experience of every mathematician.

The other point is more interesting, and of more philosophical importance. It is, that we may sometimes know a general proposition in cases where we do not know a single instance of it. Take such a case as the following: We know that any two numbers can be multiplied together, and will give a third called their *product*. We know that all pairs of integers the product of which is less than 100 have been actually multiplied together, and the value of the product recorded in the multiplication table. But we also know that the number of integers is infinite, and that only a finite number of pairs of integers ever have been or ever will be thought of by human beings. Hence it follows that there are pairs of integers which never have been and never will be thought of by human beings, and that all of them deal with integers the product of which is over 100. Hence we arrive at the proposition: 'All products of two integers, which never have been and never will be thought of by any human being, are over 100'. Here is a general proposition of which the truth is undeniable, and yet, from the very nature of the case, we can never give an instance; because any two numbers we may think of are excluded by the terms of the proposition.

This possibility, of knowledge of general propositions of which no instance can be given, is often denied, because it is not perceived that the knowledge of such propositions only requires a knowledge of the relations of universals, and does not require any knowledge of instances of the universals in question. Yet the knowledge of such general propositions is quite vital to a great deal of what is generally admitted to be known. For example, we saw, in our early chapters, that knowledge of physical objects, as opposed to sense-data, is only obtained by an inference, and that they are not things with which we are acquainted. Hence we can never know any proposition of the form 'this is a physical object', where 'this' is something immediately known. It follows that all our knowledge concerning physical objects is such that no actual instance can be given. We can give instances of the associated sense-data, but we cannot give instances of the actual physical objects. Hence our knowledge as to physical objects depends throughout upon this possibility of general knowledge where no instance can be given. And the same applies to our knowledge of other people's minds, or of any other class of things of which no instance is known to us by acquaintance.

We may now take a survey of the sources of our knowledge, as they have appeared in the course of our analysis. We have first to distinguish knowledge of things and knowledge of truths. In each there are two kinds, one immediate and one derivative. Our immediate knowledge of things, which we called *acquaintance*, consists of two sorts, according as the things known are particulars or universals. Among particulars, we have acquaintance with sense-data and (probably) with ourselves. Among universals, there seems to be no principle by which we can decide which can be known by acquaintance, but it is clear that among those that can be so known are sensible qualities, relations of space and time, similarity, and certain abstract logical universals. Our derivative knowledge of things, which we call knowledge by *description*, always involves both acquaintance with something and knowledge of truths. Our immediate knowledge of *truths* may be called *intuitive* knowledge, and the truths so known may be called *self-evident* truths. Among such truths are included those which merely state what is given in sense, and also certain abstract logical and arithmetical principles, and (though with less certainty) some ethical propositions. Our *derivative* knowledge of truths consists of everything that we can deduce from self-evident truths by the use of self-evident principles of deduction.

If the above account is correct, all our knowledge of truths depends upon our intuitive knowledge. It therefore becomes important to consider the nature and scope of intuitive knowledge, in much the same way as, at an earlier stage, we considered the nature and scope of knowledge by acquaintance. But knowledge of truths raises a further problem, which does not arise in regard to knowledge of things, namely the problem of *error*. Some of our beliefs turn out to be erroneous, and therefore it becomes necessary to consider how, if at all, we can distinguish knowledge from error. This problem does not arise with regard to knowledge by acquaintance, for, whatever may be the object of acquaintance, even in dreams and hallucinations, there is no error involved so long as we do not go beyond the immediate object: error can only arise when we regard the immediate object, i.e. the sense-datum, as the mark of some physical object. Thus the problems connected with knowledge of truths are more difficult than those connected with knowledge of things.

IV

UNIVERSALS

F. P. RAMSEY

The purpose of this paper is to consider whether there is a fundamental division of objects into two classes, particulars and universals. This question was discussed by Mr Russell in a paper printed in the Aristotelian Society's Proceedings for 1911. His conclusion that the distinction was ultimate was based upon two familiar arguments, directed against the two obvious methods of abolishing the distinction by holding either that universals are collections of particulars, or that particulars are collections of their qualities. These arguments, perfectly sound as far as they go, do not however seem to me to settle the whole question. The first, which appears again in *The Problems of Philosophy*, shows as against the nominalists that such a proposition as 'This sense-datum is white' must have as one constituent something, such as whiteness or similarity, which is not of the same logical type as the sense-datum itself. The second argument, also briefly expounded in McTaggart's *The Nature of Existence*, proves that a man cannot be identified with the sum of his qualities. But although a man cannot be one of his own qualities, that is no reason why he should not be a quality of something else. In fact material objects *are* described by Dr Whitehead as 'true Aristotelian adjectives'; so that we cannot regard these two arguments as rendering the distinction between particular and universal secure against all criticism.

What then, I propose to ask, is the difference between a particular and a universal? What can we say about one which will not also be true of the other? If we follow Mr Russell we shall have to investigate three kinds of distinction, psychological, physical, and logical. First we have the difference between a percept and a concept, the objects of two different kinds of mental acts; but this is unlikely to be a distinction of any fundamental importance, since a difference in two mental acts may not correspond to any difference whatever in their objects. Next we have various distinctions between objects based on their relations to space and time; for instance,

Written in 1925 and last published in *F. P. Ramsey: Philosophical Papers*, edited by D. H. Mellor (Cambridge: Cambridge University Press, 1990), 8–33. This article originally appeared in *Mind*, 34 (1925) and is reprinted by permission of Oxford University Press.

some objects can only be in one place at a time, others, like the colour red, can be in many. Here again, in spite of the importance of the subject, I do not think we can have reached the essence of the matter. For when, for instance, Dr Whitehead says that a table is an adjective, and Mr Johnson that it is a substantive, they are not arguing about how many places the table can be in at once, but about its logical nature. And so it is with logical distinctions that our inquiry must mainly deal.

According to Mr Russell the class of universals is the sum of the class of predicates and the class of relations; but this doctrine has been denied by Dr Stout.[1] But Dr Stout has been already sufficiently answered.[2] So I shall only discuss the more usual opinion to which Mr Russell adheres.

According to him terms are divided into individuals or particulars, qualities and relations, qualities and relations being grouped together as universals; and sometimes qualities are even included among relations as one-termed relations in distinction from two-, three-, or many-termed relations. Mr Johnson also divides terms into substantives and adjectives, including relations as transitive adjectives; and he regards the distinction between substantive and adjective as explaining that between particular and universal. But between these authorities, who agree so far, there is still an important difference. Mr Johnson holds that although the nature of a substantive is such that it can only function in a proposition as subject and never as predicate, yet an adjective can function either as predicate or as a subject of which a secondary adjective can be predicated. For example, in 'Unpunctuality is a fault' the subject is itself an adjective—the quality of unpunctuality. There is thus a want of symmetry between substantives and adjectives, for while a predicate must be an adjective, a subject may be either a substantive or an adjective, and we must define a substantive as a term which can only be a subject, but never a predicate.

Mr Russell, on the other hand, in his lectures on Logical Atomism,[3] has denied this. He says that about an adjective there is something incomplete, some suggestion of the form of a proposition; so that the adjective-symbol can never stand alone or be the subject of a proposition, but must be completed into a proposition in which it is the predicate. Thus, he says, the appropriate symbol for redness is not the word 'red' but the function 'x is red', and red can only come into a proposition through the values of this function. So Mr Russell would say 'Unpunctuality is a fault' really means

[1] 'The Nature of Universals and Propositions', *Proceedings of the British Academy*, 10 (1921–2), 157–72.

[2] See the symposium between G. E. Moore, G. F. Stout, and G. Dawes Hicks in *Aristotelian Society Supplementary Volume*, 3 (1923).

[3] [Reprinted in Bertrand Russell, *Logic and Knowledge*, edited by R. C. Marsh (London: George Allen & Unwin, 1956), 177–281.]

something like 'For all x, if x is unpunctual, x is reprehensible'; and the adjective unpunctuality is not the subject of the proposition but only comes into it as the predicate of those of its parts which are of the form 'x is unpunctual'. This doctrine is the basis of new work in the second edition of *Principia Mathematica*.

Neither of these theories seems entirely satisfactory, although neither could be disproved. Mr Russell's view does, indeed, involve difficulties in connection with our cognitive relations to universals, for which reason it was rejected in the first edition of *Principia*; but these difficulties seem to me, as now to Mr Russell, by no means insurmountable. But I could not discuss them here without embarking upon innumerable questions irrelevant to the main points which I wish to make. Neither theory, then, can be disproved, but to both objections can be raised which may seem to have some force. For instance, Mr Russell urges that a relation between two terms cannot be a third term which comes between them, for then it would not be a relation at all, and the only genuinely relational element would consist in the connections between this new term and the two original terms. This is the kind of consideration from which Mr Bradley deduced his infinite regress, of which Mr Russell apparently now approves. Mr Johnson might reply that for him the connectional or structural element is not the relation but the characterizing and coupling ties; but these ties remain most mysterious objects. It might also be objected that Mr Johnson does not make particulars and universals different enough, or take into account the peculiar incompleteness of adjectives which appears in the possibility of prefixing to them the auxiliary 'being'; 'being red', 'being a man' do not seem real things like a chair and a carpet. Against Mr Russell it might be asked how there can be such objects as his universals, which contain the form of a proposition and so are incomplete. In a sense, it might be urged, all objects are incomplete; they cannot occur in facts except in conjunction with other objects, and they contain the forms of propositions of which they are constituents. In what way do universals do this more than anything else?

Evidently, however, none of these arguments are really decisive, and the position is extremely unsatisfactory to any one with real curiosity about such a fundamental question. In such cases it is a heuristic maxim that the truth lies not in one of the two disputed views but in some third possibility which has not yet been thought of, which we can only discover by rejecting something assumed as obvious by both the disputants.

Both the disputed theories make an important assumption which, to my mind, has only to be questioned to be doubted. They assume a fundamental antithesis between subject and predicate, that if a proposition consists of two terms copulated, these two terms must be functioning in different ways, one as subject, the other as predicate. Thus in 'Socrates is wise', Socrates is the subject, wisdom the predicate. But suppose we turn the proposition round and say 'Wisdom is a characteristic of Socrates', then wisdom, formerly the predicate, is now the subject. Now it seems to me as clear as anything can be in philosophy that the two sentences 'Socrates is wise', 'Wisdom is a characteristic of Socrates' assert the same fact and express the same proposition. They are not, of course, the same sentence, but they have the same meaning, just as two sentences in two different languages can have the same meaning. Which sentence we use is a matter either of literary style, or of the point of view from which we approach the fact. If the centre of our interest is Socrates we say 'Socrates is wise', if we are discussing wisdom we may say 'Wisdom is a characteristic of Socrates'; but whichever we say we mean the same thing. Now of one of these sentences 'Socrates' is the subject, of the other 'wisdom'; and so which of the two is subject, which predicate, depends upon what particular sentence we use to express our proposition, and has nothing to do with the logical nature of Socrates or wisdom, but is a matter entirely for grammarians. In the same way, with a sufficiently elastic language any proposition can be so expressed that any of its terms is the subject. Hence there is no essential distinction between the subject of a proposition and its predicate, and no fundamental classification of objects can be based upon such a distinction.

I do not claim that the above argument is immediately conclusive; what I claim is that it throws doubt upon the whole basis of the distinction between particular and universal as deduced from that between subject and predicate, and that the question requires a new examination. It is a point which has often been made by Mr Russell that philosophers are very liable to be misled by the subject-predicate construction of our language. They have supposed that all propositions must be of the subject-predicate form, and so have been led to deny the existence of relations. I shall argue that nearly all philosophers, including Mr Russell himself, have been misled by language in a far more far-reaching way than that; that the whole theory of particulars and universals is due to mistaking for a fundamental characteristic of reality what is merely a characteristic of language.

Let us, therefore, examine closely this distinction of subject and predicate, and for simplicity let us follow Mr Johnson and include relations among predicates and their terms among subjects. The first question we have to ask is this: what propositions are they that have a subject or subjects and a predicate? Is this the case with all propositions or only with some? Before, however, we go on to answer this question, let us remind ourselves that the task on which we are engaged is not merely one of English grammar; we are not school children analysing sentences into subject, extension of the subject, complement, and so on, but are interested not so much in sentences themselves, as in what they mean, from which we hope to discover the logical nature of reality. Hence we must look for senses of subject and predicate which are not purely grammatical, but have a genuine logical significance.

Let us begin with such a proposition as 'Either Socrates is wise or Plato is foolish'. To this, it will probably be agreed, the conception of subject and predicate is inapplicable; it may be applicable to the two parts 'Socrates is wise', 'Plato is foolish', but the whole 'Either Socrates is wise or Plato is foolish' is an alternative proposition and not one with a subject or predicate. But to this someone may make the following objection: In such a proposition we can take any term we please, say Socrates, to be the subject. The predicate will then be 'being wise unless Plato is foolish' or the propositional function '$\hat{x}$ is wise or Plato is foolish'. The phrase 'being wise unless Plato is foolish' will then stand for a complex universal which is asserted to characterize Socrates. Such a view, though very frequently held, seems to me nevertheless certainly mistaken. In order to make things clearer let us take a simpler case, a proposition of the form 'aRb'; then this theory will hold that there are three closely related propositions; one asserts that the relation R holds between the terms a and b, the second asserts the possession by a of the complex property of 'having R to b', while the third asserts that b has the complex property that a has R to it. These must be three different propositions because they have different sets of constituents, and yet they are not three propositions, but one proposition, for they all say the same thing, namely that a has R to b. So the theory of complex universals is responsible for an incomprehensible trinity, as senseless as that of theology. This argument can be strengthened by considering the process of definition, which is as follows. For certain purposes 'aRb' may be an unnecessarily long symbol, so that it is convenient to shorten it into 'ϕb'. This is done by definition, $\phi x = aRx$, signifying that any symbol of the form ϕx is to be interpreted as meaning what is meant by the corresponding symbol aRx, for which it is an abbreviation. In more complicated cases such an abbreviation is often extremely useful, but it could always be dispensed with if time and paper permitted. The believer in complex universals is now confronted with a dilemma: is 'ϕ', thus defined, a name for the complex property of x which consists in a having R to x? If so, then ϕx will be the assertion that x has this property; it will be a subject-predicate proposition whose subject is x and predicate ϕ ;

and this is not identical with the relational proposition aRx. But as ϕx is by hypothesis defined to be short for aRx this is absurd. For if a definition is not to be interpreted as signifying that the definiendum and the definiens have the same meaning, the process of definition becomes unintelligible and we lose all justification for interchanging definiens and definiendum at will, on which depends its whole utility. Suppose on the other hand 'ϕ', as defined above, is not a name for the complex property; then how can the complex property ever become an object of our contemplation, and how can we ever speak of it, seeing that 'ϕ', its only possible name, is not a name for it at all but short for something else? And then what reason can there be to postulate the existence of this thing?

In spite of this *reductio ad absurdum* of the theory, it may still be worth while to inquire into its origin, and into why it is held by so many people, including formerly myself, without its occurring to them to doubt it. The chief reason for this is I think to be found in linguistic convenience; it gives us one object which is 'the meaning' of 'ϕ'. We often want to talk of 'the meaning of "ϕ"', and it is simpler to suppose that this is a unique object than to recognize that it is a much more complicated matter, and that 'ϕ' has a relation of meaning not to one complex object but to the several simple objects which are named in its definition. There is, however, another reason why this view is so popular, and that is the imaginary difficulty which would otherwise be felt in the use of a variable propositional function. How, it might be asked, are we to interpret such a statement as 'a has all the properties of b', except on the supposition that there are properties? The answer is that it is to be interpreted as being the logical product of all propositions which can be constructed in the following way: take a proposition in which a occurs, say ϕa, change a into b and obtain ϕb, and then form the proposition $\phi b . \supset . \phi a$. It is not really quite so simple as that, but a more accurate account of it would involve a lot of tiresome detail, and so be out of place here; and we can take it as a sufficient approximation that 'a has all the properties of b' is the joint assertion of all propositions of the form $\phi b . \supset . \phi a$, where there is no necessity for ϕ to be the name of a universal, as it is merely the rest of a proposition in which a occurs. Hence the difficulty is entirely imaginary. It may be observed that the same applies to any other case of apparent variables some of whose values are incomplete symbols, and this may explain the tendency to assert that some of Mr Russell's incomplete symbols are not really incomplete but the names of properties or predicates.

I conclude, therefore, that complex universals are to be rejected; and that such a proposition as 'Either Socrates is wise or Plato foolish' has neither subject nor predicate. Similar arguments apply to any compound proposition, that is any proposition containing such words as 'and', 'or', 'not', 'all', 'some'; and hence if we are to find a logical distinction between subject and predicate anywhere it will be in atomic propositions, as Mr Russell calls them, which could be expressed by sentences containing none of the above words, but only names and perhaps a copula.

The distinction between subject and predicate will then arise from the several names in an atomic proposition functioning in different ways; and if this is not to be a purely grammatical distinction it must correspond to a difference in the functioning of several objects in an atomic fact, so that what we have primarily to examine is the construction of the atomic fact out of its constituents. About this three views might be suggested; first there is that of Mr Johnson according to whom the constituents are connected together by what he calls the characterizing tie. The nature of this entity is rather obscure, but I think we can take it as something which is not a constituent of the fact but represented in language by the copula 'is', and we can describe this theory as holding that the connection is made by a real copula. Next there is the theory of Mr Russell that the connection is made by one of the constituents; that in every atomic fact there must be one constituent which is in its own nature incomplete or connective and, as it were, holds the other constituents together. This constituent will be a universal and the others particulars. Lastly there is Mr Wittgenstein's theory that neither is there a copula, nor one specially connected constituent, but that, as he expresses it, the objects hang one in another like the links of a chain.

From our point of view it is the second of these theories that demands most attention; for the first and third do not really explain any difference in the mode of functioning of subject and predicate, but leave this a mere dogma. Only on Mr Russell's theory will there be an intelligible difference between particular and universal, grounded on the necessity for there to be in each fact a copulating term or universal, corresponding to the need for every sentence to have a verb. So it is Mr Russell's theory that we must first consider.

The great difficulty with this theory lies in understanding how one sort of object can be specially incomplete. There is a sense in which any object is incomplete; namely that it can only occur in a fact by connection with an object or objects of suitable type; just as any name is incomplete, because to form a proposition we have to join to it certain other names of suitable type. As Wittgenstein says: 'The thing is independent, in so far as it can occur in all *possible* circumstances, but this form of independence is a form of connection with the atomic fact, a form of dependence. (It is impossible for words to occur in two different ways, alone and in the proposition.)[4] And Johnson: 'Ultimately a universal means an adjective that may characterize a particular, and a particular means a substantive that may be characterized by a universal.'[5] Thus we may admit that 'wise' involves the form of a proposition, but so does 'Socrates', and it is hard to see any ground for distinguishing between them. This is the substance of Mr Johnson's criticism that Mr Russell will not let the adjective stand alone, and in treating '*s* is *p*' as a function of two variables takes the arguments to be not *s* and *p*, but *s* and '$\hat{x}$ is *p*'.

In reply to this criticism Mr Russell would, I imagine, use two lines of argument, whose validity we must examine. The first would dwell on the great convenience in mathematical logic of his functional symbolism, of which he might say there was no explanation except that this symbolism corresponded to reality more closely than any other. His second line of argument would be that everyone can feel a difference between particulars and universals; that the prevalence of nominalism showed that the reality of universals was always suspected, and that this was probably because they did in fact differ from particulars by being less independent, less self-contained. Also that this was the only account of the difference between particulars and universals which made them really different kinds of objects, as they evidently were, and not merely differently related to us or to our language. For instance, Mr Johnson describes the particular as presented to thought for its character to be determined in thought, and others might say that a particular was what was meant by the grammatical subject of a sentence; and on these views what was particular, what universal would depend on unessential characteristics of our psychology or our language.

Let us take these lines of argument in reverse order, beginning with the felt difference between particular and universal, and postponing the peculiar symbolic convenience of propositional functions. Anyone, it might be said, sees a difference between Socrates and wisdom. Socrates is a real independent entity, wisdom a quality and so essentially a quality of something else. The first thing to remark about this argument is that it is not really about objects at all. 'Socrates is wise' is not an atomic proposition, and the symbols 'Socrates' and 'wise' are not the names of objects but incomplete symbols. And according to Wittgenstein, with whom I agree, this will be the case with any other instance that may be suggested, since we are not acquainted with any genuine objects or atomic propositions, but merely infer them as presupposed by other propositions. Hence the

[4] *Tractatus Logico-Philosophicus* (London: Routledge, 1922), 2·0122.
[5] W. E. Johnson, *Logic Part I* (Cambridge: Cambridge University Press, 1921), p. 11.

distinction we feel is one between two sorts of incomplete symbols, or logical constructions, and we cannot infer without further investigation that there is any corresponding distinction between two sorts of names or objects.

We can, I think, easily obtain a clearer idea of the difference between these two sorts of incomplete symbols (Wittgenstein calls them 'expressions') typified by 'Socrates' and 'wise'. Let us consider when and why an expression occurs, as it were, as an isolated unit. For instance '*aRb*' does not naturally divide into '*a*' and '*Rb*', and we want to know why anyone should so divide it and isolate the expression '*Rb*'. The answer is that if it were a matter of this proposition alone, there would be no point in dividing it in this way, but that the importance of expressions arises, as Wittgenstein points out, just in connection with generalization. It is not '*aRb*' but '$(x).xRb$' which makes *Rb* prominent. In writing $(x).xRb$ we use the expression *Rb* to collect together the set of propositions *xRb* which we want to assert to be true; and it is here that the expression *Rb* is really essential because it is this which is common to this set of propositions. If now we realize that this is the essential use of expressions, we can see at once what is the difference between Socrates and wise. By means of the expression 'Socrates' we collect together all the propositions in which it occurs, that is, all the propositions which we should ordinarily say were about Socrates, such as 'Socrates is wise', 'Socrates is just', 'Socrates is neither wise nor just'. These propositions are collected together as the values of 'ϕ Socrates', where ϕ is a variable.

Now consider the expression 'wise'; this we use to collect together the propositions 'Socrates is wise', 'Plato is wise', and so on, which are values of 'x is wise'. But this is not the only collection we can use 'wise' to form; just as we used 'Socrates' to collect all the propositions in which it occurred, we can use 'wise' to collect all those in which it occurs, including not only ones like 'Socrates is wise' but also ones like 'Neither Socrates nor Plato is wise', which are not values of 'x is wise' but only of the different function 'ϕ wise', where ϕ is variable. Thus whereas Socrates gives only one collection of propositions, wise gives two: one analogous to that given by Socrates, namely the collection of all propositions in which wise occurs; and the other a narrower collection of propositions of the form 'x is wise'.

This is obviously the explanation of the difference we feel between Socrates and wise which Mr Russell expresses by saying that with wise you have to bring in the form of a proposition. Since all expressions must be completed to form a proposition, it was previously hard to understand how wise could be more incomplete than Socrates. Now we can see that the reason for this is that whereas with 'Socrates' we only have the idea of completing it in any manner into a proposition, with 'wise' we have not only this but also an idea of completing it in a special way, giving us not merely any proposition in which wise occurs but also one in which it occurs in a particular way, which we may call its occurrence as predicate, as in 'Socrates is wise'.

What is this difference due to, and is it a real difference at all? That is to say, can we not do with 'Socrates' what we do with 'wise', and use it to collect a set of propositions narrower than the whole set in which it occurs? Is this impossible, or is it merely that we never in fact do it? These are the questions we must now try to answer. The way to do it would seem to be the following. Suppose we can distinguish among the properties of Socrates a certain subset which we can call qualities, the idea being roughly that only a simple property is a quality. Then we could form in connection with 'Socrates' two sets of propositions just as we can in connection with 'wise'. There would be the wide set of propositions in which 'Socrates' occurs at all, which we say assert properties of Socrates, but also there would be the narrower set which assert qualities of Socrates. Thus supposing justice and wisdom to be qualities, 'Socrates is wise', 'Socrates is just' would belong to the narrower set and be values of a function 'Socrates is q'. But 'Socrates is neither wise nor just' would not assert a quality of Socrates but only a compound characteristic or property, and would only be a value of the function 'ϕ Socrates', not of 'Socrates is q'.

But although such a distinction between qualities and properties may be logically possible, we do not seem ever to carry it out systematically. Some light may be thrown on this fact by a paragraph in Mr Johnson's *Logic* in which he argues that, whereas 'we may properly construct a compound adjective out of simple adjectives, yet the nature of any term functioning as a substantive is such that it is impossible to construct a genuine compound substantive'.[6] Thus from the two propositions 'Socrates is wise', 'Socrates is just' we can form the proposition 'Neither is Socrates wise nor is Socrates just', or, for short, 'Socrates is neither wise nor just'; which still, according to Mr Johnson, predicates an adjective of Socrates, is a value of 'ϕ Socrates' and would justify '$(\exists\phi).\phi$ Socrates', or 'Socrates has some property'. If, on the other hand, we take the two propositions 'Socrates is wise', 'Plato is wise' and form from them 'Neither Socrates is wise nor Plato is wise'; this is not a value of 'x is wise' and would not justify '$(\exists x).x$ is wise', or 'Someone is wise'. So inasmuch as 'Socrates is neither wise nor just' justifies 'Socrates has some adjective' we can say that 'neither wise

[6] *Part II*, p. 61.

nor just' is a compound adjective; but since 'Neither Socrates nor Plato is wise' does not justify 'something is wise', 'neither Socrates nor Plato' cannot be a compound substantive any more than nobody is a compound man.

If, however, we could form a range of qualities as opposed to properties, 'Socrates is neither wise nor just' would not justify 'Socrates has some quality' and 'neither wise nor just' would not be a quality. Against this Mr Johnson says that there is no universally valid criterion by which we can distinguish qualities from other properties; and this is certainly a very plausible contention when we are talking, as we are now, of qualities and properties of logical constructions such as Socrates. For the distinction is only really clear in connection with genuine objects; then we can say that ϕ represents a quality when ϕa is a two-termed atomic proposition, and this would distinguish qualities from other propositional functions or properties. But when the subject a is a logical construction and ϕa a compound proposition of which we do not know the analysis, it is hard to know what would be meant by asking if ϕ were simple, and calling it, if simple, a quality. It would clearly have to be a matter not of absolute but of relative simplicity.

Yet it is easy to see that, in theory, an analogous distinction can certainly be made for incomplete symbols also. Take any incomplete symbol 'α'; this will be defined not in isolation but in conjunction with any symbol of a certain sort x. Thus we might define αx to mean aRx. Then this incomplete symbol 'α' will give us two ranges of propositions: the range αx obtained by completing it in the way indicated in its definition; and the general range of propositions in which α occurs at all, that is to say, all truth-functions of the propositions of the preceding range and constant propositions not containing α. Thus in the two famous cases of descriptions and classes, as treated in *Principia Mathematica*, the narrower range will be that in which the description or class has primary occurrence, the wider range that in which it has any sort of occurrence primary or secondary, where the terms 'primary' and 'secondary' occurrence have the meanings explained in *Principia*. In brief with regard to any incomplete symbol we can distinguish its primary and secondary occurrences, and this is fundamentally the same distinction which we found to be characteristic of the adjective. So that any incomplete symbol is really an adjective, and those which appear substantives only do so in virtue of our failing whether through inability or neglect to distinguish their primary and secondary occurrences. As a practical instance let us take the case of material objects; these we are accustomed to regard as substantives, that is to say we use them to define ranges of propositions in one way only, and make no distinction between their primary and secondary occurrences. At least no one made such a distinction until Dr Whitehead declared that material objects are adjectives of the events in which they are situated, so that the primary occurrence of a material object A is in a proposition 'A is situated in E'. From such propositions as this we can construct all other propositions in which A occurs. Thus 'A is red' will be 'For all E, A is situated in E implies redness is situated in E', in which A has secondary occurrence. So the distinction between primary and secondary occurrence is not merely demonstrated as logically necessary, but for this case effected practically.

The conclusion is that, as regards incomplete symbols, the fundamental distinction is not between substantive and adjective but between primary and secondary occurrence; and that a substantive is simply a logical construction between whose primary and secondary occurrences we fail to distinguish. So that to be a substantive is not an objective but a subjective property in the sense that it depends not indeed on any one mind but on the common elements in all men's minds and purposes.

This is my first conclusion, which is I think of some importance in the philosophy of nature and of mind; but it is not the conclusion which I most want to stress, and it does not answer the question with which I began my paper. For it is a conclusion about the method and possibility of dividing certain logical constructions into substantives and adjectives, it being in connection with these logical constructions that the idea of substantive and adjective traditionally originated. But the real question at issue is the possibility of dividing not logical constructions but genuine objects into particulars and universals, and to answer this we must go back and pick up the thread of the argument, where we abandoned it for this lengthy digression about logical constructions.

We saw above that the distinction between particular and universal was derived from that between subject and predicate which we found only to occur in atomic propositions. We then examined the three theories of atomic propositions or rather of atomic facts, Mr Johnson's theory of a tie, Mr Russell's that the copulation is performed by universals, of which there must be one and only one in each atomic fact, and Mr Wittgenstein's that the objects hang in one another like the links of a chain. We observed that of these theories only Mr Russell's really assigned a different function to subject and predicate and so gave meaning to the distinction between them, and we proceeded to discuss this theory. We found that to Mr Johnson's criticisms Mr Russell had two possible answers; one being to argue that his theory alone took account of the difference we feel there to be between Socrates and wisdom, the other that his notation was far more convenient than any other and must therefore correspond more closely to the facts. We then took the first of these arguments, and examined the difference between Socrates and wisdom. This we found to consist in the fact that whereas Socrates determined only one range of propositions in which it occurred, wise determined two such ranges, the complete range 'f wise', and the narrower range 'x is wise'. We then examined the reason for this difference between the two incomplete symbols Socrates and wise, and decided that it was of a subjective character and depended on human interests and needs.

What we have now to consider is whether the difference between Socrates and wise has any such bearing on the composition of atomic facts as Mr Russell alleges it to have. This we can usefully combine with the consideration of Mr Russell's other possible argument from the superior convenience of his symbolism. The essence of this symbolism, as Mr Johnson has observed, consists in not letting the adjective stand alone, but making it a propositional function by attaching it to a variable x. A possible advantage of this procedure at once suggests itself in terms of our previous treatment of the difference between substantive and adjective; namely, that attaching the variable x helps us to make the distinction we require to make in the case of the adjective, but not in the case of the substantive, between the values of ϕx and those of $f(\phi\hat{z})$ where f is variable. Only so, it might be said, can we distinguish $(x).\phi x$ from $(f).f(\phi\hat{z})$. But very little consideration is required to see that this advantage is very slight and of no fundamental importance. We could easily make the distinction in other ways; for instance by determining that if the variable came after the ϕ it should mean what we now express by ϕx, but if before the ϕ what we express by $f(\phi\hat{z})$; or simply by deciding to use the letters 'x', 'y', 'z', in one case, 'f', 'g', 'h', in the other.

But, although this supposed advantage in the functional symbolism is imaginary, there is a reason which renders it absolutely indispensable. Take such a property as 'either having R to a, or having S to b'; it would be absolutely impossible to represent this by a simple symbol 'ϕ'. For how then could we define ϕ? We could not put $\phi=Ra. \vee .Sb$ because we should not know whether the blanks were to be filled with the same or different arguments, and so whether ϕ was to be a property or relation. Instead we must put $\phi x.=.xRa. \vee .xSb$; which explains not what is meant by ϕ by itself but that followed by any symbol x it is short for $xRa. \vee .xSb$. And this is the reason which makes inevitable the introduction of propositional functions. It simply means that in such a case 'ϕ' is not a name but an incomplete symbol and cannot be defined in isolation or allowed to stand by itself.

But this conclusion about $xRa. \vee .xSb$ will not apply to all propositional functions. If ϕa is a two-termed atomic proposition, 'ϕ' is a name of the term other than a, and can perfectly well stand by itself; so, it will be asked, why do we write 'ϕx' instead of 'ϕ' in this case also? The reason for this lies in a fundamental characteristic of mathematical logic, its extensionality, by which I mean its primary interest in classes and relations in extension. Now if in any proposition whatever we change any individual name into a variable, the resulting propositional function defines a class; and the class may be the same for two functions of quite different forms, in one of which 'ϕ' is an incomplete symbol, in the other a name. So mathematical logic, being only interested in functions as a means to classes, sees no need to distinguish these two sorts of functions, because the difference between them, though all-important to philosophy, will not correspond to any difference between the classes they define. So because some ϕ's are incomplete and cannot stand alone, and all ϕ's are to be treated alike in order to avoid useless complication, the only solution is to allow none to stand alone.

Such is the justification of Mr Russell's practice; but it is also the refutation of his theory, which fails to appreciate the distinction between those functions which are names and those which are incomplete symbols, a distinction which, as remarked above, though immaterial for mathematics is essential for philosophy. I do not mean that Mr Russell would now deny this distinction; on the contrary it is clear from the second edition of *Principia* that he would accept it; but I think that his present theory of universals is the relic of his previous failure to appreciate it.

It will be remembered that we found two possible arguments for his theory of universals. One was from the efficiency of the functional notation; this clearly lapses because, as we have seen, the functional notation merely overlooks an essential distinction which happens not to interest the mathematician, and the fact that some functions cannot stand alone is no argument that all cannot. The other argument was from the difference we feel between Socrates and wise, which corresponds to a difference in his logical system between individuals and functions. Just as Socrates determines one range of propositions, but wise two, so a determines the one range ϕa, but $\phi \hat{z}$ the two ranges ϕx and $f(\phi \hat{z})$. But what is this difference between individuals and functions due to? Again simply to the fact that certain things do not interest the mathematician. Anyone who was interested not only in classes of things, but also in their qualities, would want to distinguish from among the others those functions which were names; and if we called the objects of which they are names qualities, and denoted a variable quality by q, we should have not only the range ϕa but also the narrower range qa, and the difference analogous to that between 'Socrates' and 'wisdom' would have disappeared. We should have complete symmetry between qualities and individuals; each could have names which could stand alone, each would determine two ranges of propositions, for a would determine the ranges qa and ϕa, where q and ϕ are variables, and q would determine the ranges qx and fq, where x and f are variables.

So were it not for the mathematician's biased interest he would invent a symbolism which was completely symmetrical as regards individuals and qualities; and it becomes clear that there is no sense in the words individual and quality; all we are talking about is two different types of objects, such that two objects, one of each type, could be sole constituents of an atomic fact. The two types being in every way symmetrically related, nothing can be meant by calling one type the type of individuals and the other that of qualities, and these two words are devoid of connotation.

To this, however, various objections might be made which must be briefly dealt with. First it might be said that the two terms of such an atomic fact must be connected by the characterizing tie and/or the relation of characterization, which are asymmetrical, and distinguish their relata into individuals and qualities. Against this I would say that the relation of characterization is simply a verbal fiction. 'q characterizes a' means no more and no less than 'a is q', it is merely a lengthened verbal form; and since the relation of characterization is admittedly not a constituent of 'a is q' it cannot be anything at all. As regards the tie, I cannot understand what sort of thing it could be, and prefer Wittgenstein's view that in the atomic fact the objects are connected together without the help of any mediator. This does not mean that the fact is simply the collection of its constituents but that it consists in their union without any mediating tie. There is one more objection suggested by Mr Russell's treatment in the new edition of *Principia*. He there says that all atomic propositions are of the forms $R_1(x)$, $R_2(x,y)$, $R_3(x,y,z)$, etc., and so can *define* individuals as terms which can occur in propositions with any number of terms; whereas of course an n-termed relation could only occur in a proposition with $n+1$ terms. But this assumes his theory as to the constitution of atomic facts, that each must contain a term of a special kind, called a universal; a theory we found to be utterly groundless. The truth is that we know and can know nothing whatever about the forms of atomic propositions; we do not know whether some or all objects can occur in more than one form of atomic proposition; and there is obviously no way of deciding any such question. We cannot even tell that there are not atomic facts consisting of two terms of the same type. It might be thought that this would involve us in a vicious circle contradiction, but a little reflection will show that it does not, for the contradictions due to letting a function be its own argument only arise when we take for argument a function containing a negation which is therefore an incomplete symbol not the name of an object.

In conclusion let us describe from this new point of view the procedure of the mathematical logician. He takes any type of objects whatever as the subject of his reasoning, and calls them individuals, meaning by that simply that he has chosen this type to reason about, though he might equally well have chosen any other type and called them individuals. The results of replacing names of these individuals in propositions by variables he then calls functions, irrespective of whether the constant part of the function is a name or an incomplete symbol, because this does not make any difference to the class which the function defines. The failure to make this distinction has led to these functional symbols, some of which are names and some incomplete, being treated all alike as names of incomplete objects or properties, and is responsible for that great muddle the theory of universals. Of all philosophers Wittgenstein alone has seen through this muddle and declared that about the forms of atomic propositions we can know nothing whatever.

NOTE ON THE PRECEDING PAPER[7]

When I wrote my article I was sure that it was impossible to discover atomic propositions by actual analysis. Of this I am now very doubtful, and I cannot therefore be sure that they may not be discovered to be all of one or other of a series of forms which can be expressed by $R_1(x)$, $R_2(x,y)$, $R_3(x,y,z)$, etc., in which case we could, as Mr Russell has suggested, define individuals as terms which can occur in propositions of any of these forms, universals as terms which can only occur in one form. This I admit may be found to be the case, but as no one can as yet be certain what sort of atomic propositions there are, it cannot be positively asserted; and there is no strong presumption in its favour, for I think that the argument of my article establishes that nothing of the sort can be known *a priori*.

And this is a matter of some importance, for philosophers such as Mr Russell have thought that, although they did not know into what ultimate terms propositions are analysable, these terms must nevertheless be divisible into universals and particulars, categories which are used in philosophical investigations as if it were certain *a priori* that they would be applicable. This certainly seems to be derived primarily from the supposition that there must be a difference between ultimate objects

---

[7] [Part of Ramsey's contribution to a symposium on 'Universals and the "Method of Analysis"', *Aristotelian Society Supplementary Volume*, 6 (1926), 17–26.]

analogous to one felt to subsist between such terms as Socrates and wise; and to see if this can reasonably be maintained, we must discover what difference there is between Socrates and wise analogous to the distinction made in Mr Russell's system between particulars and universals.

If we consider the development of Mr Russell's system of logic, as expounded in the Introduction to the second edition of *Principia Mathematica*, we can see what difference there is in his treatment of particulars and universals. We find that universals always occur as propositional functions, which serve to determine ranges of propositions, especially the range of values of the function ϕx, and the range of functions of the function $f(\phi \hat{x})$ (where f is variable). Individuals also serve to determine ranges of propositions, but in this case there is only one principal range, the range of functions of the individual ϕa (ϕ variable). We could make a narrower range, as Mr Russell points out, by using a variable quality, but we have no need to do so. Now this is the only difference between the way individuals and universals function in his system, and as we find that there is a precisely similar difference between Socrates and wise, it is probable that we have here the essence of the matter. Wise, like a ϕx in Mr Russell's system, determines the narrower range of propositions 'x is wise' and the wider one 'f wise', where the last range includes all propositions whatever in which wise occurs. Socrates, on the other hand, is only used to determine the wider range of propositions in which it occurs in any manner; we have no precise way of singling out any narrower range. We cannot do it by limiting it to propositions in which Socrates occurs as subject, because in any proposition in which he occurs he can be regarded as the subject: we can always regard the proposition as saying 'It is true of Socrates that — '. The point is that with Socrates the narrower range is missing. . . .

Nevertheless this difference between Socrates and wise is illusory, because it can be shown to be theoretically possible to make a similar narrower range for Socrates, though we have never needed to do this. Nevertheless, once this fact is observed, the difference between Socrates and wise lapses, and we begin, like Dr Whitehead, to call Socrates an adjective. If you think all or nearly all propositions about material objects are truth-functions of propositions about their location in events, then, on my view, you will regard material objects as adjectives of events. For that is the real meaning of the distinction between adjective and substantive. I do not say that the distinction has arisen from explicit reflection about the difference in regard to ranges of propositions, but that this difference obscurely felt is the source of the distinction. My view is strikingly confirmed by the case of Dr Whitehead, who, having made material objects analogous to wise in the way in question, then declared that they were adjectives.

V

ON WHAT THERE IS

W. V. QUINE

A curious thing about the ontological problem is its simplicity. It can be put in three Anglo-Saxon monosyllables: 'What is there?' It can be answered, moreover, in a word—'Everything'—and everyone will accept this answer as true. However, this is merely to say that there is what there is. There remains room for disagreement over cases; and so the issue has stayed alive down the centuries.

Suppose now that two philosophers, McX and I, differ over ontology. Suppose McX maintains there is something which I maintain there is not. McX can, quite consistently with his own point of view, describe our difference of opinion by saying that I refuse to recognize certain entities. I should protest, of course, that he is wrong in his formulation of our disagreement, for I maintain that there are no entities, of the kind which he alleges, for me to recognize; but my finding him wrong in his formulation of our disagreement is unimportant, for I am committed to considering him wrong in his ontology anyway.

When *I* try to formulate our difference of opinion, on the other hand, I seem to be in a predicament. I cannot admit that there are some things which McX countenances and I do not, for in admitting that there are such things I should be contradicting my own rejection of them.

It would appear, if this reasoning were sound, that in any ontological dispute the proponent of the negative side suffers the disadvantage of not being able to admit that his opponent disagrees with him.

This is the old Platonic riddle of nonbeing. Nonbeing must in some sense be, otherwise what is it that there is not? This tangled doctrine might be nicknamed *Plato's beard*; historically it has proved tough, frequently dulling the edge of Occam's razor.

It is some such line of thought that leads philosophers like McX to impute being where they might otherwise be quite content to recognize that there is nothing. Thus, take Pegasus. If Pegasus *were* not, McX argues,

First published in *Review of Metaphysics*, 2 (1948), 21–38, and reprinted in W. V. Quine, *From a Logical Point of View* (Cambridge, Mass.: Harvard University Press, 1953), 1–19. Reprinted by permission.

we should not be talking about anything when we use the word; therefore it would be nonsense to say even that Pegasus is not. Thinking to show thus that the denial of Pegasus cannot be coherently maintained, he concludes that Pegasus is.

McX cannot, indeed, quite persuade himself that any region of space-time, near or remote, contains a flying horse of flesh and blood. Pressed for further details on Pegasus, then, he says that Pegasus is an idea in men's minds. Here, however, a confusion begins to be apparent. We may for the sake of argument concede that there is an entity, and even a unique entity (though this is rather implausible), which is the mental Pegasus-idea; but this mental entity is not what people are talking about when they deny Pegasus.

McX never confuses the Parthenon with the Parthenon-idea. The Parthenon is physical; the Parthenon-idea is mental (according anyway to McX's version of ideas, and I have no better to offer). The Parthenon is visible; the Parthenon-idea is invisible. We cannot easily imagine two things more unlike, and less liable to confusion, than the Parthenon and the Parthenon-idea. But when we shift from the Parthenon to Pegasus, the confusion sets in—for no other reason than that McX would sooner be deceived by the crudest and most flagrant counterfeit than grant the nonbeing of Pegasus.

The notion that Pegasus must be, because it would otherwise be nonsense to say even that Pegasus is not, has been seen to lead McX into an elementary confusion. Subtler minds, taking the same precept as their starting point, come out with theories of Pegasus which are less patently misguided than McX's, and correspondingly more difficult to eradicate. One of these subtler minds is named, let us say, Wyman. Pegasus, Wyman maintains, has his being as an unactualized possible. When we say of Pegasus that there is no such thing, we are saying, more precisely, that Pegasus does not have the special attribute of actuality. Saying that Pegasus is not actual is on a par, logically, with saying that the Parthenon is not red; in either case we are saying something about an entity whose being is unquestioned.

Wyman, by the way, is one of those philosophers who have united in ruining the good old word 'exist'. Despite his espousal of unactualized possibles, he limits the word 'existence' to actuality—thus preserving an illusion of ontological agreement between himself and us who repudiate the rest of his bloated universe. We have all been prone to say, in our common-sense usage of 'exist', that Pegasus does not exist, meaning simply that there is no such entity at all. If Pegasus existed he would indeed be in space and time, but only because the word 'Pegasus' has spatio-temporal connotations, and not because 'exists' has spatio-temporal connotations. If spatio-temporal reference is lacking when we affirm the existence of the cube root of 27, this is simply because a cube root is not a spatio-temporal kind of thing, and not because we are being ambiguous in our use of 'exist'.[1] However, Wyman, in an ill-conceived effort to appear agreeable, genially grants us the nonexistence of Pegasus and then, contrary to what *we* meant by nonexistence of Pegasus, insists that Pegasus *is*. Existence is one thing, he says, and subsistence is another. The only way I know of coping with this obfuscation of issues is to *give* Wyman the word 'exist'. I'll try not to use it again; I still have 'is'. So much for lexicography; let's get back to Wyman's ontology.

Wyman's overpopulated universe is in many ways unlovely. It offends the aesthetic sense of us who have a taste for desert landscapes, but this is not the worst of it. Wyman's slum of possibles is a breeding ground for disorderly elements. Take, for instance, the possible fat man in that doorway; and, again, the possible bald man in that doorway. Are they the same possible man, or two possible men? How do we decide? How many possible men are there in that doorway? Are there more possible thin ones than fat ones? How many of them are alike? Or would their being alike make them one? Are no *two* possible things alike? Is this the same as saying that it is impossible for two things to be alike? Or, finally, is the concept of identity simply inapplicable to unactualized possibles? But what sense can be found in talking of entities which cannot meaningfully be said to be identical with themselves and distinct from one another? These elements are well-nigh incorrigible. By a Fregean therapy of individual concepts, some effort might be made at rehabilitation; but I feel we'd do better simply to clear Wyman's slum and be done with it.

Possibility, along with the other modalities of necessity and impossibility and contingency, raises problems upon which I do not mean to imply that we should turn our backs. But we can at least limit modalities to whole statements. We may impose the adverb 'possibly' upon a statement as a whole, and we may well worry about the semantical analysis of such usage; but little real advance in such analysis is to be hoped for in expanding our universe to include so-called *possible entities*. I suspect that the main motive for this expansion is simply the old notion that Pegasus, for

---

[1] The impulse to distinguish terminologically between existence as applied to objects actualized somewhere in space-time and existence (or subsistence or being) as applied to other entities arises in part, perhaps, from an idea that the observation of nature is relevant only to questions of existence of the first kind. But this idea is readily refuted by counter-instances such as 'the ratio of the number of centaurs to the number of unicorns'. If there were such a ratio, it would be an abstract entity, viz. a number. Yet it is only by studying nature that we conclude that the number of centaurs and the number of unicorns are both 0 and hence that there is no such ratio.

example, must be because otherwise it would be nonsense to say even that he is not.

Still, all the rank luxuriance of Wyman's universe of possibles would seem to come to naught when we make a slight change in the example and speak not of Pegasus but of the round square cupola on Berkeley College. If, unless Pegasus were, it would be nonsense to say that he is not, then by the same token, unless the round square cupola on Berkeley College were, it would be nonsense to say that it is not. But, unlike Pegasus, the round square cupola on Berkeley College cannot be admitted even as an un-actualized *possible*. Can we drive Wyman now to admitting also a realm of unactualizable impossibles? If so, a good many embarrassing questions could be asked about them. We might hope even to trap Wyman in contradictions, by getting him to admit that certain of these entities are at once round and square. But the wily Wyman chooses the other horn of the dilemma and concedes that it is nonsense to say that the round square cupola on Berkeley College is not. He says that the phrase 'round square cupola' is meaningless.

Wyman was not the first to embrace this alternative. The doctrine of the meaninglessness of contradictions runs away back. The tradition survives, moreover, in writers who seem to share none of Wyman's motivations. Still, I wonder whether the first temptation to such a doctrine may not have been substantially the motivation which we have observed in Wyman. Certainly the doctrine has no intrinsic appeal; and it has led its devotees to such quixotic extremes as that of challenging the method of proof by *reductio ad absurdum*—a challenge in which I sense a *reductio ad absurdum* of the doctrine itself.

Moreover, the doctrine of meaninglessness of contradictions has the severe methodological drawback that it makes it impossible, in principle, ever to devise an effective test of what is meaningful and what is not. It would be forever impossible for us to devise systematic ways of deciding whether a string of signs made sense—even to us individually, let alone other people—or not. For it follows from a discovery in mathematical logic, due to Church, that there can be no generally applicable test of contradictoriness.[2]

I have spoken disparagingly of Plato's beard, and hinted that it is tangled. I have dwelt at length on the inconveniences of putting up with it. It is time to think about taking steps.

Russell, in his theory of so-called singular descriptions, showed clearly how we might meaningfully use seeming names without supposing that

[2] Alonzo Church, 'A Note on the Entscheidungsproblem', *Journal of Symbolic Logic*, 1 (1936), pp. 40 f., 101 f.

there be the entities allegedly named. The names to which Russell's theory directly applies are complex descriptive names such as 'the author of *Waverley*', 'the present King of France', 'the round square cupola on Berkeley College'. Russell analyses such phrases systematically as fragments of the whole sentences in which they occur. The sentence 'The author of *Waverley* was a poet', for example, is explained as a whole as meaning 'Someone (better: something) wrote *Waverley* and was a poet, and nothing else wrote *Waverley*'. (The point of this added clause is to affirm the uniqueness which is implicit in the word 'the', in '*the* author of *Waverley*'.) The sentence 'The round square cupola on Berkeley College is pink' is explained as 'Something is round and square and is a cupola on Berkeley College and is pink, and nothing else is round and square and a cupola on Berkeley College'.

The virtue of this analysis is that the seeming name, a descriptive phrase, is paraphrased in *context* as a so-called incomplete symbol. No unified expression is offered as an analysis of the descriptive phrase, but the statement as a whole which was the context of that phrase still gets its full quota of meaning—whether true or false.

The unanalysed statement 'The author of *Waverley* was a poet' contains a part, 'the author of *Waverley*', which is wrongly supposed by McX and Wyman to demand objective reference in order to be meaningful at all. But in Russell's translation, 'Something wrote *Waverley* and was a poet and nothing else wrote *Waverley*', the burden of objective reference which had been put upon the descriptive phrase is now taken over by words of the kind that logicians call bound variables, variables of quantification, namely, words like 'something', 'nothing', 'everything'. These words, far from purporting to be names specifically of the author of *Waverley*, do not purport to be names at all; they refer to entities generally, with a kind of studied ambiguity peculiar to themselves. These quantificational words or bound variables are, of course a basic part of language, and their meaningfulness, at least in context, is not to be challenged. But their meaningfulness in no way presupposes there being either the author of *Waverley* or the round square cupola on Berkeley College or any other specifically preassigned objects.

Where descriptions are concerned, there is no longer any difficulty in affirming or denying being. 'There *is* the author of *Waverley*' is explained by Russell as meaning 'Someone (or, more strictly, something) wrote *Waverley* and nothing else wrote *Waverley*'. 'The author of *Waverley* is not' is explained, correspondingly, as the alternation 'Either each thing failed to write *Waverley* or two or more things wrote *Waverley*'. This alternation is false, but meaningful; and it contains no expression purporting to name the author of *Waverley*. The statement 'The round square cupola on

Berkeley College is not' is analysed in similar fashion. So the old notion that statements of nonbeing defeat themselves goes by the board. When a statement of being or nonbeing is analysed by Russell's theory of descriptions, it ceases to contain any expression which even purports to name the alleged entity whose being is in question, so that the meaningfulness of the statement no longer can be thought to presuppose that there be such an entity.

Now what of 'Pegasus'? This being a word rather than a descriptive phrase, Russell's argument does not immediately apply to it. However, it can easily be made to apply. We have only to rephrase 'Pegasus' as a description, in any way that seems adequately to single out our idea; say, 'the winged horse that was captured by Bellerophon'. Substituting such a phrase for 'Pegasus', we can then proceed to analyse the statement 'Pegasus is', or 'Pegasus is not', precisely on the analogy of Russell's analysis of 'The author of *Waverley* is' and 'The author of *Waverley* is not'.

In order thus to subsume a one-word name or alleged name such as 'Pegasus' under Russell's theory of description, we must, of course, be able first to translate the word into a description. But this is no real restriction. If the notion of Pegasus had been so obscure or so basic a one that no pat translation into a descriptive phrase had offered itself along familiar lines, we could still have availed ourselves of the following artificial and trivial-seeming device: we could have appealed to the *ex hypothesi* unanalysable, irreducible attribute of *being Pegasus*, adopting, for its expression, the verb 'is-Pegasus', or 'pegasizes'. The noun 'Pegasus' itself could then be treated as derivative, and identified after all with a description: 'the thing that is-Pegasus', 'the thing that pegasizes'.

If the importing of such a predicate as 'pegasizes' seems to commit us to recognizing that there is a corresponding attribute, pegasizing, in Plato's heaven or in the minds of men, well and good. Neither we nor Wyman nor McX have been contending thus far, about the being or nonbeing of universals, but rather about that of Pegasus. If in terms of pegasizing we can interpret the noun 'Pegasus' as a description subject to Russell's theory of descriptions, then we have disposed of the old notion that Pegasus cannot be said not to be without presupposing that in some sense Pegasus is.

Our argument is now quite general. McX and Wyman supposed that we could not meaningfully affirm a statement of the form 'So-and-so is not', with a simple or descriptive singular noun in place of 'so-and-so', unless so-and-so is. This supposition is now seen to be quite generally groundless, since the singular noun in question can always be expanded into a singular description, trivially or otherwise, and then analysed out *à la* Russell.

We commit ourselves to an ontology containing numbers when we say there are prime numbers larger than a million; we commit ourselves to an ontology containing centaurs when we say there are centaurs; and we commit ourselves to an ontology containing Pegasus when we say Pegasus is. But we do not commit ourselves to an ontology containing Pegasus or the author of *Waverley* or the round square cupola on Berkeley College when we say that Pegasus or the author of *Waverley* or the cupola in question is *not*. We need no longer labor under the delusion that the meaningfulness of a statement containing a singular term presupposes an entity named by the term. A singular term need not name to be significant.

An inkling of this might have dawned on Wyman and McX even without benefit of Russell if they had only noticed—as so few of us do—that there is a gulf between *meaning* and *naming* even in the case of a singular term which is genuinely a name of an object. The following example from Frege will serve.[3] The phrase 'Evening Star' names a certain large physical object of spherical form, which is hurtling through space some scores of millions of miles from here. The phrase 'Morning Star' names the same thing, as was probably first established by some observant Babylonian. But the two phrases cannot be regarded as having the same meaning; otherwise that Babylonian could have dispensed with his observations and contented himself with reflecting on the meanings of his words. The meanings, then, being different from one another, must be other than the named object, which is one and the same in both cases.

Confusion of meaning with naming not only made McX think he could not meaningfully repudiate Pegasus; a continuing confusion of meaning with naming no doubt helped engender his absurd notion that Pegasus is an idea, a mental entity. The structure of his confusion is as follows. He confused the alleged *named object* Pegasus with the *meaning* of the word 'Pegasus', therefore concluding that Pegasus must be in order that the word have meaning. But what sorts of things are meanings? This is a moot point; however, one might quite plausibly explain meanings as ideas in the mind, supposing we can make clear sense in turn of the idea of ideas in the mind. Therefore Pegasus, initially confused with a meaning, ends up as an idea in the mind. It is the more remarkable that Wyman, subject to the same initial motivation as McX, should have avoided this particular blunder and wound up with unactualized possibles instead.

Now let us turn to the ontological problem of universals: the question whether there are such entities as attributes, relations, classes, numbers,

---

[3] Gottlob Frege, 'On Sense and Nomination', in *Readings in Philosophical Analysis*, edited by Herbert Feigl and Wilfrid Sellars (New York: Appleton-Century-Crofts, 1949), 85–102. Translation of 'Ueber Sinn und Bedeutung', *Zeitschrift für Philosophie und Philosophische Kritik*, 100 (1892), 25–50.

functions. McX, characteristically enough, thinks there are. Speaking of attributes, he says: 'There are red houses, red roses, red sunsets; this much is prephilosophical common sense in which we must all agree. These houses, roses, and sunsets, then, have something in common; and this which they have in common is all I mean by the attribute of redness.' For McX, thus, there being attributes is even more obvious and trivial than the obvious and trivial fact of there being red houses, roses, and sunsets. This, I think, is characteristic of metaphysics, or at least of that part of metaphysics called ontology: one who regards a statement on this subject as true at all must regard it as trivially true. One's ontology is basic to the conceptual scheme by which he interprets all experiences, even the most commonplace ones. Judged within some particular conceptual scheme—and how else is judgement possible?—an ontological statement goes without saying, standing in need of no separate justification at all. Ontological statements follow immediately from all manner of casual statements of commonplace fact, just as—from the point of view, anyway, of McX's conceptual scheme—'There is an attribute' follows from 'There are red houses, red roses, red sunsets'.

Judged in another conceptual scheme, an ontological statement which is axiomatic to McX's mind may, with equal immediacy and triviality, be adjudged false. One may admit that there are red houses, roses, and sunsets, but deny, except as a popular and misleading manner of speaking, that they have anything in common. The words 'houses', 'roses', and 'sunsets' are true of sundry individual entities which are houses and roses and sunsets, and the word 'red' or 'red object' is true of each of sundry individual entities which are red houses, red roses, red sunsets; but there is not, in addition, any entity whatever, individual or otherwise, which is named by the word 'redness', nor, for that matter, by the word 'househood', 'rosehood', 'sunsethood'. That the houses and roses and sunsets are all of them red may be taken as ultimate and irreducible, and it may be held that McX is no better off, in point of real explanatory power, for all the occult entities which he posits under such names as 'redness'.

One means by which McX might naturally have tried to impose his ontology of universals on us was already removed before we turned to the problem of universals. McX cannot argue that predicates such as 'red' or 'is-red', which we all concur in using, must be regarded as names each of a single universal entity in order that they be meaningful at all. For we have seen that being a name of something is a much more special feature than being meaningful. He cannot even charge us—at least not by *that* argument—with having posited an attribute of pegasizing by our adoption of the predicate 'pegasizes'.

However, McX hits upon a different stratagem. 'Let us grant', he says, 'this distinction between meaning and naming of which you make so much. Let us even grant that "is red", "pegasizes", etc., are not names of attributes. Still, you admit they have meanings. But these *meanings*, whether they are *named* or not, are still universals, and I venture to say that some of them might even be the very things that I call attributes, or something to much the same purpose in the end.'

For McX, this is an unusually penetrating speech; and the only way I know to counter it is by refusing to admit meanings. However, I feel no reluctance toward refusing to admit meanings, for I do not thereby deny that words and statements are meaningful. McX and I may agree to the letter in our classification of linguistic forms into the meaningful and the meaningless, even though McX construes meaningfulness as the *having* (in some sense of 'having') of some abstract entity which he calls a meaning, whereas I do not. I remain free to maintain that the fact that a given linguistic utterance is meaningful (or *significant*, as I prefer to say so as not to invite hypostasis of meanings as entities) is an ultimate and irreducible matter of fact; or, I may undertake to analyse it in terms directly of what people do in the presence of the linguistic utterance in question and other utterances similar to it.

The useful ways in which people ordinarily talk or seem to talk about meanings boil down to two: the *having* of meanings, which is significance, and *sameness* of meaning, or synonymy. What is called *giving* the meaning of an utterance is simply the uttering of a synonym, couched, ordinarily, in clearer language than the original. If we are allergic to meanings as such, we can speak directly of utterances as significant or insignificant, and as synonymous or heteronymous one with another. The problem of explaining these adjectives 'significant' and 'synonymous' with some degree of clarity and rigor—preferably, as I see it, in terms of behavior— is as difficult as it is important. But the explanatory value of special and irreducible intermediary entities called meanings is surely illusory.

Up to now I have argued that we can use singular terms significantly in sentences without presupposing that there are the entities which those terms purport to name. I have argued further that we can use general terms, for example, predicates, without conceding them to be names of abstract entities. I have argued further that we can view utterances as significant, and as synonymous or heteronymous with one another, without countenancing a realm of entities called meanings. At this point McX begins to wonder whether there is any limit at all to our ontological immunity. Does *nothing* we may say commit us to the assumption of universals or other entities which we may find unwelcome?

I have already suggested a negative answer to this question, in speaking of bound variables, or variables of quantification, in connection with Russell's theory of descriptions. We can very easily involve ourselves in ontological commitments by saying, for example, that *there is something* (bound variable) which red houses and sunsets have in common; or that *there is something* which is a prime number larger than a million. But this is, essentially, the *only* way we can involve ourselves in ontological commitments: by our use of bound variables. The use of alleged names is no criterion, for we can repudiate their namehood at the drop of a hat unless the assumption of a corresponding entity can be spotted in the things we affirm in terms of bound variables. Names are, in fact, altogether immaterial to the ontological issue, for I have shown, in connection with 'Pegasus' and 'pegasize', that names can be converted to descriptions, and Russell has shown that descriptions can be eliminated. Whatever we say with the help of names can be said in a language which shuns names altogether. To be assumed as an entity is, purely and simply, to be reckoned as the value of a variable. In terms of the categories of traditional grammar, this amounts roughly to saying that to be is to be in the range of reference of a pronoun. Pronouns are the basic media of reference; nouns might better have been named propronouns. The variables of quantification, 'something', 'nothing', 'everything', range over our whole ontology, whatever it may be; and we are convicted of a particular ontological presupposition if, and only if, the alleged presuppositum has to be reckoned among the entities over which our variables range in order to render one of our affirmations true.

We may say, for example, that some dogs are white and not thereby commit ourselves to recognizing either doghood or whiteness as entities. 'Some dogs are white' says that some things that are dogs are white; and, in order that this statement be true, the things over which the bound variable 'something' ranges must include some white dogs, but need not include doghood or whiteness. On the other hand, when we say that some zoological species are cross-fertile we are committing ourselves to recognizing as entities the several species themselves, abstract though they are. We remain so committed at least until we devise some way of so paraphrasing the statement as to show that the seeming reference to species on the part of our bound variable was an avoidable manner of speaking.

Classical mathematics, as the example of primes larger than a million clearly illustrates, is up to its neck in commitments to an ontology of abstract entities. Thus it is that the great mediaeval controversy over universals has flared up anew in the modern philosophy of mathematics. The issue is clearer now than of old, because we now have a more explicit standard whereby to decide what ontology a given theory or form of discourse is committed to: a theory is committed to those and only those entities to which the bound variables of the theory must be capable of referring in order that the affirmations made in the theory be true.

Because this standard of ontological presupposition did not emerge clearly in the philosophical tradition, the modern philosophical mathematicians have not on the whole recognized that they were debating the same old problem of universals in a newly clarified form. But the fundamental cleavages among modern points of view on foundations of mathematics do come down pretty explicitly to disagreements as to the range of entities to which the bound variables should be permitted to refer.

The three main mediaeval points of view regarding universals are designated by historians as *realism, conceptualism*, and *nominalism*. Essentially these same three doctrines reappear in twentieth-century surveys of the philosophy of mathematics under the new names *logicism, intuitionism*, and *formalism*.

Realism, as the word is used in connection with the mediaeval controversy over universals, is the Platonic doctrine that universals or abstract entities have being independently of the mind; the mind may discover them but cannot create them. *Logicism*, represented by Frege, Russell, Whitehead, Church, and Carnap, condones the use of bound variables to refer to abstract entities known and unknown, specifiable and unspecifiable, indiscriminately.

Conceptualism holds that there are universals but they are mind-made. *Intuitionism*, espoused in modern times in one form or another by Poincaré, Brouwer, Weyl, and others, countenances the use of bound variables to refer to abstract entities only when those entities are capable of being cooked up individually from ingredients specified in advance. As Fraenkel has put it, logicism holds that classes are discovered while intuitionism holds that they are invented—a fair statement indeed of the old opposition between realism and conceptualism. This opposition is no mere quibble; it makes an essential difference in the amount of classical mathematics to which one is willing to subscribe. Logicists, or realists, are able on their assumptions to get Cantor's ascending orders of infinity; intuitionists are compelled to stop with the lowest order of infinity, and, as an indirect consequence, to abandon even some of the classical laws of real numbers. The modern controversy between logicism and intuitionism arose, in fact, from disagreements over infinity.

Formalism, associated with the name of Hilbert, echoes intuitionism in deploring the logicist's unbridled recourse to universals. But formalism also finds intuitionism unsatisfactory. This could happen for either of two opposite reasons. The formalist might, like the logicist, object to the crippling of classical mathematics; or he might, like the *nominalists* of old, object to admitting abstract entities at all, even in the restrained sense of mind-made entities. The upshot is the same: the formalist keeps classical mathematics as a play of insignificant notations. This play of notations can still be of utility—whatever utility it has already shown itself to have as a crutch for physicists and technologists. But utility need not imply significance, in any literal linguistic sense. Nor need the marked success of mathematicians in spinning out theorems, and in finding objective bases for agreement with one another's results, imply significance. For an adequate basis for agreement among mathematicians can be found simply in the rules which govern the manipulation of the notations—these syntactical rules being, unlike the notations themselves, quite significant and intelligible.[4]

I have argued that the sort of ontology we adopt can be consequential—notably in connection with mathematics, although this is only an example. Now how are we to adjudicate among rival ontologies? Certainly the answer is not provided by the semantical formula 'To be is to be the value of a variable'; this formula serves rather, conversely, in testing the conformity of a given remark or doctrine to a prior ontological standard. We look to bound variables in connection with ontology not in order to know what there is, but in order to know what a given remark or doctrine, ours or someone else's, *says* there is; and this much is quite properly a problem involving language. But what there is is another question.

In debating over what there is, there are still reasons for operating on a semantical plane. One reason is to escape from the predicament noted at the beginning of this essay: the predicament of my not being able to admit that there are things which McX countenances and I do not. So long as I adhere to my ontology, as opposed to McX's, I cannot allow my bound variable to refer to entities which belong to McX's ontology and not to mine. I can, however, consistently describe our disagreement by characterizing the statements which McX affirms. Provided merely that my ontology countenances linguistic forms, or at least concrete inscriptions and utterances, I can talk about McX's sentences.

Another reason for withdrawing to a semantical plane is to find common

[4] Nelson Goodman and W. V. Quine, 'Steps Toward a Constructive Nominalism', *Journal of Symbolic Logic*, 12 (1947), 105–22. For further discussion of the general matters touched on in the past two pages, see Paul Bernays, 'Sur le Platonisme dans les Mathématiques', *L'Enseignement Mathématique*, 34 (1935–6), 52–69; A. A. Fraenkel, 'Sur la Notion d'Existence dans les Mathématiques', *L'Enseignement Mathématique*, 34 (1935–6), 18–32; and Max Black, *The Nature of Mathematics* (London: Kegan Paul, 1933).

ground on which to argue. Disagreement in ontology involves basic disagreement in conceptual schemes; yet McX and I, despite these basic disagreements, find that our conceptual schemes converge sufficiently in their intermediate and upper ramifications to enable us to communicate successfully on such topics as politics, weather, and, in particular, language. In so far as our basic controversy over ontology can be translated upward into a semantical controversy about words and what to do with them, the collapse of the controversy into question-begging may be delayed.

It is no wonder, then, that ontological controversy should tend into controversy over language. But we must not jump to the conclusion that what there is depends on words. Translatability of a question into semantical terms is no indication that the question is linguistic. To see Naples is to bear a name which, when prefixed to the words 'sees Naples', yields a true sentence; still there is nothing linguistic about seeing Naples.

Our acceptance of an ontology is, I think, similar in principle to our acceptance of a scientific theory, say a system of physics: we adopt, at least in so far as are reasonable, the simplest conceptual scheme into which the disordered fragments of raw experience can be fitted and arranged. Our ontology is determined once we have fixed upon the over-all conceptual scheme which is to accommodate science in the broadest sense; and the considerations which determine a reasonable construction of any part of that conceptual scheme, for example, the biological or the physical part, are not different in kind from the considerations which determine a reasonable construction of the whole. To whatever extent the adoption of any system of scientific theory may be said to be a matter of language, the same—but no more—may be said of the adoption of an ontology.

But simplicity, as a guiding principle in constructing conceptual schemes, is not a clear and unambiguous idea; and it is quite capable of presenting a double or multiple standard. Imagine, for example, that we have devised the most economical set of concepts adequate to the play-by-play reporting of immediate experience. The entities under this scheme—the values of bound variables—are, let us suppose, individual subjective events of sensation or reflection. We should still find, no doubt, that a physicalistic conceptual scheme, purporting to talk about external objects, offers great advantages in simplifying our over-all reports. By bringing together scattered sense events and treating them as perceptions of one object, we reduce the complexity of our stream of experience to a manageable conceptual simplicity. The rule of simplicity is indeed our guiding maxim in assigning sense data to objects: we associate an earlier and a later round sensum with the same so-called penny, or with two different so-called pennies, in obedience to the demands of maximum simplicity in our total world-picture.

Here we have two competing conceptual schemes, a phenomenalistic one and a physicalistic one. Which should prevail? Each has its advantages; each has its special simplicity in its own way. Each, I suggest, deserves to be developed. Each may be said, indeed, to be the more fundamental, though in different senses: the one is epistemologically, the other physically, fundamental.

The physical conceptual scheme simplifies our account of experience because of the way myriad scattered sense events come to be associated with single so-called objects; still there is no likelihood that each sentence about physical objects can actually be translated, however deviously and complexly, into the phenomenalistic language. Physical objects are postulated entities which round out and simplify our account of the flux of experience, just as the introduction of irrational numbers simplifies laws of arithmetic. From the point of view of the conceptual scheme of the elementary arithmetic of rational numbers alone, the broader arithmetic of rational and irrational numbers would have the status of a convenient myth, simpler than the literal truth (namely, the arithmetic of rationals) and yet containing that literal truth as a scattered part. Similarly, from a phenomenalistic point of view, the conceptual scheme of physical objects is a convenient myth, simpler than the literal truth and yet containing that literal truth as a scattered part.[5]

Now what of classes or attributes of physical objects, in turn? A platonistic ontology of this sort is, from the point of view of a strictly physicalistic conceptual scheme, as much a myth as that physicalistic conceptual scheme itself is for phenomenalism. This higher myth is a good and useful one, in turn, in so far as it simplifies our account of physics. Since mathematics is an integral part of this higher myth, the utility of this myth for physical science is evident enough. In speaking of it nevertheless as a myth, I echo that philosophy of mathematics to which I alluded earlier under the name of formalism. But an attitude of formalism may with equal justice be adopted toward the physical conceptual scheme, in turn, by the pure aesthete or phenomenalist.

The analogy between the myth of mathematics and the myth of physics is, in some additional and perhaps fortuitous ways, strikingly close. Consider, for example, the crisis which was precipitated in the foundations of mathematics, at the turn of the century, by the discovery of Russell's paradox and other antinomies of set theory. These contradictions had to

---

[5] The arithmetical analogy is due to Philipp Frank, *Modern Science and its Philosophy* (Cambridge, Mass.: Harvard University Press, 1949), pp. 108 f.

be obviated by unintuitive, *ad hoc* devices; our mathematical myth-making became deliberate and evident to all. But what of physics? An antinomy arose between the undular and the corpuscular accounts of light; and if this was not as out-and-out a contradiction as Russell's paradox, I suspect that the reason is that physics is not as out-and-out as mathematics. Again, the second great modern crisis in the foundations of mathematics—precipitated in 1931 by Gödel's proof that there are bound to be undecidable statements in arithmetic[6]—has long had its companion piece in physics in Heisenberg's indeterminacy principle.

In earlier pages I undertook to show that some common arguments in favor of certain ontologies are fallacious. Further, I advanced an explicit standard whereby to decide what the ontological commitments of a theory are. But the question what ontology actually to adopt still stands open, and the obvious counsel is tolerance and an experimental spirit. Let us by all means see how much of the physicalistic conceptual scheme can be reduced to a phenomenalistic one; still, physics also naturally demands pursuing, irreducible *in toto* though it be. Let us see how, or to what degree, natural science may be rendered independent of platonistic mathematics; but let us also pursue mathematics and delve into its platonistic foundations.

From among the various conceptual schemes best suited to these various pursuits, one—the phenomenalistic—claims epistemological priority. Viewed from within the phenomenalistic conceptual scheme, the ontologies of physical objects and mathematical objects are myths. The quality of myth, however, is relative; relative, in this case, to the epistemological point of view. This point of view is one among various, corresponding to one among our various interests and purposes.

---

[6] Kurt Gödel, 'Ueber formale unentscheidbare Sätze der Principia Mathematica und verwandte Systeme', *Monatshefte für Mathematik und Physik*, 38 (1931), 173–98.

VI

STATEMENTS ABOUT UNIVERSALS

FRANK JACKSON

A feature of many versions of Nominalism is the claim that all statements putatively about universals can be translated as statements about particulars. This is certainly possible in some cases, for instance, 'Wisdom was a characteristic of Plato' is equivalent to 'Plato was wise'. I will argue that it is not, however, always possible; in particular, that it is not possible for 'Red is a colour' and 'Red resembles pink more than blue'.

The usual nominalist suggestion is that 'Red is a colour' is equivalent to something like 'Everything red is coloured'. There is a standard objection to this translation.[1] Consider the scattered location, L, of all the red things. Everything L-located is coloured, but evidently L-location is not a colour. Likewise, everything red might have been triangular and vice-versa, so that everything triangular was coloured; but triangularity still would not have been a colour.

The nominalist particularist can, however, side-step this objection by offering 'Necessarily, everything red is coloured' as his translation of 'Red is a colour'. For it is, at best, only contingently true that everything L-located or triangular is coloured. This reply gives a hostage to fortune, namely, the ontic commitments of such assertions of necessity. But it is arguable that these do not include a commitment to universals.

It is, thus, important that the following, apparently decisive, objection is available to the realist about universals. Everything red is both shaped and extended, but red is neither a shape nor an extension. And, further, it is necessarily true that everything red is shaped and extended. This is not to deny that 'Red is a colour' entails that necessarily everything red is coloured. But the former says more than the latter. If red's being a colour were nothing more than a matter of every red thing necessarily being coloured, then red's being a shape and an extension would be nothing more than the fact that necessarily every red thing is shaped and extended.

Reprinted from *Mind*, 86 (1977), 427–9, by permission of Oxford University Press.
[1] See, for example, A. N. Prior, 'Existence', *Encyclopedia of Philosophy*, edited by Paul Edwards (New York: Macmillan, 1967), volume 3, p. 146.

And red is not a shape and not an extension. It seems that 'Red is a colour' says, as realists maintain, something about red not reducible to something about red things.

The nominalist might have recourse at this point to the distinction between *analytic* truth in the Fregean sense of reducibility to a logical truth by synonymy substitution and necessity in the wide sense. He might, that is, suggest 'It is analytic that everything red is coloured' as his translation. However, there are difficulties in the way of reducing 'Everything red is coloured' to a logical truth. For instance, one cannot replace 'is coloured' by 'is yellow or red or . . .'. Because one cannot complete the disjunction, there being no finite list of all the possible colours; and further, the nominalist cannot explicate the dots by saying 'and so on for all the colours' for this ontically commits him to all the colours (as well as being circular).

In general, appeal to relations (of synonymy or whatever) between linguistic entities is beside the point when seeking an analysis of red being a colour. Red did not become a colour the day we first commented on the fact in our languages, and its being a colour is in no way dependent on the existence of English or French or whatever language the linguistic entities may belong to.

Similar difficulties face nominalist attempts to give a particularist translation of:

> (1) Red resembles pink more than blue.

Following Arthur Pap,[2] (1) is not equivalent to 'Anything red resembles anything pink more than anything blue'. For some red things resemble some blue things more than some pink things because of factors other than colour. For example, a red ball resembles a blue ball more than a pink elephant. The nominalist must offer instead:

> (2) Anything red colour-resembles anything pink more than any-
>   thing blue.

The standard realist objection to (2) (again from Pap, *ibid.*) is that 'x colour-resembles y' is analysable as 'x resembles y in colour', where the latter is obtained from 'x resembles y in z' by substitution for 'z'. Hence (2) is ontically committed to universals, albeit in disguise, for it contains a three-place relation with a place for designations of universals. Notoriously, the trouble with this objection is that it is hard to *prove* the realist's analysis of colour-resemblance without begging the question of the

---

[2] 'Nominalism, Empiricism and Universals: I', *Philosophical Quarterly*, 9 (1959), 330–40.

existence of universals. There is, however, a further objection to (2) which avoids this difficulty.

Consider the possible world in which 'red' and 'triangular' are co-extensive, 'pink' and 'sweet' are co-extensive, and 'blue' and 'square' are co-extensive. In this world, anything triangular colour-resembles anything sweet more than anything square. But no one will want to say that in this world triangularity resembles sweetness more than squareness. Hence, arguing along the same lines as before, there is more to red's resembling pink more than blue than the fact that red things colour-resemble pink things more than blue things. For triangular things might colour-resemble sweet things more than square things without triangularity resembling sweetness more than squareness.

It may be suggested that I am here misconstruing the nominalist's suggestion. It is not that 'Anything F ϕ-resembles anything G more than anything H' is invariably equivalent to 'F resembles G more than H', it is only equivalent to the latter when F, G, H are all ϕ. Now I have no doubt this is true, but it is not something a nominalist can say. It re-introduces universals, for it is *they* which are required all to be ϕ.

The obvious response for the nominalist is to point out that (2) is true in all worlds, and so to advocate 'Necessarily, anything red colour-resembles anything pink more than anything blue' as his translation of (1). (This also has the advantage of avoiding difficulties arising from the possibility of there being no red, pink, or blue things making (2) trivially true in some worlds.)

This response has, however, a crucial shortcoming. It cannot handle 'The colour of ripe tomatoes resembles the colour associated with girl babies more than the colour associated with boy babies'. For this statement is true, while 'Necessarily, anything with the colour of ripe tomatoes colour-resembles anything with the colour associated with girl babies more than anything with the colour associated with boy babies' is *false*. The statement governed by 'necessarily' is true, but only contingently so— tomatoes and baby lore might have been such that it was false. (Of course, the nominalist will want to write, for example, 'anything same-coloured as ripe tomatoes' rather than 'anything with the colour of ripe tomatoes', but this is not germane to the present point.)

Finally, the line of argument just outlined can be modified to apply to our first statement, 'Red is a colour'. Red is, let us suppose, the most conspicuous property of ripe tomatoes; then the most conspicuous property of ripe tomatoes is a colour. This cannot be nominalistically translated as 'Everything with the most conspicuous property of ripe tomatoes is coloured'. (I leave aside the question of what further translation the

nominalist might attempt to eliminate 'the most conspicuous property
. . .'.) Because the most conspicuous property of ripe tomatoes might have
been their smell while it remained true that all tomatoes were coloured
(though not so conspicuously); then 'Everything with the most conspicuous
property of ripe tomatoes is coloured' would be true together with the
falsity of 'The most conspicuous property of ripe tomatoes is a colour'.
And, of course, it would be wrong to offer 'Necessarily, everything with
the most conspicuous property of ripe tomatoes is coloured' as the translation of 'The most conspicuous property of ripe tomatoes is a colour'.
The former is false, there is no *necessity* about it: the most conspicuous
property of ripe tomatoes might have been, as we have just noted, their
smell, and some things with that smell might have been transparent, so
that some things with the most conspicuous property of ripe tomatoes
might not have been coloured. On the other hand 'The most conspicuous
property of ripe tomatoes is a colour' is true.

It seems then that—though some criticisms in the literature of particularist translations of 'Red is a colour' and 'Red resembles pink more than
blue' and the like may not be decisive—there are decisive criticisms of
these translations available to the realist.

VII

'OSTRICH NOMINALISM' OR 'MIRAGE REALISM'?

MICHAEL DEVITT

David Armstrong's approach to 'the problem of universals' has a contemporary gloss: he leaves it to 'total science ... to determine what universals there are'. Nevertheless his conception of the problem shows him to be a devotee of the 'old-time' metaphysics. The problem is the traditional one allegedly posed by the premise of Plato's One over Many argument: 'Many different particulars can all have what appears to be the same nature' (p. xiii).[1] It is a pity that Armstrong takes no serious account of the 'new' metaphysics of W. V. Quine and others, according to which there is no such problem as Armstrong seeks to solve.[2] In my view this Quinean position is a much stronger rival to Armstrong's Realism about universals than the many others he carefully demolishes.

The universals we are concerned with here are properties (what Quine calls 'attributes') and relations. 'Realists' believe in them, 'Nominalists' don't. After outlining five versions of Nominalism, Armstrong mentions the Quinean position as a possible sixth under the title 'Ostrich or Cloak-and-dagger Nominalism'.

I have in mind those philosophers who refuse to countenance universals but who at the same time see no need for any reductive analyses of the sorts just outlined. There are no universals but the proposition that *a* is *F* is perfectly all right as it is. Quine's refusal to take predicates with any ontological seriousness seems to make him a Nominalist of this kind (p. 16).

Worse, these philosophers are guilty of trying to have it both ways: denying universals whilst, *prima facie*, unashamedly making use of them. They

Reprinted by permission of Blackwell Publishers from *Pacific Philosophical Quarterly*, 61 (1980), 433–9. ©1980 by University of Southern California.
*I am indebted to Elizabeth Prior for help with the first draft of this paper and to David Armstrong and Frank Jackson for helpful comments on that draft.
    [1] Such references are to *Nominalism and Realism: Universals and Scientific Realism, Volume 1* (Cambridge: Cambridge University Press, 1978).
    [2] See particularly Quine's discussion in 'On What There Is' [chapter V in this volume]. Quine's discussion is largely aimed at a position like Armstrong's ('For "McX" read "McArmstrong"': Elizabeth Prior).

commit the sin of failing to answer 'a compulsory question in the examination paper' (p. 17). In Quinean language, they fail to face up to their ontological commitments.

Ostriches are reputed to ignore problems by putting their heads in the sand. Mirages are another feature of desert life: people see things that aren't there. An 'Ostrich Nominalist' is a person who maintains Nominalism whilst ignoring a problem. A 'Mirage Realist' is a person who adopts Realism because he sees a problem that isn't there. My major thesis is as follows:

> 1. To maintain Nominalism whilst ignoring the One over Many argument is not to be an Ostrich Nominalist; rather to adopt Realism because of that argument is to be a Mirage Realist.

Establishing this thesis would not, of course, show Realism to be unjustified (let alone false): there might be problems independent of the One over Many argument for which Realism is a possible solution. Armstrong thinks there are. I agree. To the extent that he is responding to those problems he is not a Mirage Realist. My thesis about him is as follows:

> 2. Armstrong is largely though not entirely a Mirage Realist.

Correspondingly, a Nominalist could be an Ostrich by putting his head in the sand as *real* problems loom. However correct his stand on the One over Many argument he could *otherwise* commit the sin that Armstrong complains of. I don't know whether there are any Ostrich Nominalists, but the only philosopher Armstrong alleges (tentatively) to be one, Quine, is not:

> 3. Quine is not an Ostrich Nominalist.

ARGUMENT FOR THESIS 1

According to Armstrong, the problem posed by the One over Many argument is that of explaining 'how numerically different particulars can nevertheless be identical in nature, all be of the same "type"' (p. 41). What phenomena are supposed to need explaining here? I take it that what Armstrong is alluding to is the common habit of expressing, assenting to, and believing, statements of the following form:

> (1) a and b have the same property (are of the same type), F-ness.

To settle ontological questions we need a criterion of ontological commitment. Perhaps Quine's criterion has difficulties, but something along that line is mandatory. The key idea is that a person is committed to the existence of those things that must exist for the sentences he accepts to be true. What must exist for a given sentence to be true is a semantic question to which our best theory may give no answer in which we have confidence. Furthermore the sentence may, by its use of quantifiers or singular terms, suggest an answer which the person would want to resist. Hence, in my view, the importance of Quine's mention of paraphrase in this context. Suppose the given sentence *seems* to require for its truth the existence of Gs yet the person can offer another sentence, which serves his purposes well enough, and which is known not to have that requirement. This is known because our semantic theory can be applied to this other sentence, in a way that it cannot to the given sentence, to show that the sentence can be true even though Gs do not exist. We can then say that the person's apparent commitment to Gs in the given sentence arises from 'a mere manner of speaking'; he is not really committed to them.

Now in the ordinary course of conversation a Quinean is prepared to express or assent to the likes of (1). (1) seems to require the existence of an F-ness for it to be true. So he appears committed to that existence. To this extent the One over Many argument does pose a problem to the Quinean Nominalist, but it is a negligible extent. He has a suitable paraphrase readily to hand:

(2) *a* and *b* are both *F*.

When the ontological chips are down, he can drop (1). There is no problem about identities in nature beyond a trivial one of paraphrase.

Armstrong will not be satisfied by this, of course: 'You have simply shifted the problem. In virtue of what are *a* and *b* both *F*?' The Quinean sees only a trivial problem here too. It is in virtue of the following:

(3) *a* is *F*;
(4) *b* is *F*.

Armstrong will still be dissatisfied: 'In virtue of what is *a* (or *b*) *F*?' If the One over Many argument poses a problem it is this. That was historically the case and, though Armstrong always *states* the problem in terms of identities in nature, it is the case for him too.[3] If there is no problem for the Nominalist in (3) and (4) *as they stand* then he has an easy explanation of identities in nature.

The Realist who accepts the One over Many problem attempts to solve

---

[3] See, e.g., his remarks on Ostrich Nominalism (quoted above) and his discussion of the varieties of Nominalism, pp. 12–16.

it here by claiming the existence of a universal, F-ness, which both a and b have. The Nominalist who accepts the problem attempts to solve it without that claim. The Quinean rejects the problem.

The Quinean sees no problem for Nominalism in the likes of (3) because there is a well-known semantic theory which shows that (3) can be true without there being any universals:

> (3) is true if and only if there exists an x such that 'a' designates x and 'F' applies to x.

So (3) can be true without the existence of F-ness. There is no refusal here 'to take predicates with any ontological seriousness'. The Quinean thinks that there *really must exist something* (said as firmly as you like) that the predicate 'F' applies to. However that thing is not a universal but simply an object. Further, in denying that this object need have properties, the Quinean is not denying that it *really is* F (or G, or whatever). He is not claiming that it is 'a bare particular'. He sees no need to play that game.

The Realist may reply that this is a mistaken statement of the truth conditions of (3) and that the correct one *does* require the existence of F-ness for (3)'s truth. Until a good argument for this reply is produced the Quinean is entitled to go on thinking he has no problem.

All of this is not to say that there is nothing further about (3), or about a being F, that might need explanation. I can think of four possible problems here. None of them pose any special difficulty for the Nominalist: they are irrelevant to 'the problem of universals'.

(i) We might need to explain what *caused a* to be F. (ii) We might need to explain what was *the purpose* of a being F. Nobody interested in 'the problem of universals' is likely to confuse their problem with (i) or (ii) and so I shall set them aside immediately.

It is not so easy to keep the next two problems distinct from 'the problem of universals'. (iii) If 'F' is not a fundamental predicate then as reductivists we might need to explain what *constitutes a* being F: perhaps we will want to be told that it is in virtue of being G, where 'G' is some physical predicate (a is a gene in virtue of being a DNA molecule). (iv) We might need to explain the *semantics* of 'F': we might want to know what makes it the case that 'F' applies to a.

The traditional 'problem of universals' has often appeared in a misleading semantic guise: how can 'F' 'be applied to an indefinite multiplicity of particulars' (p. xiii; Armstrong does not approve of this way of putting the problem)? The strictly semantic problem of multiplicity does not have anything to do with universals. We need to explain the link between 'F' and all F things in virtue of which the former applies to the latter. This is not different *in principle* from explaining the link between '*a*' and one object, *a*, in virtue of which the former designates the latter. The explanation of '*F*''s application depends on a theory of one semantic relation, application, the explanation of '*a*''s designation depends on a theory of another, designation. A feature of the explanations will be that it is *F* things that are linked to '*F*', and *a* that is linked to '*a*'. The *F*-ness of *F* things and the *a*-ness of *a* need not go unexplained in the semantics. Thus I think it is part of a good explanation of the link between 'tiger' and the many objects that it applies to that those objects are genetically of a certain sort. So the semantic problem may require *some* answer to the question: in virtue of what is *a F*? But the answer required is of type (iii), a reductivist answer.

In denying that there is any problem for the Nominalist about (3) it is important to see that we are not denying the reductivist problem (iii), nor the semanticist problem (iv), nor some combination of (iii) and (iv). What we are denying can be brought out vividly by taking '*F*' to be a fundamental predicate, say a physical predicate. Then there is no problem (iii): we have nothing to say about what makes *a F*, it just *is F*; that is a basic and inexplicable fact[4] about the universe. Problem (iv) remains: it is the problem of explaining the link between the predicate '*F*' and that basic fact. Nothing else remains to be explained.

Why be dissatisfied with this? Explanation must stop somewhere. What better place than with a fundamental physical fact of our world?

Armstrong feels that we need to go further. How can we tell who is right? There is one sure sign that explanation has not gone far enough: an explanation that goes further. Thus if Armstrong's Realist response to the One over Many argument is a genuine explanation then there must be a genuine problem here to be explained. My final remarks in support of thesis 1 will consider Armstrong's response.

One Realist response, but not Armstrong's, to the One over Many argument runs as follows: *a* is *F* in virtue of having the property *F*-ness. We explain (3) by

(5) *a* has *F*-ness.

An obvious question arises: how is (5) to be explained? The Realist feels that the one-place predication (3) left something unexplained, yet all he has done to explain it is offer a two-place predication (a relational statement). If there is a problem about *a being F* then there is at least an equal

---

[4] Lest an uncharitable reader should take this talk as committing me to the existence of facts, let me hasten to add that such talk is a mere manner of speaking, eliminable at the cost of style and emphasis.

problem about *a having F*-ness. Furthermore, the point of this manoeuvre for the Realist is to commit us to universals. In ontology, the less the better. Therefore this sort of Realist makes us ontologically worse off without explanatory gain. Any attempt by him to achieve explanatory power by explaining (5) seems doomed before it starts: it will simply raise the same problem as (5); he is in a vicious regress. If there is a problem about (3) this sort of Realist *cannot* solve it.

Armstrong calls the doctrine we have just considered 'relational Immanent Realism', and rejects it for reasons not unconnected to mine (pp. 104–7). In its place he offers us 'non-relational Immanent Realism'. This doctrine is obscure. Armstrong offers us (5), or the similar, '*F*-ness is *in a*,' and simply *declares* it to be non-relational and inexplicable: particulars are not *related* to universals but bonded to them in a metaphysical unity (pp. 108–11). We have just seen that (5), taken at face value, cannot explain any problem about (3): it is a relational statement and so any problem for (3) is a problem for it. Armstrong avoids this grievous difficulty for Realism by fiat: (5) is not to be taken at face value. How then is it to be taken? Do we have even the remotest idea of what the words 'in' and 'have' mean here if they are not construed as relational predicates? Armstrong's Realism replaces the explanatory failings of relational Realism with a complete mystery. I suspect that Armstrong views sentences like (5) as attempts to speak the unspeakable: to talk about 'the link' between particulars and universals without saying they are related. (Note the scare-quotes around 'in' on p. 108 and the use of a special hyphenating device on p. 111.)

Talk of 'particulars' and 'universals' clutters the landscape without adding to our understanding. We should rest with the basic fact that *a* is *F*. Even the alleged unity of particular and universal can be captured without mystery: a predication must involve both a singular term and a predicate; drop either partner and you say nothing. For the Nominalist the unity of predication is an unexciting linguistic fact. The move to relational Realism loses the unity. Armstrong's non-relational Realism attempts to bring it back with metaphysical glue. These are 'degenerating problem shifts' (Lakatos).

Armstrong sees the One over Many argument as posing a problem for Nominalism and offers a Realist solution. If his solution were real then the problem would be real. The solution is not real. So it throws no doubt on my earlier argument that the problem is not real.

Indeed the Quinean can gain much comfort from Armstrong's book: it is a powerful argument for thesis 1. We have just demonstrated the failings of Armstrong's response to the One over Many argument. Armstrong himself carefully, and convincingly, demolishes every other known response to it. This chronicle of two thousand years of failure makes the task seem hopeless. The alternative view that there is no problem to solve becomes very attractive.

I take my major thesis to be established:

1. To maintain Nominalism whilst ignoring the One over Many argument is not to be an Ostrich Nominalist; rather to adopt Realism because of that argument is to be a Mirage Realist.

Even if there *are* universals they cannot form part of a solution to the One over Many problem, because that problem is a mirage.

ARGUMENT FOR THESIS 2

The arguments for theses 2 and 3 will be brief. It follows from thesis 1 that in so far as Armstrong adopts Realism because of the One over Many argument, he is a Mirage Realist. At the beginning of his book he indicates that he sees that argument as the main one for universals (p. xiii). When he talks of 'the problem of universals' it is the problem allegedly posed by that argument that he is referring to (e.g. p. 41). Almost the whole book is taken up with the consideration of responses to that argument. Armstrong is largely a Mirage Realist.

In one chapter, drawing on the ideas of Arthur Pap and Frank Jackson, Armstrong offers quite independent reasons for Realism (pp. 58–63).[5] We all assent to, express, believe, statements like the following:

(6) Red resembles orange more than it resembles blue;
(7) Red is a colour;
(8) He has the same virtues as his father;
(9) The dresses were of the same colour.

Unlike (3) these seem to require the existence of properties for them to be true. Whether or not they are sufficient for Realism depends on whether or not we can find acceptable paraphrases without that commitment. There is nothing illusory about this problem for a Nominalist. Armstrong is not entirely a Mirage Realist. So,

(2) Armstrong is largely though not entirely a Mirage Realist.

[5] Given the importance Armstrong attaches to the One over Many argument for Realism, this chapter's title, 'Arguments for Realism', is misleading.

ARGUMENT FOR THESIS 3

For Quine to be an Ostrich Nominalist would be for him to ignore the ontological problem posed by his acceptance of statements like (6) to (9). *A priori* it is unlikely that this would be so. Quine, more than any other philosopher, has pointed out what constitutes an ontological commitment and has preached against ignoring such. Philosophers, like others, can fail to practise what they preach, but I suggest that it is unlikely that Quine would fail here, about as unlikely as that he would confuse use and mention.

A quick glance through *Word and Object* [6] shows that he does not fail. In a section on abstract terms he considers, e.g., the sentence,

(10) Humanity is a virtue,

a sentence that raises much the same problem as Armstrong's (8), and sees it as committing him to the existence of 'an abstract object' (p. 119), in fact to 'an attribute', what Armstrong would call 'a property'. He goes on to 'deplore the facile line of thought' that allows us to ignore this (pp. 119–20). He considers ways to paraphrase away this apparent commitment to attributes and admits the difficulties (pp. 121–3). The issues are postponed until chapter VII. He does not there discuss sentences like (6) to (10) directly, so far as I can see, but his strategy for them is clear enough: all talk of attributes is to be dispensed with in favour of talk of eternal open sentences or talk of classes (p. 209). Whatever the merits of this approach it is not the behaviour of an Ostrich. So,

(3) Quine is not an Ostrich Nominalist.

[6] W. V. Quine, *Word and Object* (Cambridge, Mass.: M.I.T., 1960).

VIII

AGAINST 'OSTRICH' NOMINALISM: A REPLY TO MICHAEL DEVITT

D. M. ARMSTRONG

I am dissatisfied with my treatment, in Volume 1 of *Universals and Scientific Realism*,[1] of what I there called 'Ostrich' Nominalism. Michael Devitt's vigorous defence of Quine, whom I accused of being such a Nominalist, gives me a second opportunity. (I should like to thank Devitt for comments on earlier drafts, and for the pleasant spirit in which this controversy has been conducted.)

1. QUINE AND THE 'ONE OVER MANY'

I think that the main argument for the existence of universals is Plato's 'One over Many'. I do not think that it proves straight off that there are universals. But I think that it shows that there is a strong preliminary case for accepting universals. There are various sorts of Nominalists (I spoke of Predicate, Concept, Class, Mereological, and Resemblance Nominalists) who seem to perceive the strength of the 'One over Many' but who maintain their Nominalism nevertheless. There are, however, Nominalists who deny that the argument has any force. These I christened, tendentiously enough, Ostrich Nominalists. Quine is certainly one who denies the force of the 'One over Many'.

In chapter 1 of *From a Logical Point of View* (1953), that is, the well-known paper 'On What There Is' [chapter V in this volume], Quine makes a philosopher whom he calls 'McX'[2] advance the 'One over Many':

Speaking of attributes, he [McX] says: 'There are red houses, red roses, and red sunsets; this much is prephilosophical common sense in which we must all agree.

Reprinted by permission of Blackwell Publishers from *Pacific Philosophical Quarterly*, 61 (1980), 440–9. © 1980 by University of Southern California.

[1] [D. M. Armstrong, *Nominalism and Realism* (Cambridge: Cambridge University Press, 1978).]

[2] Devitt, following E. Prior, suggests that for the variable 'X' be substituted the name 'Armstrong'. However, Devitt and Prior overlook the fact that 'McArmstrong' is ill-formed. 'Armstrong' is a *Lowland* Scottish name.

These houses, roses and sunsets, then, have something in common: and this which
they have in common is all I mean by the attribute of redness.' For McX, thus,
there being attributes is even more obvious and trivial than the obvious and trivial
fact of there being red houses, roses, and sunsets (p. 81).

In my view, Quine has here made McX considerably overplay his hand.
I would wish to start in a much more cautious way by saying, as I say on
p. xiii, that:

many different particulars can all have what appears to be the same nature.

and draw the conclusion that, as a result, there is a *prima facie* case for
postulating universals.

Quine, I think, admits or half-admits the truth of this premiss, though in
a back-handed way, when he says, in the course of his assault on McX:

One may admit that there are red houses, roses and sunsets, but deny, except as a
popular and misleading manner of speaking, that they have anything in common
(p. 81).

Quine here allows that there is a popular manner of speaking in which
different red things are said to have something in common. But he does
not seem to realize just how ubiquitous such manners of speaking are. We
(that is, everybody) are continually talking about the *sameness* of things.
And most of the time when we talk about the sameness of things we are
talking about the sameness of *different* things. We are continually talking
about different things having the same property or quality, being of the
same sort or kind, having the same nature, and so on.

Philosophers have formalized the matter a little. They draw the enor-
mously useful Peircean distinction between sameness of token and sameness of type. But they are only formalizing, making explicit, a distinction
which ordinary language (and so, ordinary thought) perfectly recognizes.

G. E. Moore thought, correctly I believe, that there are many facts
which even philosophers should not deny, whatever philosophical account
or analysis they gave of these facts. He gave as an example the existence of
his hands. We can argue about the philosophical account which ought to
be given of material objects, such as Moore's hands. But we should not
deny that there are such things. (He was not arguing that their existence
was a logically necessary or logically indubitable truth.) I suggest that the
fact of sameness of type is a Moorean fact.

Any comprehensive philosophy must try to give some account of
Moorean facts. They constitute the compulsory questions in the philosophical examination paper. If sameness of type is a Moorean fact, then,
because Quine sees no need to give an account of it, he is refusing to
answer a compulsory question.

Here is one answer to the question. When we speak of sameness of token, the sameness of the Morning and the Evening star to coin an example, we are speaking of *identity*. But when we speak of sameness of type, of two dresses being the same shade of colour for instance, sameness is merely a matter of *resemblance* (on one view between the dresses, on another between two property-instances). Resemblance is not to be analysed in terms of identity. Hence *sameness* with respect to token is not the same as (is not identical with) sameness with respect to type. The word 'same' is fundamentally ambiguous.

This is not a view which I accept. But it is an attempt to grapple with the problem.

Again, it may be held that sameness of token and sameness of type is sameness in exactly the same sense, *viz.* identity. This Realist view seems to be nearer the truth of the matter. I think it is a bit crude as it stands, because it appears to require recognition of a universal wherever we recognize sameness of type, a universal corresponding to each general word. However, the rightness or wrongness of the answer is not what is in debate here. The point is that the philosophical problem of the nature of sameness of type is faced, not evaded.

By comparison, what does Quine offer us? He simply says:

That the houses and roses and sunsets are all of them red may be taken as ultimate and irreducible, . . . (p. 81).

What does he mean by this? This remark might be made by a Realist, or at any rate by a Realist who believes that *redness* is a property. But, of course, Quine is engaged in rejecting Realism, personified by the unfortunate McX.

It is natural to interpret him instead as saying that, although these tokens are all of the same type, yet we have no need to consider what sameness of type is. (And, *a fortiori*, sameness of type is not a matter of identity of property.)

If this is the way to interpret Quine, then is he not an ostrich about types? Like an Oxford philosopher of yore, he keeps on saying that he does not deny that many different objects are all of them red, but what this ostensible sameness is he refuses to explain (except to say it is ultimate and irreducible). Instead, he thrusts his head back into his desert landscape.

But perhaps there is a still deeper level of scepticism in Quine. Perhaps he would object to this foisting upon him of talk about types. Suppose *a* is red and *b* is red, then, Quine might say, we can by a convenient abbreviation say that *a* and *b* are *both* red. If *a* is red and *b* is red and *c* is red, we can by a convenient abbreviation say that *a*, *b* and *c* are *all of them* red. But nothing here justifies talking of sameness of type, unless this too is mere abbreviation.

Such scepticism cannot be maintained. It is true that '*a* and *b* are both red' is an abbreviation of '*a* is red and *b* is red.' But the abbreviation does not hold just for these particular sentences (much less for the above sentence-tokens), but is a rule-governed, projectible, transformation which we are capable of applying to an indefinite multiplicity of sentences. And what is the rule? It goes something like this. Suppose that we are given a sentence of the form '*a* is — and *b* is —.' If but only if the two blanks are filled by the *same* predicate, it is permitted to rewrite the sentence as '*a* and *b* are both —,' with that same predicate in the new blank. But 'same predicate' here is a type-notion. It is not meant that the very same predicate-token be plugged successively into three gaps!

It appears, then, that just to understand phrases like 'are both red' requires that we understand at least what a *predicate*-type is. And if this notion is understood, and at least at a Moorean level accepted, then there can be no bar to understanding, and at least at the Moorean level accepting, type-notions generally. Some account must then be given, reductive or otherwise, of what sameness of type is.

But perhaps Quine failed to appreciate this point when he wrote 'On What There Is'. The insight on which the argument of the penultimate paragraph is based was not available to contemporary philosophers until the work of Donald Davidson. For this, see Davidson, who criticises Quine for a similar failure to appreciate the projectible semantic structure of sentences attributing beliefs in *Word and Object*.[3]

It may be, then, that Quine did not perceive at least the full urgency of the need to give an account of types. But however it was with Quine (or is with Devitt), the distinction between tokens and types cannot be ignored. Hence a philosophical account of a general sort is required of what it is for different tokens to be of the same type. To refuse to give such an account is to be a metaphysical ostrich.

2. QUINE'S CRITERION OF ONTOLOGICAL COMMITMENT

But there is, of course, something else which insulates Quine from the full impact of the problem of types, from the problem of the One over Many. The insulating material is his extraordinary doctrine that predicates

---

[3] Donald Davidson (1965), 'Theories of Meaning and Learnable Languages', in his *Inquiries into Truth and Interpretation* (Oxford: Clarendon Press, 1984), 3–36; W. V. O. Quine, *Word and Object* (Cambridge, Mass.: M.I.T. Press, 1960).

involve no ontological commitment. In a statement of the form '*Fa*', he holds, the predicate '*F*' need not be taken with ontological seriousness. Quine gives the predicate what has been said to be the privilege of the harlot: power without responsibility. The predicate is informative, it makes a vital contribution to telling us what is the case, the world is different if it is different, yet ontologically it is supposed not to commit us. Nice work: if you can get it.

It is at this very point, however, that Quine may protest, as Devitt does on his behalf, that his Nominalism is at least not an *Ostrich* Nominalism. For although Quine is perfectly cavalier about predicates, he is deadly serious about referring expressions. Suppose that a statement meets three conditions. (1) It makes ostensible *reference* to universals. (2) We account it true. (3) It is impossible to find a satisfactory paraphrase of the statement in which this reference to universals is eliminated. Under these conditions, Quine allows, indeed insists, we ought to admit universals into our ontology. Perhaps the three conditions cannot be met, but if they can be met, why then Quine will turn Realist.

I grant freely that to put forward such a set of conditions is not the behaviour of a philosophical ostrich. On the other hand, I do think that Quine is an ostrich *with respect to the One over Many argument*. Furthermore I think that Quine (and his followers) have been distinctly perfunctory in considering the many statements which answer to conditions (1) and (2) and which *appear* to answer to condition (3).

In chapter 6 of my book[4] I consider the statements:

(1) Red resembles orange more than it resembles blue
(2) Red is a colour
(3) He has the same virtues as his father.

Basing myself upon work by Pap and Jackson, I argue that these statements cannot be analyzed in a way which removes their ostensible reference to universals, or at least to property-instances.[5] (I try to show the incoherence of the doctrine of property-instances, that is, particularized properties, in chapter 8.)

It would in fact have been desirable also to have made reference to Hilary Putnam's 'On Properties'[6] which considers the statement:

---

[4] Devitt correctly noted that it was misleading to call the chapter 'Arguments for Realism' in spite of the fact that what I take to be the main argument for Realism, the One over Many, is deployed in earlier chapters and is not deployed in chapter 6. As Frank Jackson has pointed out, the title should really be 'Arguments for Realism that work even if Quine is right about ontological commitment'.

[5] Arthur Pap, 'Nominalism, Empiricism and Universals: I', *Philosophical Quarterly*, 9 (1959), 330–40; Frank Jackson, 'Statements About Universals [chapter VI of this volume].

[6] [*Essays in Honor of Carl G. Hempel*, edited by Nicholas Rescher (Dordrecht: Reidel, 1970), 235–54].

(4) There are undiscovered fundamental physical properties.

To this might be added an example suggested by David Stove:

(5) Acquired characteristics are never inherited,

and many others.

Now we might expect reasonably extended discussions of examples of this sort in Quine. Our expectation, however, is disappointed. In 'On What There Is' he does mention:

(6) Some zoological species are cross-fertile

and says that, unless we can paraphrase it in some way, it commits us to 'abstract'[7] objects, *viz.* species. But he does not say what account he would give of (6).

As Devitt points out, in §25 of *Word and Object*, Quine does give brief consideration to:

(7) Humility is a virtue

along with:

(8) Redness is a sign of ripeness.

For (8) he suggests

(8′) Red fruits are ripe

which perhaps may be allowed to pass. But (7), which resembles (2), cannot be rendered, as he seems to suggest, by:

(7′) Humble persons are virtuous.

First, the truth of (7) is compatible with there being humble persons who are not virtuous. Indeed, it is compatible with *no* humble persons being virtuous. For it may be that every humble person is so full of glaring faults that, although they have the virtue of humility, they are not virtuous persons.

---

[7] Quine appears to mean by an 'abstract' entity one that is outside space and time. This is a misuse of the term, on a par with using 'disinterested' to mean the same as 'uninterested'. An abstract object is one which can be *considered* apart from something else, but cannot *exist* apart from that thing. Being outside space and time has no special connection with abstraction. He holds that both classes, if they exist, and universals, if they exist, are abstract in his sense. He also says that classes *are* universals (pp. 115–23), probably because he takes 'universal' to be a convenient synonym for 'abstract'. In fact classes are particulars, even if, as Quine claims, non-spatio-temporal particulars. This is because unlike universals, they are not ones which may run through many. There can be many instances of redness, but not many instances of the class of men or the class of colours. A 'Nominalist', for Quine, is simply one who does not recognize abstract objects in his sense, a 'Platonist' is one who does recognize them. So when he reluctantly admitted classes Quine became a 'Platonist'. The misuse of all these terms has contributed to muddling a whole philosophical generation about the Problem of Universals.

Second, and more seriously, the truth of (7') is compatible with humility not being a virtue. Consider an example suggested by Graham Nerlich. Suppose it was true, and well known to be true, that tall people are always virtuous.

(7'') Tall persons are virtuous

is exactly parallel to:

(7') Humble persons are virtuous.

But nobody would wish to suggest that it would then be a truth that:

(7''') Tallness is a virtue.[8]

So not only does (7) fail to entail (7') which was the first objection, but (7') fails to entail (7).

As Devitt says, Quine then postpones general discussion of the problems of 'abstract objects' until chapter VII. In that chapter, Quine, without discussing examples, suggests that all apparent reference to attributes and relations should be dispensed with in favour of talk of 'eternal' open sentences (or general terms) and/or talk of classes.

Here, I agree, he has moved beyond his original position to some form of Predicate and/or Class Nominalism. But he does not discuss the rather well-known difficulties for these varieties of Nominalism. (Devitt, it may be noticed, appears to think that the difficulties are insoluble.)

It seems, then, that Quine is in trouble, even under his own rules. But the more important question, I think, is why we should grant him his rules. Devitt can only say that:

... we need a criterion of ontological commitment. Perhaps Quine's criterion has difficulties, but something along that line is mandatory (pp. 94–5).

After this less than full-blooded defence, one can only ask 'Why not a criterion which allows predicates a role in ontological commitment?'

At this point, appeal may be made to semantics. Devitt makes such an appeal. He says that one can give the truth conditions of 'Fa' by saying that it is true if and only if 'a' denotes some particular which 'F' applies to. He says that this shows that 'Fa' can be true even though the 'F' carries no ontological commitment. But two points may be made in reply. First, there may be alternative, and perhaps more satisfying, ways of giving the semantics for 'Fa'. Devitt offers no argument against this possibility. Second, and

---

[8] Equally, supposing it to be true that:

(7'''') Humble persons are amphibious

it does not follow that:

(7''''') Humility is an amphibian.

more important, the semantics of 'applies' has been left totally obscure.
The Realist may well argue, correctly I believe, that a convincing account
of the semantics of 'applies' cannot be given without appeal to the properties and/or relations of the object *a*. (I owe this point to John Bishop.)

3. PROBLEMS FOR REALISM

Besides supporting Quine in his rejection of the One over Many argument,
Devitt also argues directly against Realism. He confines himself to the
problem, familiar to all Realists, of how particulars stand to universals. I
agree with Devitt that this is the central difficulty in the Realist position.
So I will finish what I have to say by making some remarks about it. But
Devitt's own remarks are brief, and I think it best to expound the problem
anew.

The problem is a sub-problem of the problem about the nature of
particulars. For one who denies the existence of properties *in re* (whether
these properties be universals or particulars), particulars are a sort of
structureless blob. They can have parts. Predicates can be hung on them,
concepts applied to them, they can be herded into classes, they may even
have resemblances to other particulars if a Resemblance Nominalism is
adopted, but they lack real internal structure. For those who accept
properties *in re*, however, particulars are sort of layer-cake. The *one*
particular somehow unites within itself *many* different properties (another
One over Many). The question is: how is this possible?

The problem divides at this point because a defender of properties *in re*
may develop the theory of particulars in different ways. According to one
view, a particular is nothing but its properties. It is not, of course, a mere
class of properties, but is a certain *bundling* of properties. A certain
relation holds between all and only the properties of a particular, and the
holding of this relation is what makes it a particular. This 'Bundle' view in
turn divides into two, because the properties in the bundle may be conceived either as universals or as property-instances. Russell held the
Bundle view in its first form, Donald Williams in its second.

However, the more orthodox view among those who accept properties
in re is that, besides their properties, particulars involve a factor of
particularity, an individuating component. This view in turn divides into
two in the same way as before. There are those who make the properties
into particulars. Locke is a probable example. However, the more orthodox version of this more orthodox view takes the properties to be
universals.

Since our special concern here is with the problems of *Realism*, we may ignore the views which give an account of particulars by appealing to property-instances. The view that a particular is nothing but a bundle of universals is exposed to many grave difficulties (some of which I try to spell out in chapter 9 of my book), but I do not think that the difficulty raised by Devitt is among them. The problem proposed by Devitt only arises, I think, if one holds (as I do hold) that a particular involves a factor of particularity (*haeccitas*, thisness) together with properties which are universals. The question is then this: how are the two components of a particular to be put together?

There are, broadly, two sorts of answer to the question which Realists have given. According to the first, the factor of particularity stands in a certain *relation* to the properties. It really is correct to speak of the *related components* of a full-blooded particular. For this line of thought it is quite natural to reify the factor of particularity and to think of it as a 'bare particular'. This line of thought, it seems further, ought to be reasonably sympathetic to the idea that bare particulars might exist without any properties, and properties might exist which are not properties of any particular. For why should not the relation fail to hold? A synthetic necessity could be postulated to ensure that the factors only exist in relation, but it is hard to see the necessity for this necessity.

But whether or not bare particulars can exist apart from properties, or properties from bare particulars, difficulties arise for this conception of a particular. Let the relation be I, a bare particular be B, and wholly distinct properties of the particular be P', P''. ... An ordinary particular containing B will then be constituted by a conjunction of states of affairs $I(B,P)$, $I(B,P')$ ... etc. The difficulty then is that I is a *relation* and so, on this view, is a universal. As a result, a *new* relation of instantiation will be required to hold between I, on the one hand, and the elements which it relates, on the other. The new relation will then be involved in the same difficulty. The difficulty has been appreciated at least since the work of F. H. Bradley.

Various shifts may be attempted in the face of this regress, for instance, it may be suggested that the regress exists, but is not vicious. Without arguing the matter here, I will just say that I do not think that this way out, or any other, succeeds.

In common with many other Realists, I therefore favour the view that, while we can *distinguish* the particularity of a particular from its properties, nevertheless the two 'factors' are too intimately together to speak of a *relation* between them. The thisness and the nature are incapable of existing apart from each other. Bare particulars and uninstantiated universals are vicious abstractions (in the non-Quinean sense of 'abstraction', of course!) from what may be called states of affairs: this-of-a-certain-nature. The thisness and the nature are therefore not related.

Frege says of his concepts that they are 'unsaturated'. Fregean concepts are not something mental. They are close to being the Realist's properties and relations. His idea, I think, was that the concepts have, as it were, a gap in their being, a gap which must be filled by particulars. If we think of the particularity of particulars as *also* 'unsaturated', then I think Frege's metaphor is helpful.

All this is profoundly puzzling. As a result, Devitt is able to claim, not implausibly, that all I have done is to substitute inexplicable mystery for the relational view. Realism requires a relation between particularity and universality. Yet to postulate such a relation appears to lead to insoluble problems. So, he says, I simply 'unite' the two factors in an incomprehensible manner.

I accept some of the force of this. But I have three things to say which I think ought to make Devitt look upon this 'Non-Relational Immanent Realism' with a little more sympathy.

First, as was made clear already, the problem arises not simply where a particular has a property, but where two or more particulars are related. Suppose a has R to b. If R is a universal, and a and b are particulars, and if we think that a relation is needed to link a universal to its particulars, then we shall require a further relation or relations to link R to a and b. This seems intolerable. It seems much better, therefore, to say that, while we can distinguish the relation from the particulars, yet the three 'entities' are together in a way which does not require any further relation to *get* them together. Now, if we think this way about the polyadic case, it seems to me that when we go back to the monadic case we ought in consistency to take the same line, and deny that the particularity of a particular is related to the properties of the particular. Contrariwise, if we admit a relation in the monadic case, should we not admit an extra relation in the polyadic case?

I hope that this generalization of the problem will at least show Devitt how strong an intellectual pressure there is for a Realist to adopt a non-relational view. It may be crooked, but it looks to be the best (Realist) game in town.

Second, I appeal to what Devitt says himself. He says:

Talk of 'particulars' and 'universals' clutters the landscape without adding to our understanding. We should rest with the basic fact that a is F (p. 98).

Now, of course, I accept the *second* sentence just as much as Devitt. (There is, as it were, *f.a.* in my philosophy as much as there is in Devitt's.)

Let us consider the sentence. Devitt will surely admit that '*a*' is a token-word, picking out just this thing *a*, while '*F*' is a type-word, applicable, potentially at least, to many things. Now why should we need two words of just this semantic sort to record the basic fact? Does not some explanation seem called for? Is it so very extreme an hypothesis that, while '*a*' names a particular, '*F*' captures something repeatable, something universal, about the situation?

I might add that I think that the dispute between Devitt and myself here is an instance of a very deep dispute indeed. There are those who, apparently like Devitt, think of reality as made up of *things*. There are others who, like me, think of it as made up of *facts* or *states of affairs*. We cannot expect any easy resolution of such an argument. (All the more reason to try to argue it of course.)

Third, I offer a second *ad hominem* criticism of Devitt's position. Devitt rejects the 'One over Many'. But he agrees that the problems posed for Quine by the arguments of Arthur Pap and Frank Jackson, retailed by me in the chapter 'Arguments for Realism', are hard to solve. He makes no attempt to improve upon the unsatisfactory paraphrases suggested by Quine of statements ostensibly referring to universals. So it seems that he thinks that it may be necessary to postulate universals. If he does have to postulate them, how will *he* solve the problem of how universals stand to their particulars? I think he will end up saying something similar to what I (and indefinitely many other Realists) have had to say.

IX

ON THE ELEMENTS OF BEING: I

DONALD C. WILLIAMS

First philosophy, according to the traditional schedule, is analytic ontology, examining the traits necessary to whatever is, in this or any other possible world. Its cardinal problem is that of substance and attribute, or at any rate something cognate with this in that family of ideas which contains also subsistence and inherence, subject and predicate, particular and universal, singular and general, individual and class, and matter and form. It is the question how a thing can be an instance of many properties while a property may inhere in many instances, the question how everything is a *case* of a *kind*, a this-such, an essence endowed with existence, an existent differentiated by essence, and so forth. Concerned with what it means to be a thing or a kind at all, it is in some wise prior to and independent of the other great branch of metaphysics, speculative cosmology: what kinds of things are there, what stuff are they made of, how are they strung together? Although 'analytic ontology' is not much practised as a unit under that name today, its problems, and especially the problem of subsistence and inherence, are as much alive in the latest manifestos of the logical analysts, who pretend to believe neither in substances nor in universals, as they were in the counsels of Athens and of Paris. Nothing is clear until that topic is clear, and in this essay I hope to clarify it in terms of a theory or schema which over a good many years I have found so serviceable that it may well be true.

Metaphysics is the thoroughly empirical science. Every item of experience must be evidence for or against any hypothesis of speculative cosmology, and every experienced object must be an exemplar and test case for the categories of analytic ontology. Technically, therefore, one example ought for our present theme to be as good as another. The more dignified examples, however, are darkened with a patina of tradition and partisanship, while some frivolous ones are peculiarly perspicuous. Let us therefore imagine three lollipops, made by a candy man who buys sticks from a big supplier and molds candy knobs on them. Lollipop No. 1 has a

Reprinted from *Review of Metaphysics*, 7 (1953), 3–18; by permission.

red round peppermint head, No. 2 a brown round chocolate head, No. 3 a red square peppermint head. The circumstance here which mainly provokes theories of subsistence and inherence is similarity with difference: each lollipop is partially similar to each other and partially different from it. If we can give a good account of this circumstance in this affair we shall have the instrument to expose the anatomy of everything, from an electron or an apple to archangels and the World All.

My chief proposal to that end may be put, to begin with, as nothing more tremendous than that we admit literally and seriously that to say that *a* is partially similar to *b* is to say that a part of *a* is wholly or completely similar to a part of *b*. This is a truism when we construe it with respect to ordinary concrete parts, for example, the sticks in the lollipops. On physical grounds, to be sure, it is not likely that any three solid objects, not even three sticks turned out by mass industry, are exactly similar, but they often look as if they were, and we can intelligibly stipulate for our argument that our exemplary sticks do exactly resemble each other through and through. To say then that each of the lollipops is partially similar to each other, that is, with respect to stick, is to say that there is a stick in each which is perfectly similar to the stick in every other, even though each stick remains as particular and distinct an individual as the whole lollipop. We would seldom give a proper name to a lollipop, and still more seldom to the stick in one, but we might easily do so—'Heraplem' for lollipop No. 1, for example, 'Paraplete' for its stick, 'Boanerp' for No. 2 and 'Merrinel' for its stick. Heraplem and Boanerp are partially similar because Paraplete and Merrinel are perfectly similar.

But what now of the rest of each lollipop and what of their more subtle similarities, of color, shape, and flavor? My proposal is that we treat them in exactly the same way. Since we can not find more parts of the usual gross sort, like the stick, to be wholly similar from lollipop to lollipop, let us discriminate subtler and thinner or more diffuse parts till we find some of these which *are* wholly similar. This odd-sounding assignment, of course, is no more than we are accustomed to do, easily and without noticing. Just as we can distinguish in the lollipops Heraplem and Boanerp the gross parts called 'sticks', namely, Paraplete and Merrinel, so we can distinguish in each lollipop a finer part which we are used to call its 'color' and another called its 'shape'—not its kind of color or shape, mind you, but these particular cases, this reddening, this occurrence or occasion of roundness, each as uniquely itself as a man, an earthquake, or a yell. With only a little more hardihood than christened the lollipops and sticks we can christen our finer components: 'Harlac' and 'Bantic' for the respective color components, let us say, and 'Hamis' and 'Borcas' for the respective shape components. In these four new names the first and last letters are initials of 'Heraplem' and 'Boanerp', and of 'color' and 'shape', respectively, but this is a mnemonic device for us, irrelevant to their force as names. 'Harlac', for example, is not to be taken as an abbreviation for the description, 'the color component of Heraplem'. In a real situation like the one we are imagining, 'Harlac' is defined ostensively, as one baptizes a child or introduces a man, present in the flesh; the descriptive phrase is only a scaffolding, a temporary device to bring attention to bear on the particular entity being denoted, as a mother of twins might admonish the vicar, 'Boadicea is the cross-looking one'. Heraplem and Boanerp are partially similar, then, not merely because the respective gross parts Paraplete and Merrinel (their sticks) are wholly similar, but also because the respective fine parts, Hamis and Borcas (their 'shapes'), are wholly similar—all this without prejudice to the fact that Hamis is numerically as distinct from Borcas, to which it is wholly similar, and from Harlac, with which it is conjoined in Heraplem, as Harlac is from Bantic to which it is neither similar nor conjoined, and as the stick Paraplete is from the stick Merrinel, and as the whole lollipop, Heraplem, is from the whole Boanerp. The sense in which Heraplem and Boanerp 'have the same shape', and in which 'the shape of one is identical with the shape of the other', is the sense in which two soldiers 'wear the same uniform', or in which a son 'has his father's nose', or our candy man might say 'I use the same identical stick, Ledbetter's Triple-X, in all my lollipops'. They do not 'have the same shape' in the sense in which two children 'have the same father', or two streets have the same manhole in the middle of their intersection, or two college boys 'wear the same tuxedo' (and so can't go to dances together). But while similar in the indicated respects, Heraplem and Boanerp are partially dissimilar in as much as their knobs or heads are partially dissimilar, and these are partially dissimilar because some of their finer parts, for example, Harlac and Bantic, their colors, are dissimilar.

In like manner, to proceed, we note that Harlac, the color component of No. 1 (Heraplem), though numerically distinct from, is wholly similar to the color component of No. 3. But No. 1 has not only a color component which is perfectly similar to the color component of No. 3; it has also a flavor component perfectly similar to the flavor component of No. 3. (It does not matter whether we think of the flavor as a phenomenal quality or as a molecular structure in the stuff of the candy.) The flavor-plus-color of No. 1 (and likewise of No. 3) is a complex whose own constituents are the flavor and the color, and so on for innumerable selections and combinations of parts, both gross and fine, which are embedded in any one such object or any collection thereof.

Crucial here, of course, is the admission of a 'fine' or 'subtle' part, a 'diffuse' or 'permeant' one, such as a resident color or occurrent shape, to at least as good standing among the actual and individual items of the world's furniture as a 'gross' part, such as a stick. The fact that one part is thus finer and more diffuse than another, and that it is more susceptible of similarity, no more militates against its individual actuality than the fact that mice are smaller and more numerous than elephants makes them any the less real. To borrow now an old but pretty appropriate term, a gross part, like the stick, is 'concrete', as the whole lollipop is, while a fine or diffuse part, like the color component or shape component, is 'abstract'. The color-cum-shape is less abstract or more concrete or more nearly concrete than the color alone but it is more abstract or less concrete than color-plus-shape-plus-flavor, and so on till we get to the total complex which is wholly concrete.

I propose now that entities like our fine parts or abstract components are the primary constituents of this or any possible world, the very alphabet of being. They not only are actual but are the only actualities, in just this sense, that whereas entities of all other categories are literally composed of them, they are not in general composed of any other sort of entity. That such a crucial category has no regular name is quite characteristic of first principles and is part of what makes the latter worth pursuing. A description of it in good old phraseology has a paradoxical ring: our thin parts are 'abstract particulars'.[1] We shall have occasion to use 'parts' for concreta and 'components' for our abstracta (and 'constituent' for both), as some British philosophers use 'component' for property and 'constituent' for concrete part. Santayana, however, used 'trope' to stand for the *essence* of an *occurrence*;[2] and I shall divert the word, which is almost useless in either his or its dictionary sense, to stand for the abstract particular which is, so to speak, the *occurrence* of an *essence*. A trope then is a particular entity either abstract or consisting of one or more concreta in combination with an abstractum. Thus a cat and the cat's tail are not tropes, but a cat's smile is a trope, and so is the whole whose constituents are the cat's smile plus her ears and the aridity of the moon.

Turning now briefly from the alphabet of being to a glimpse of its syllabary, we observe two fundamental ways in which tropes may be connected with one another: the way of location and the way of similarity. These are categorially different, and indeed systematic counterparts of

---

[1] I argued the general legitimacy of such a category in 'The Nature of Universals and of Abstractions', *The Monist*, (1931), 583–93.

[2] *The Realm of Matter* (London: Constable & Co., 1930), chapter VI.

one another—mirror images, as it were. Location is external in the sense that a trope *per se* does not entail or necessitate or determine its location with respect to any other trope, while similarity is internal in the sense that, given any two tropes, there are entailed or necessitated or determined whether and how they are similar. (What further this *prima facie* difference amounts to we cannot pursue here.) Location is easiest thought of as position in physical space-time, but I intend the notion to include also all the analogous spreads and arrangements which we find in different conscious fields and indeed in any realm of existence which we can conceive—the whole interior stretch and structure of a Leibnizian monad, for example. Both modes of connection are describable in terms of 'distance' and 'direction'. We are very familiar in a general way with the numberless distances and directions which compose locations in space and time, somewhat less familiar with the idea of what I suggest is the limiting value of such location (though very familiar with the phenomenon itself): the collocation, or peculiar interpretation, the unique congress in the same volume, which we call 'belonging to (or inhering in, or characterizing) the same thing'. With various interests and intentions, this nexus has been mentioned by Russell as 'compresence', by Mill as 'co-inherence', by G. F. Stout as 'concresence', by Professor Goodman as 'togetherness', and by Whitehead, Keynes, and Mill again as 'concurrence'.[3] With respect to similarity, on the other hand, we are comparatively familiar with the notion of its limiting value, the precise, or almost precise, similarity such as obtained between the colors of our first and third lollipops, less familiar with the idea of the lesser similarity which obtains between a red and a purple, and rather uncertain, unless we are psychologists or phenomenologists, about such elaborate similarity distances and directions as are mapped on the color cone.

Any possible world, and hence, of course, this one, is completely constituted by its tropes and their connections of location and similarity, and any others there may be. (I think there are no others, but that is not necessary to the theory of tropes.) Location and similarity (or whatever else there is) provide all the relations, as the tropes provide the terms, but the total of the relations is not something over and above the total of the terms, for a relation R between tropes a and b is a constitutive trope of the complex $r'(a, b)$, while conversely the terms a and b will be in general

[3] See Russell, *Human Knowledge* (London: George Allen & Unwin), pp. 294, 297, 304, etc.; Stout, 'The Nature of Universals and Propositions' (note 7 below); Nelson Goodman, *The Structure of Appearance* (Cambridge, Mass.: Harvard University Press, 1951), p. 178; Whitehead, *Concept of Nature* (Cambridge: Cambridge University Press, 1920), pp. 157–8; J. M. Keynes, *Treatise on Probability* (London: Macmillan, 1921), p. 385; J. S. Mill, *A System of Logic* (London: Longmans, 1930), p. 67. Mills is quoting Bain.

composed of constituents in relation—though perhaps no more than the spread of a smooth or 'homoeomerous' quale such as a color.

Any trope belongs to as many sets or sums of tropes as there are ways of combining it with other tropes in the world. Of special interest however are (1) the set or sum of tropes which have to it the relation of *concurrence* (the limiting value of location), and (2) the set or sum of those which have to it the relation of *precise similarity* (the limiting value of similarity, sometimes mischievously called 'identity'). For a given trope, of course, one or both of these sets or sums might contain nothing except the trope itself, but it is hard to imagine a world in which there would not be many tropes that belong to well populated sets or sums of both sorts, and in our world such sets or sums are very conspicuous. Speaking roughly, now, the set or sum of tropes concurrent with a trope, such as our color component Harlac, is the concrete particular or 'thing' which it may be said to 'characterize', in our example the lollipop Heraplem, or, to simplify the affair, the knob of the lollipop at a moment. Speaking roughly, again, the set or sum of tropes precisely similar to a given trope, say Harlac again, is the abstract universal or 'essence' which it may be said to exemplify, in our illustration a definite shade of Redness. (The tropes approximately similar to the given one compose a less definite universal.)

The phrase 'set or sum' above is a deliberate hedge. A set is a *class* of which the terms are members; a sum is a whole of which the terms are parts, in the very primitive sense of 'part' dealt with by recent calculi of individuals.[4] In the accompanying figure, for instance, the class of six squares, the class of three rows, and the class of two columns are different from each other and from the one figure; but the sum of squares, the sum of rows, and the sum of columns are identical with one another and with the whole.

What a difference of logical 'type' amounts to, particularly in the philosophy of tropes, is far from clear, but everybody agrees that a sum is of the same type with its terms, as a whole is of the same type with its parts, a man of the same type with his arms and legs. The concept of a class or set, on the other hand, is notably more complex and questionable. A class is surely not, in any clear sense, what it is too often called,[5] 'an abstract entity', but there is some excuse for considering it of a different 'type' from its members. Convinced that tropes compose a concretum in a

[4] Nelson Goodman and Henry Leonard, 'The Calculus of Individuals and Its Uses', *Journal of Symbolic Logic*, 5 (1940), 45–55; Goodman, *The Structure of Appearance*, pp. 42 ff.; Appendix E, by Alfred Tarski, in J. H. Woodger, *The Axiomatic Method in Biology* (Cambridge: Cambridge University Press, 1937), 161–72.

[5] Goodman, *The Structure of Appearance*, p. 150; W. V. Quine, *Methods of Logic* (New York: Holt, 1950), p. 204.

manner logically no different from that in which any other exhaustive batch of parts compose it, we have every incentive to say that the concretum is not the set but the sum of the tropes; and let us so describe it. Whether the counterpart concept of the universal can be defined as the sum of similars —all merely grammatical difficulties aside—is not so clear. There is little doubt that the set or class will do the job. For all the paradoxes which attend the fashionable effort to equate the universal Humanity, for example, with the class of concrete men (including such absurdities as that being a featherless biped is the same as having a sense of humor) disappear when we equate it rather with our new set, the class of abstract humanities—the class whose members are not Socrates, Napoleon, and so forth, but the human trope in Socrates, the one in Napoleon, and so forth. Still wilder paradoxes resulted from the more radical nominalistic device of substituting the *sum* of concrete men for their class,[6] and most even of these are obviated by taking our sum of similar tropes instead. I suspect, however, that some remain, and because concurrence and similarity are such symmetrical counterparts, I shall not be surprised if it turns out that while the concurrence complex must be a sum, the similarity complex must be a set.

In suggesting how both concrete particulars and abstract universals are composed of tropes, I aver that those two categories do not divide the world between them. It does not consist of concrete particulars in addition to abstract universals, as the old scheme had it, nor need we admit that it must be 'constructible' *either* from concrete particulars *or* from abstract universals as recent innovators argue (Carnap and Goodman, respectively, for example). The notions of the abstract and the universal (and hence of the concrete and the particular) are so far independent that their combinations box the logical compass. Socrates is a concrete particular; the component of him which is his wisdom is an abstract particular or 'trope'; the total Wisdom of which all such wisdoms are components or members is an abstract universal; and the total Socratesity of which all creatures exactly like him are parts or members is a 'concrete universal', not in the idealistic but in a strictly accurate sense. It was because of the unfortunate limitation of ordinary philosophic discourse to the two combinations, concrete particular and abstract universal, that in order to call attention to our tropes we had to divert such phrases as 'the humanity of Socrates' or 'the redness of the lollipop', which normally would stand for kinds of degrees of humanity and redness, to stand for their particular cases of Humanity and Redness, respectively, and so we have been driven in turn

---

[6] Witness the doughty struggle of Quine and Goodman in 'Steps Toward a Constructive Nominalism', *Journal of SymbolicLogic*, 12 (1947), 105–22.

to using the capital letters in 'Humanity' and 'Redness' to restore the 'abstract nouns' to their normal duty of naming the respective universals. A similar explanation, but a longer one, would have to be given of our less definite phrases like 'the shape of Boanerp' or 'the color of it'.

Having thus sorted out the rubrics, we can almost automatically do much to dispel the ancient mystery of predication, so influential in the idea of logical types. The prevalent theory has been that if y can be 'predicated' of x, or 'inheres in' or 'characterizes' x, or if x is an 'instance' of y, then x and y must be sundered by a unique logical and ontological abyss. Most of the horror of this, however, which has recently impelled some logicians to graceless verbalistic contortions, is due to taking predication as one indissoluble and inscrutable operation, and vanishes when our principles reveal predication to be composed of two distinct but intelligible phases. 'Socrates is wise', or generically 'a is φ', means that the concurrence sum (Socrates) includes a trope which is a member of the similarity set (Wisdom). When we contrast a thing with a property or 'characteristic' of it, a 'substantive' with an 'adjective', we may intend either or both of these connections. The particular wisdom in Socrates is in one sense 'characteristic', i.e., it is a component, of him—this is the sense in which Stout held, quite properly to my way of thinking, that 'characters are abstract particulars which are predicable of concrete particulars'.[7] The universal Wisdom is in the second sense the 'characteristic' of each such wisdom—this is the sense in which Moore could hold plausibly that even an event, such as a sneeze, *has* characteristics and is not one.[8] In the third or ordinary sense, however, the universal Wisdom 'characterizes' the whole Socrates. From this imbroglio emerge at least two senses of 'instance', the sense in which Socrates is a (concrete) 'instance' of Wisdom and that in which his wisdom component is an (abstract) 'instance' of it, and the two notions of class, the ordinary concreta class consisting of Socrates, Plato, and all other whole wise creatures, and the abstracta class of their wisdoms, our similarity set.

Raying out around the problem of predication is many another half-magical notion about essence and existence which we now can prosily clarify. Thus Mr Broad and Mr Dawes Hicks, while believing in 'Abstracta', have described them in the same fantastic terms in which

---

[7] 'Are the Characteristics of Particular Things Universal or Particular?', a symposium by G. E. Moore, G. F. Stout, and G. Dawes Hicks, *Aristotelian Society Supplementary Volume*, 3 (1923), 95–128, p. 114. His theory of abstract particulars, here and in 'The Nature of Universals and Propositions', *Proceedings of the British Academy*, 10 (1921–23), is almost identical with the one I am defending; if there is a difference it is in his obscure idea of the class as a unique form of unity not reducible to similarity.

[8] *Loc. cit.*, p. 98. Mr Moore, I cannot help thinking, already a very uncommonplace minion of the commonplace, almost fiercely resists understanding the Stout theory.

Santayana described his essences, as placeless and timeless, and hence 'real but non-existent'.[9] This remarkable but not unusual proposition might for a Platonist be grounded in a whole theory of universals *ante rem*, but mostly it results from not distinguishing between its two principal sources: the specious eternity a *universal* has because, as Stout put it, it 'spreads undivided, operates unspent',[10] which for us is just the fact that similarity is a 'saltatory' relation, overleaping spatial and temporal distances undiminished and without cost in stuff or energy; and the specious eternity an *abstractum* has because in attending to it we normally 'abstract from' its spatiotemporal location (which nevertheless it has and keeps). As the obscurity of Essence is thus mostly resolved by looking at it stereoscopically, to distinguish the dimensions of the universal and of the abstract, so too that dark mingling of glory and degradation which haunts Existence and the individual is mostly resolved by the ideas of concreteness and particularity. The Individual is hallowed both by the utter self-identity and self-existence of the particular occurrent and by the inexhaustible richness and the inimitability of the concrete. At the same time, however, it is debased by the very same factors. It seems ignobly arbitrary and accidental, *qua* particular, with respect to its mere self in its external relations, because it thus lacks the similarity, classification, and generalization which could interpret it; and it has the confusion and unfathomability of the concrete, wherein every form struggles in a melee of forms so stupendous that the Aristotelians mistook it for formless matter.

A philosophy of tropes calls for completion in a dozen directions at once. Some of these I must ignore for the present because the questions would take us too far, some because I do not know the answers. Of the first sort would be a refinement and completion of our account of substance and of the similarity manifold. Of the second sort would be an assimilation of the very categories of our theory—concurrence, similarity, abstractness, and so forth—to the theory itself, as tropes like the rest, instead of relegating them to the anomalous immunities of 'transcendentals' (as the old Scholastics said) and 'metalanguage' (as the new scholastics say). What in fact I shall do here is to defend the fundamental notion that there are entities at once abstract, particular, and actual, and this in two ways: the affirmative way of showing how experience and nature evince them over and over, and the negative way of settling accounts with old dialectical objections to them.

[9] Broad, *Mind and Its Place in Nature* (London: Routledge & Kegan Paul, 1925), p. 19; Dawes Hicks, *Critical Realism* (London: Macmillan, 1938), pp. 76–8. Broad can justly marvel that we can cognize what is mental or physical only by 'cognizing objects which are neither' (p. 5).

[10] 'Are the Characteristics, etc.,' p. 116.

I deliberately did not use the word 'abstract' to describe our tropes till we had done our best to identify them in other ways, lest the generally derogatory connotation of the word blind us to the reality of objects as plain as the sunlight (for indeed the sunlight *is* an abstract existent). The many meanings of 'abstract' which make it repulsive to the empirical temper of our age suggest that an abstractum is the product of some magical feat of mind, or the denizen of some remote immaterial eternity. Dictionaries, journalists, and philosophical writers are almost equally vague and various about it. Santayana has it that 'abstract' means imprecise, but also 'verbal, unrealizable, or cognitively secondary'.[11] The abstract is equated with the abstruse, the ethereal, the mental, the rational, the incorporeal, the ideally perfect, the non-temporal, the primordial or ultimate, the purely theoretical, the precariously speculative and visionary; or again with the empty, the deficient, the non-actual or merely potential, the downright imaginary, and the unreal. In some quarters 'abstract' means symbolical, figurative, or merely representative, in contrast with what is real in its own right. On the same page the word may connote alternately the two extremes of precious precision and the vague, confused, or indefinite. Mathematics or logic is called 'abstract' partly because it is about formal structures, partly because it treats them only hypothetically;[12] but a symbolic calculus is called 'abstract' because it isn't about anything. Semanticists and professors of composition shudder away from statements on such 'high levels of abstraction' as 'Herbivority is conducive to bovine complacency' in contrast with the 'concrete' virility of 'Cows like grass', though the two sentences describe exactly the same state of affairs. Logical philosophers proclaim their 'renunciation of abstract entities' without making clear either what makes an entity 'abstract' or how one goes about 'renouncing' an entity.

One wonders, in view of this catalog, if there is anything which would not on occasion be called 'abstract'. Most people would deny that a cat is abstract, but an idealist would say she is. Yet it would be a mistake to infer that 'abstract' has been a wholly indiscriminate epithet. All the uses we have observed, and doubtless others, have stemmed from two roots which in turn are related in a very intimate way. They represent what various persons believed, often mistakenly, is implied by those root ideas. One of them is the use of 'abstract' to mean *transcending individual existence*, as a universal, essence, or Platonic idea is supposed to transcend it. But even though this use of 'abstract' is probably as old as the word itself, I think it

[11] *Realms of Being*, p. 32.
[12] C. I. Lewis, *Mind and the World-Order* (London: Charles Scribner's Sons, 1929), pp. 242, 249.

was in fact derived, by the natural mistake which we earlier noted, from the other aboriginal use, more literally in accord with the word's Latin construction, which is virtually identical with our own. At its broadest the 'true' meaning of 'abstract' is *partial, incomplete,* or *fragmentary,* the trait of what is less than its including whole. Since there must be, for everything but the World All, at least something, and indeed many things, of which it is a proper part, everything but the World All is 'abstract' in this broad sense. It is thus that the idealist can denounce the cat as 'abstract'. The more usual practice of philosophers, however, has been to require for 'abstractness' the more special sort of incompleteness which pertains to what we have called the 'thin' or 'fine' or 'diffuse' sort of constituent, like the color or shape of our lollipop, in contrast with the 'thick', 'gross', or chunky sort of constituent, like the stick in it.[13]

If now one looks at things without traditional prepossessions, the existence of abstracta seems as plain as any fact could be. There is something ironically archaic in the piety with which the new nominalists abhor abstract entities in favor of that 'common-sense prejudice pedantically expressed',[14] the dogma of Aristotle that there can be no real beings except 'primary substances', concrete individuals, as absolute and 'essential' units, and thus turn their backs on one of the greatest insights of the Renaissance, that the apparent primacy of such chunky middle-sized objects is only a function of our own middle size and practical motivation. The great modern philosophies have rather sought the real in putative 'simple natures' at one end of the scale and the one great ocean of action at the other end. I have no doubt that whole things like lollipops, trees, and the moon, do exist in full-blooded concreteness, but it is not they which are 'present to the senses',[15] and it is not awareness of abstracta which is 'difficult, . . . not to be attained without pains and study'.[16] To claim primacy for our knowledge of concreta is 'mysticism' in the strict sense, that is, a claim to such acquaintance with a plethoric being as no

[13] Although this has been for centuries the root meaning of 'abstract', the nearest to a straightforward statement of it which I have found is by Professor Ledger Wood in the *Dictionary of Philosophy,* edited by D. D. Runes (London: Routledge, 1944), p. 2: 'a designation applied to a partial aspect or quality considered in isolation from a total object, which is, in contrast, designated concrete.' Even here the word 'isolation', as we shall see, is delusive.

[14] Russell, *History of Western Philosophy* (London: George Allen & Unwin, 1946), p. 163.

[15] I have in mind Willard Quine's epistemological ballad about Homo javanensis, whose simple faculties 'could only treat of things concrete and present to the senses'. 'Identity, Ostension, and Hypostasis', *Journal of Philosophy,* 47 (1950), 621–33, p. 631 n.

[16] This is Berkeley on abstract ideas, *The Principles of Human Knowledge* (London: 1710), Introduction, §10. It is cited at length by William James, *The Principles of Psychology* (London: Macmillan, 1901), volume 1, p. 469, who argues, correctly I think, that what is difficult is not the recognition of abstracta but the recognition that they are abstract, and the conception of the universal, and that these are at worst no more laborious than the counterpart conception of the concretum.

conceivable stroke of psychophysics could account for. What we primarily *see* of the moon, for example, is its shape and color and not at all its whole concrete bulk—generations lived and died without suspecting it had a concrete bulk; and if now we impute to it a solidity and an aridity, we do it item by item quite as we impute wheels to a clock or a stomach to a worm. Evaluation is similarly focussed on abstracta. What most men value the moon for is its brightness; what a child wants of a lollipop is a certain flavor and endurance. He would much rather have these abstracta without the rest of the bulk than the bulk without the qualities. Integral to the debate between the metaphysical champions of the concrete particular and of the abstract universal has been a discussion whether the baby's first experiences are of whole concrete particulars (his ball, his mother, and so forth) or of abstract universals (redness, roundness, and so forth). For what it may be worth, perhaps not much, a little observation of a baby, or oneself in a babyish mood, will convince the candid and qualified that the object of such absorption is not the abstract universal (the infant does not 'fall from the clouds upon the top-most twig of the tree of Porphyry')[17] and certainly not the concrete particular (that 'foreign thing and a marvel to the spirit'[18] which a lifetime of observation and twenty centuries of research hardly begin to penetrate), but is in sooth the abstract particular or trope, *this* redness, *this* roundness, and so forth.

Though the uses of the trope to account for substances and universals are of special technical interest, the impact of the idea is perhaps greater in those many regions not so staled and obscured by long wont and old opinion and not so well supplied with alternative devices. While substances and universals can be 'constructed' out of tropes, or apostrophized *in toto* for sundry purposes, the trope cannot well be 'constructed' out of them and provides the one rubric which is hospitable to a hundred sorts of entity which neither philosophy, science, nor common sense can forego. This is most obvious in any attempt to treat of the mind, just because the mind's forte is the tuning, focussing, or spotlighting which brings abstracta into relief against a void or nondescript background. A pain is a trope *par excellence*, a mysterious bright pain in the night, for example, without conscious context or classification, yet as absolutely and implacably its particular self as the Great Pyramid. But all other distinguishable contents are of essentially the same order: a love, or a sorrow, or 'a single individual pleasure'.[19]

[17] Brand Blanshard, *The Nature of Thought* (New York: Humanities Press, 1964), volume I, p. 569.

[18] Santayana, *The Unknowable* (Oxford: Clarendon Press, 1923), p. 29.

[19] C. S. Peirce, without the notion of trope, denounces this perfectly intelligible phrase as 'words without meaning', *Collected Papers*, edited by C. Hartshorne and P. Weiss (Cambridge, Mass.: Harvard University Press, 1931), volume I, p. 172.

The notion, however, gets its best use in the theory of knowledge. The 'sensible species' of the Scholastics, the 'ideas' of Locke and Berkeley, the ideas and impressions of Hume, the sense data of recent epistemology— once they are understood as tropes, and as neither things nor essences, a hundred riddles about them dissolve, and philistine attacks on theory of knowledge itself lose most of their point. We need not propose that a red sensum, for example, is perfectly abstract (whatever that might be). But even though it have such distinguishable components as a shape and a size as well as a color, and though the color itself involve the 'attributes' of hue, brightness, and saturation, still it is abstract in comparison with a whole colored solid. According to reputable psychologists, furthermore, there can be data much more abstract, professed 'empiricists' to the contrary notwithstanding: data which have color and no other character, or even hue and no other 'attribute'. The person who uses the theory of tropes to sharpen his sight of what really is present and what is not may not credit such still more delicate components, attributed to the mind, as the imageless thought of the old German schools, or the non-imaginal ideas of Descartes, or the pure concepts of the Scholastics, or the ethereal Gestalten of more recent German evangels; but if any of these do exist, they exist as tropes. The same is to be said, I suppose, of the still darker categories of pure mental act, intentionalities, dispositions, and powers. Such actual but relatively complex mental processes as trains of thought, moral decisions, beliefs, and so forth, taken as particular occurrents, whether comparatively brief or lifelong, and not (as nearly all phrases in this department at least equally suggest) as recurrent kinds, are tropes and compounded of tropes—and the kinds too, of course, are compounds of tropes in their own way. A whole soul or mind, if it is not a unique immaterial substance on its own, is a trope.

X

THE METAPHYSIC OF ABSTRACT PARTICULARS

KEITH CAMPBELL

1. THE CONCEPTION OF PROPERTIES AS PARTICULAR

A classic tradition in first philosophy, descending from Plato and Aristotle, and recently reaffirmed by D. M. Armstrong,[1] proposes two equally essential, yet mutually exclusive, categories of reality: substances (or particulars), which are particular and concrete, and properties (and relations), which are universal and abstract. Material bodies are the most familiar examples of concrete particulars, and their characteristics, conceived of as repeatable entities common to many different objects, are paradigms of abstract universals.

Particular being's distinguishing mark is that it is exhausted in the one embodiment, or occasion, or example. For the realm of space, this restricts particulars to a single location at any one time. Particulars thus seem to enjoy a relatively unproblematic mode of being.

Universals, by contrast, are unrestricted in the plurality of different locations in space-time at which they may be wholly present. Altering the number of instances of a universal (*being a bee*, for example), increasing or decreasing it by millions, in no way either augments or diminishes the universal itself. In my opinion, the difficulty in comprehending how any item could enjoy this sort of reality has been the scandal which has motivated much implausible nominalism in which, with varying degrees of candor, the existence of properties and relations is denied.

The scandal would disappear if properties were not really universal after all. In modern times, it was G. F. Stout who first explicitly made the proposal that properties and relations are as particular as the substances that they qualify.[2] Recently others have given the notion some

Reprinted by permission of the University of Minnesota Press and the author from P. French et al., editors, *Midwest Studies in Philosophy VI: The Foundations of Analytical Philosophy* (Minneapolis: University of Minnesota Press, 1981), 477–88.

[1] D. M. Armstrong, *Universals and Scientific Realism* (Cambridge: Cambridge University Press, 1978).
[2] G. F. Stout, 'The Nature of Universals and Propositions', *Proceedings of the British Academy*, 10 (1921–3), 157–72.

countenance,[3] but its most wholehearted advocate, perhaps, has been D. C. Williams.[4] What are its merits?

In the first place, that a property should, in some sense, enjoy particular being, is not a contradiction in terms. The opposite of *particular* is *universal*, whereas the opposite of *concrete* is *abstract*. In this context, an item is abstract if it is got before the mind by an act of abstraction, that is, by concentrating attention on some, but not all, of what is presented. A complete material body, a shoe, ship, or lump of sealing wax, is concrete; all of what is where the shoe is belongs to the shoe—its color, texture, chemical composition, temperature, elasticity, and so on are all aspects or elements included in the being of the shoe. But these features or characteristics considered individually, e.g., the shoe's color or texture, are by comparison abstract.

The distinction between abstract and concrete is different from that between universal and particular, and logically independent of it. That some particulars as well as universals should be abstract, and that, specifically, cases or instances of properties should be particulars, is at least a formal possibility.

In the second place, it is plain that one way or another, properties must take on or meet particularity in their instances. Consider two pieces of red cloth. There are two pieces of cloth, *ex hypothesi*. Each is red. So there are two occurrences of redness. Let them be two occurrences of the very same shade of redness, so that difference in quality between them does not cloud the issue. We can show that there really are two pieces of cloth (and not, for example, that one is just a reflection of the other) by selective destruction—burn one, leaving the other unaffected. We can show that there really are two cases of redness in the same sort of way; dye one blue, leaving the other unaffected. In this case there remain two pieces of cloth. But there do *not* remain two cases of redness. So the cases of redness here are not to be identified with the pieces of cloth. They are a pair of somethings, distinct from the pair of pieces of cloth. A pair of what? The fact that there are two of them, each with its bounded location, shows that they are particulars. The fact that they are a pair of *rednesses* shows them to be qualitative in nature. The simplest thesis about them is that they are

[3] G. E. L. Owen, 'Inherence', *Phronesis*, 10 (1965), 97–108; Nicholas Wolterstorff, 'Qualities', *Philosophical Review*, 69 (1960), 183–200, and *On Universals* (Chicago: Chicago University Press, 1970); Anthony Quinton, 'Objects and Events', *Mind*, 87 (1979), 197–214; Jerrold Levinson, 'The Particularisation of Attributes', *Australasian Journal of Philosophy*, 58 (1980), 102–15. Panayot Butchvarov, *Being Qua Being* (Bloomington: Indiana University Press, 1979), 184–206, discusses but rejects the view.

[4] D. C. Williams, 'The Elements of Being' [part I is chapter IX of this volume; for part II, see 'Tropes' in the Select Bibliography].

not the compound or intersection of two distinct categories, but are as they seem to be, items both abstract and particular. Williams dubs abstract particulars *tropes*.

The argument above is to the effect that tropes are required in any proper understanding of the nature of concrete particulars (in this case specimen material bodies, pieces of cloth) and that this becomes evident in the analysis of local qualitative change.

A third ground for admitting tropes in our ontology is to be found in the problem of universals itself. The problem of universals is the problem of determining the minimum ontological schedule adequate to account for the similarities between different things, or the recurrence of like qualities in different objects. Take a certain shade of red as an example. Many different items are the same color, this certain shade of red. There is a multiple occurrence involved. But what, exactly, is multiple? The *universal* quality, the shade of red, is common to all the cases but is not plural. On the other hand, the red *objects* are plural enough, but they are heterogeneous. Some are pieces of cloth, others bits of skin of berries, others exotic leaves, dollops of paint, bits of the backs of dangerous spiders, and so on. There is no common recurrent substance.

What does recur, the only element that does recur, is the color. But it must be the color as a particular that is involved in the recurrence, for only particulars can be many in the way required for recurrence.

It is the existence of resembling tropes which poses the problem of universals. The accurate expression of that problem is: What, if anything, is common to a set of resembling tropes?

2. TROPES AS INDEPENDENT EXISTENCES

Williams claims more for tropes than just a place in our ontology; he claims a fundamental place. Tropes constitute, for him, 'the very alphabet of being', the independent, primitive elements which in combination constitute the variegated and somewhat intelligible world in which we find ourselves.

To take this line, we must overcome a longstanding and deeply in-grained prejudice to the effect that *concrete* particulars, atoms or molecules or larger swarms, are the minimal beings logically capable of independent existence.

We are used to the idea that the redness of our piece of cloth, or Julius Caesar's baldness, if they are beings at all, are essentially dependent ones. Without Julius Caesar to support it, so the familiar idea runs, his baldness would be utterly forlorn. Without the cloth, no redness of the cloth. On this view, concrete particulars are the basic particulars. Tropes are at best parasitic.

Being used to an idea, of course, is not a sufficient recommendation for it. When it is conceded that, as a matter of fact, tropes tend to come in clusters and that a substantial collection of them, clinging together in a clump, is the normal minimum which we do in fact encounter, we have conceded all that this traditional point of view has a right to claim. The question at issue, however, is not what is in fact the ordinary minimum in what is 'apt for being', but what that minimum is of metaphysical necessity. The least which could exist on its own may well be less than a whole man or a whole piece of cloth. It may be just a single trope or even a minimal part of a single trope.

And some aspects of experience encourage the view that abstract particulars are capable of independent existence. Consider the sky; it is, to appearance at least, an instance of color quite lacking the complexity of a concrete particular. The color bands in a rainbow seem to be tropes dissociated from any concrete particular.

All Williams requires here, of course, is that dissociated tropes be possible (capable of independent existence), not that they be actual. So the possibility of a Cheshire Cat face, as areas of color, or a massless, inert, impenetrable zone as a solidity trope, or free-floating sounds and smells, are sufficient to carry the point.

The way concrete particularity dissolves in the subatomic world, and in the case of black holes, suggests that dissociated tropes are not just possibilities but are actually to be encountered in this world.

On the view that tropes are the basic particulars, concrete particulars, the whole man and the whole piece of cloth, count as dependent realities. They are collections of co-located tropes, depending on these tropes as a fleet does upon its component ships.

3. THE ANALYSIS OF CAUSATION

D. Davidson has provided powerful reasons why some singular causal statements, like

> The short circuit caused the fire,

are best interpreted as making reference to events.[5] Davidson's example is a specimen of an *event-event* singular causal claim.

[5] Donald Davidson, 'Causal Relations', *Journal of Philosophy*, 64 (1967), 691–703; 'The Logical Form of Action Sentences', in *Logic of Decision and Action*, edited by Nicholas Rescher (Pittsburgh: Pittsburgh University Press, 1966).

But by no means all singular causal statements are of this type. Many involve *conditions* as terms in causal connections. For example:

Condition-event:	The weakness of the cable caused the collapse of the bridge.
Event-condition:	The firing of the auxiliary rocket produced the eccentricity in the satellite's orbit.
Condition-condition:	The high temperature of the frying pan arises from its contact with the stove.

Now the conditions referred to in these examples, the cable's weakness, the orbit's eccentricity, the frying pan's temperature, are properties, but the particular cases of properties involved in particular causal transactions. It is the weakness of this particular cable, not weakness in general or the weakness of anything else, which is involved in the collapse of this bridge on this occasion. And it is not the cable's steeliness, rustiness, mass, magnetism, or temperature, which is at all involved. To hold that the whole cable, as concrete particular, is the cause of the collapse is to introduce a mass of irrelevant characteristics.

The cause of the collapse is the weakness of this cable (and not any other), the whole weakness, and nothing but the weakness. It is a particular, a specific condition at a place and time: so it is an abstract particular. It is, in short, a trope.

Events, the other protagonists in singular causal transactions, are widely acknowledged to be particulars. They are plainly not ordinary concrete particulars.[6] They are, in my opinion, best viewed as trope-sequences, in which one condition gives way to others. Events, on this view, are changes in which tropes replace one another. This is a promising schema for many sorts of change.

Attempts to avert reference to tropes by use of *qua*-clauses do not succeed. If we affirm that

The cable *qua* weak caused the collapse

yet deny that

The cable *qua* steely caused the collapse,

then we are committed to the view that

The cable *qua* weak ≠ the cable *qua* steely.

---

[6] If Quine is right, they are four-dimensional concrete particulars whose boundaries are determined not by material discontinuities but by discontinuities in other respects, which we pre-theoretically describe as discontinuities in *activity*.

So at least one of these terms refers to something other than the cable. What could it be referring to?—only the weakness (or steeliness) of the cable, that is, only to the trope.

The philosophy of cause calls for tropes. That on its own is virtually sufficient recommendation for a place in the ontological sun.

4. PERCEPTION AND EVALUATION

The introduction of tropes into our ontology gives us an extremely serviceable machinery for analyzing any situation in which specific *respects* of concrete particulars are involved.

In the philosophy of perception, tropes appear not only as terms of the causal relations involved but also, epistemically, as the immediate objects of perception. The difficulties involved in direct realism with material objects disappear. Notoriously, we do not see an entire cat, all there is to a cat, for a cat has a back not now perceived and an interior never perceived. The immediate object of vision cannot even be part of the front surface of the cat, for that front surface has a texture and temperature which are not visible, and a microscopic structure not perceptible by any means. So that when you look at a cat what you most directly see is neither the cat nor part of its front surface. This conclusion has, to say the least, encouraged idealist claims that the immediate object of perception is of a mental nature, a percept or representation standing in some special relation to the cat.

In the trope philosophy, a direct realist theory of perception would hold that not cats, but tropes of cats, are what is seen, touched, and so on. The cat's shape and color, but not its temperature or the number of molecules it contains, are objects of vision. Some of the tropes belonging to the cat are perceptible, some not. On any one occasion, some of the perceptible ones are perceived, others are hidden. That is the way in which the senses are selectively sensitive; that is why there is no need for embarrassment in admitting that the senses can give us knowledge only of certain aspects of concrete particulars.

Evaluation is another field in which the admission of tropes does away with awkwardness. Concrete particulars can be simultaneously subject to conflicting evaluations—in different respects, of course. A wine's flavor can be admirable and its clarity execrable, a pole vaulter's strength be splendid and his manners ill. On a trope analysis, the immediate object of evaluation is the trope, so that strictly speaking, different objects are being evaluated when we consider the flavor and the clarity of the wine, and thus the incompatible evaluations give rise to no problem at all.

5. THE PROBLEM OF CONCRETE INDIVIDUALS

The problem of concrete individuals is the problem of how it is possible for many different qualities to belong to one and the same thing. To answer it is to give the constitution of a single individual. For convenience's sake, we tend to discuss the issue in terms of items of medium scale, such as books, chairs, or tables, although we know such objects are not really single units but assemblies of parts which are themselves also individuals. The question of the constitution of a single individual is, of course, quite distinct from the relationship between complex wholes and their simpler parts. To avoid confusion we might do better to use as an example some more plausible specimen of a single concrete individual, such as one corpuscle in classical atomism. Our question is: what is it, in the reality of one corpuscle, in virtue of which it is one, single, complete, distinct individual?

In an ontology that recognizes properties and relations only as *universals*, no satisfactory solution to this question can be found. There are two ways of tackling it:

(i) A complete individual is the union of universal properties with some additional, particularizing reality. For Aristotelians, this will be the Prime Matter that qualities inform, for Lockeans the substratum in which qualities inhere. The common ground of objection to solutions of this type lies in their introduction of a somewhat which, because it lies beyond qualities, lies by its very nature beyond our explorations, describings, and imaginings, all of which are of necessity restricted to the qualities things have. We do well to postpone as long as possible the admission into our ontology of elements essentially elusive and opaque to the understanding.

To avoid such elements, we must deny that in the ontic structure of an individual is to be found any non-qualitative element. Which is precisely the course followed in the other main tradition:

(ii) A complete individual is no more than a bundle of qualities, viz., all and only the qualities that, as we would ordinarily say, the thing has. In banishing 'metaphysical' particularizers, such views are appealing to empiricists, for as long as they can forget their nominalism, which is, of course, incompatible with any bundle theory.

Where the bundle is a bundle of universals, the very same repeatable item crops up in many different bundles (the same property occurs in many different instances). And herein lies the theory's downfall. For it is a necessary truth that each individual is distinct from each other individual. So each bundle must be different from every other bundle. Since the bundles contain nothing but qualities, there must be at least one qualitative difference between any two bundles. In short, this theory requires that the Identity of Indiscernibles be a necessary truth.

Unfortunately, the Identity of Indiscernibles is not a necessary truth. There are possible worlds in which it fails, ranging from very simple worlds with two uniform spheres in a non-absolute space to very complex ones, without temporal beginning or end, in which the same sequence of events is cyclically repeated, with non-identical indiscernibles occurring in the different cycles.

Bundle theories with elements that are universal qualities thus come to grief over the status of the Identity of the Indiscernibles. But where the elements in the bundle are not repeatable universals but particular cases of qualities, not smoothness-in-general but the particular smoothness here, in this place, qualifying this particular tile, the situation is quite different. Now the elements in the bundles are tropes, and no matter how similar they are to one another, the smoothness trope in one tile is quite distinct from the smoothness trope in every other tile. So the bundles can never have any common elements, let alone coincide completely. The question of the Identity of Indiscernibles becomes the question whether all the elements in one bundle match perfectly with all the elements in any other, which is, as it should be, an *a posteriori* question of contingent fact.

Tropes of different sorts can be *compresent* (present at the same place). In being compresent they, in common speech, 'belong to the same thing.' Taken together, the maximal sum of compresent tropes constitutes a complete being, a fully concrete particular. Each fully concrete individual is, of necessity, distinct from every other.

There is no need for any non-qualitative particularizer, nor any problem over the Identity of Indiscernibles. In the trope philosophy, the Problem of Individuals has an elegant solution.

A. Quinton recently proposed that an individual is the union of a group of qualities and a position, and D. M. Armstrong has endorsed a similar view.[7] If we take this as a version of the Lockean *substratum* strategy, it invites the criticism that it involves an *a priori* commitment to absolute space or space-time, anterior to the placing of qualities. To avoid such objectionable *a priori* cosmology, we must hold not that place and the

---

[7] Anthony Quinton, *The Nature of Things* (London: Routledge & Kegan Paul, 1973), part 1; D. M. Armstrong, *Universals*, chapter 11.

quality present at that place are distinct beings, one the particularizer and the other a universal, but that quality-at-a-place is itself a single, particular, reality. And this second view is just the trope doctrine re-expressed.

6. THE PROBLEM OF UNIVERSALS

Tropes can be compresent; this makes possible a solution to the problem of individuals. Tropes can also resemble one another, more or less closely. Williams holds that this facilitates a solution to the problem of universals. I regret to report that I cannot fully share his optimism.

The Problem of Universals is the problem of how the same property can occur in any number of different instances. 'The Problem of Universals' is not really a good name, since the principal issue is whether there *are* any universals; the problem is: what ontological structure, what array of real entities, is necessary and sufficient to account for the likeness among different objects which ground the use on different occasions of the same general term, 'round', 'square', 'blue', 'black', or whatever. 'The Problem of Resemblance' would thus be a better name; proposed solutions consist in theories of the nature of properties.

As with the problem of individuals, philosophical tradition exhibits an ominous unstable oscillation between unsatisfactory alternatives. Realism claims the existence of a new category of entities, not particular, not having any restricted location, literally completely present, the very same item, in each and every different circular object, or square one, or blue one, or whatever. Nominalism holds that roundness and squareness are no more than shadows cast by the human activity of classifying together, and applying the same description to, sundry distinct particular objects. The classic objection to realism is Locke's *dictum* that all things that exist are only particulars. This amounts to the difficulty of believing in universal beings. The objection to nominalism is its consequence that if there were no human race (or other living things), nothing would be like anything else.

Can a philosophy of abstract particulars be of any assistance? Williams claims that a property, such as smoothness, is a set of resembling tropes. Members of this set are instances of the property. Tile A's smoothness, tile B's smoothness, tile C's smoothness, in so far as they resemble one another, all belong to a set S. There are no *a priori* limits on how many members S should have, or how they should be distributed through space and time. So in this respect S behaves as a universal must. Moreover, since the members of S are particular smoothnesses, each of them is fully smooth, not merely partly smooth. This is again a condition which anything proposed as a universal must meet.

The closeness of resemblance between the tropes in a set can vary. These variations correspond to the different degrees to which different properties are specific. According to this view, Resemblance is taken as an unanalyzable primitive, and there are no non-particular realities beyond the sets of resembling tropes. So this view holds that there is *no* entity literally common to the resembling tropes; it is a version of particularism.

Can we take Resemblance as a primitive? Resemblance between tropes, rather than between concrete particulars, avoids two classic objections to this line.

Objection 1. The Companionship Difficulty[8]

Attempts to construct a property as a Resemblance-Class of the items that 'have the property' face this objection: there could be two *different* properties (say, *having a heart* and *having a kidney*), which, as a matter of fact, happen to be present in the very same objects. But if each property is no more than the Resemblance-Class containing all and only those objects, since these two different properties determine the same Resemblance-Class it will turn out that the 'two' properties are not different after all. The theory falsely identifies *having a heart* with *having a kidney*, and indeed any pair of co-extensive properties.

This problem cannot arise where the members of the Resemblance-Class are *tropes* rather than whole concrete particulars. Although the *animals* that have hearts coincide with the animals with kidneys, the instances of having a heart, as abstract particulars, are quite different items from the instances of having a kidney. The Resemblance-Classes for the two properties have no members in common, and there is no basis for the objectionable identification.

Objection 2. The Difficulty of Imperfect Community[9]

In constructing a Resemblance-Class, we cannot just select some object O and take all the objects that resemble O in some way or other. That would yield an utterly heterogeneous collection, with 'nothing in common', as we would intuitively put it.

To avoid saying that the members of the Resemblance-Class must all resemble O in the same respect, which introduces *respects* as realistically conceived universals, we have to require that all the members of the

---

[8] See Nelson Goodman, *The Structure of Appearance*, 2nd edition (Indianapolis: Bobbs-Merrill, 1966), chapter 5.

[9] Nelson Goodman, *The Structure of Appearance*, chapters 5 and 6.

Resemblance-Class must not only resemble O but must also resemble one another.

But although necessary, this restriction is not sufficient. For consider the case where

O_1 has features $P Q R$
O_2 has features $Q R S$
O_3 has features $R S T$
O_4 has features $S T P$

Each of these objects does resemble all the others. But they share no common property. This is the phenomenon of *imperfect community*. Family resemblance classes are examples. Not all resemblance classes pick out a genuine universal property. More precisely, this is the case where the members of the resemblance classes are objects with many different features.

The problem of imperfect community cannot arise where our resemblance sets are sets of tropes. For tropes, by their very nature and mode of differentiation *can* only resemble in one respect. An instance of solidity, unlike a complete material object, does not resemble a host of different objects in a host of heterogeneous ways. The difficulty of imperfect community springs from the complexity of concrete particulars. The simplicity of tropes puts a stop to it.

Although the prospects for a resolution of the problem of universals through appeal to resemblances between tropes are better than those for resemblance between concrete particulars, it is by no means plain that this line succeeds.

The difficulty is that we have an answer to the question: What do two smooth tiles have in common, in virtue of which they are both smooth? They both contain a trope of smoothness; *matching* tropes occur in their makeup. But then we at once invite the question: What do two smooth tropes have in common, in virtue of which they match? And now we have no answer, or only answers that restate the situation: These tropes resemble, or are alike, in virtue of their nature, in virtue of what they are. This leaves us with no answer to the question: Why isn't the way a rough trope is, a ground for matching a smooth trope? We cannot say it is the wrong *sort* of thing. We must just say: because it isn't.

Now explanations must stop somewhere. But is this a satisfactory place to stop?

7. THE ROLE OF SPACE IN A FIRST PHILOSOPHY

The metaphysic of abstract particulars gives a central place to space, or space-time, as the frame of the world. It is through *location* that tropes get their particularity. Further, they are identified, and distinguished from one another, by location. Further yet, the continuing identity over time of the tropes that can move is connected with a continuous track in space-time.

Still further, space (and time) are involved in *co-location*, or compresence, which is essential to the theory's account of concrete particulars. So the theory seems to be committed to the thesis that every reality is a spatio-temporal one. This would make a clean sweep of transcendent gods, Thomist angels, Cartesian minds, Kantian noumena, and Berkeley's entire ontology. But that is too swift, too dismissive.

There is, in fact, a less drastic possibility open. That is, that to the extent that there can be non-spatial particulars, to that extent there must be some analogue of the locational order of space.[10] And in that case, there will be an analogue of location to serve as the principle of individuation for non-spatial abstract particulars.

To concede that there can be non-spatial particulars to the extent that they belong in an array analogous to space is generous enough toward such dubious items.

We are, however, not yet at the end of the special status of space. The geometric features of things, their form and volume, have a special role. Form and volume are not tropes like any others. Their presence in any particular sum of tropes is not an optional, contingent, matter. For the color, taste, solidity, salinity, and so on, which any thing has are essentially spread out. They exist, if they exist at all, *all over* a specific area or volume. They cannot be present except by being present in a formed volume. Tropes are, of their essence, regional. And this carries with it the essential presence of shape and size in any trope occurrence. The often-noticed fact that shape and size, like Siamese twins, are never found except together, is part of this special status of the geometrical features.

Color, solidity, strength are never found except as the-color-of-this-region, the-solidity-of-this-region, and so on. So wherever a trope is, there is formed volume. Conversely, shape and size are not genuinely found except in company with other characteristics. A mere region, a region whose boundaries mark no material distinction whatever, is only artificially a single and distinct being.

[10] Cf. P. F. Strawson, *Individuals* (London: Methuen, 1959), chapter 2.

So the geometric features are doubly special; they are essential to ordinary tropes and in themselves insufficient to count as proper beings. Form and volume are therefore best considered not as tropes in their own right at all. Real tropes are qualities-of-a-formed-volume. The distinctions we can make between color, shape, and size are distinctions in thought to which correspond no distinctions in reality. A change in the size or shape of an occurrence of redness is not the association of the same red trope with different size and shape tropes, but the occurrence of an (at least partly) different trope of redness.

There is no straightforward correlation between distinct *descriptions* and distinct tropes. That predicates may not go hand-in-hand with tropes is important, for therein lies the possibility of reduction, exhibiting one trope as consisting in tropes which before the discovery of the reduction would have been considered 'other' tropes. Reduction is the life and soul of any scientific cosmology. Reductions involving elements in familiar human-scale material bodies provide the best of explanations why tropes ordinarily occur in compresent bundles which cannot be dissociated and whose members resist independent manipulation.

8. THE PHILOSOPHY OF CHANGE AND MODERN COSMOLOGY

The admission of abstract particulars as the basic ontological category gives us a way into the philosophy of change. We all feel in our bones that there is a quite radical distinction to be made between the sorts of changes involved in becoming bald and the sorts involved in becoming a grandfather. The first sort are closer to home. They are intrinsic, whereas the others are in some way derivative, dependent, or secondary. If we content ourselves with an analysis of change in terms of the applicability of descriptions, however, the two sorts of change seem to be on a par.

We can do justice to the feeling in our bones by distinguishing changes in which different descriptions apply to *O* in virtue of a new trope situation at *O* itself, from changes in which the new descriptions apply as a consequence of a new trope situation elsewhere. Trope changes become the metaphysical base from which other sorts of change derive.

We can recognize three basic types of change into which tropes enter:

1. *Motions*, the shifting about of tropes which retain their identity. When a cricket ball moves from the bat to the boundary, it retains its identity, and the tropes that constitute it retain their identity

also. Many *instances of relations*, of being so far, in such direction, from such and such, are involved. For all that has been said so far, these are tropes too. Many such enjoy a brief occurrence during any motion. Because there cannot be relations without terms, in a metaphysic that makes first-order tropes the terms of all relations, relational tropes must belong to a second, derivative order.

2. *Substitutions*, in which one, or more, trope passes away and others take its place. Burning is a classic case. The object consumed does not retain its identity. Its constituent tropes are no more. In their place are others which formerly had no existence.

3. *Variations*. An object gets harder or softer, warmer or cooler. With such qualities which admit of degree, I think we should allow that the same trope, determinable in character though determinate at any given point in time, is involved. Call an abstract element in a situation, extending over time, a *thread*. Variations are homogeneous threads; processes, such as burning, are heterogeneous ones.

The concept of a thread is very useful in ordering categories. Stability is represented by the most homogeneous threads of all. Variations in a quantity, as we have seen, involve no deep discontinuity; different parts of the thread are plainly instances of the same type of property. *Events* are of various sorts: a rise in temperature is a quantitative alteration along a homogeneous thread: an explosion terminates many threads and initiates many different ones. Events, processes, stabilities, and continuities are all explicable as variations in the pattern of presence of tropes. All these are categories constructable from the same basis in abstract particulars.

Attempts to relate these three kinds of change are of course a perfectly proper part of cosmology. Classical atomism, for example, the very apotheosis of concrete particularism, involves the thesis that all three types of change resolve, on finer analysis, into motions, in particular the motions of corpuscles.

But classical atomism is false, and any type of atomism looks unpromising at the present time. The cosmology of General Relativity takes a holistic view of space-time. And it seems positively to call for a trope metaphysic and a break with concrete particularism. The distinction between 'matter' and 'space' is no longer absolute. All regions have, to some degree, those quantities which in sufficient measure constitute the matter of the objects among which we live and move and have our being.

The world is resolved into six quantities, whose values at each point specify the tensor for curved space-time at that point. Material bodies are zones of relatively high curvature.

The familiar concept of a complex, distinct, concrete individual dissolves. In its place we get the concept of quantities with values in regions. Such quantities, at particular locations, are dissociated abstract particulars, or tropes. Considered in their occurrence and variation across all space and time, they are pandemic homogeneous threads.

The metaphysic of abstract particulars thus finds a vindication in providing the most suitable materials for the expression of contemporary cosmology.

XI

TROPES

CHRIS DALY

1. INTRODUCING TROPES

Trope theory is a theory of particularized properties and particularized relations. D. C. Williams in chapter IX, and Keith Campbell in chapter X (and his book *Abstract Particulars*,[1] hereafter *AP*), take it to be an alternative to the theory of universals.[2] The theory of universals posits substances and universals. There are so-called Platonist and Aristotelian versions of this theory, but, for simplicity, I will assume the Aristotelian version when discussing it. According to the theory of universals, properties and relations are universals. That is, they are entities which can be identical between numerically distinct particulars. For instance, consider the property *being red*. According to the theory of universals, if the particulars *a*, *b*, and *c* are each red, one and the same property, the universal *being red*, is identical between them. Trope theory denies this. If *a*, *b*, and *c* are each red, there are three particularized properties here. There is *a*'s particularized property of being red, or *a*'s red trope, there is *b*'s red trope, and there is *c*'s. Each of these red tropes is a distinct particularized property.

The theory of universals also posits substances. Substances are particulars which can have any number of properties or relations. But although tropes are particulars, they are not substances. For each trope there is just the one particularized property or relation. Furthermore, a trope does not have a particularized property or a relation. It just is a particularized property or relation: a property- or a relation-at-a-place-at-a-time. So, for instance, a trope might be the blue of the sky this afternoon or the present weight of this page.

This is a specially rewritten version of a paper first published in the *Proceedings of the Aristotelian Society*, 94 (1994–5), 253–61. Reprinted by courtesy of the Editor of the Aristotelian Society: © 1994–95.

[1] Keith Campbell, *Abstract Particulars* (Oxford: Blackwell, 1990).

[2] Page references to Williams and Campbell in this chapter are to chapters IX and X unless otherwise stated.

2. DEFINING TROPES

The previous section introduced the notion of a trope by contrasting it with the notions of a universal and a substance. This leaves open the question of how, if at all, the notion of a trope should be defined.

Two rival interpretations of tropes are available. On the first, tropes are taken to be both particularized properties and fundamental entities.[3] On the second, tropes are taken to be particularized properties but not fundamental entities. Williams (p. 115) and Campbell (p. 127; *AP*, pp. xi, 4, 20, 81) hold the first interpretation. The second interpretation takes a trope to be a complex entity which can be understood in other terms. For instance, on this interpretation it might be held that a trope is a substance having a universal.

The availability of these two different interpretations of tropes matters for the following reason. Williams and Campbell present certain arguments which are intended to show that there are tropes according to the first interpretation. These arguments, however, show only that there are tropes according to one or other of these interpretations. Specifically, these arguments can be accommodated by the theory of universals. This theory can take these arguments as showing that there are tropes, but where tropes are understood as substances having universals.[4] Therefore, these arguments by Williams and Campbell fail to show that there are tropes according to the first interpretation.

As an illustration of these arguments, consider Campbell's account of causal statements. Campbell takes causal statements, such as 'the weakness of the cable caused the collapse of the bridge' or 'the high temperature of the frying pan arises from contact with the stove', and claims that

the conditions referred to in these examples, the cable's weakness, . . ., the frying pan's temperature, are . . . the particular cases of properties involved in particular causal transactions (p. 129).

A realist about universals, however, could accept the claim made in this passage, and yet take these particular cases to be certain substances having certain universals, namely a cable's having a certain *weakness* universal, and a frying pan's having a certain *temperature* universal. So this argument fails to show that the particular cases referred to are tropes according to Williams and Campbell's chosen interpretation.

---

[3] For simplicity, I will concentrate on particularized properties. What I will say about them carries over straightforwardly to particularized relations.

[4] For this strategy, see also D. M. Armstrong, *Nominalism and Realism: Universals and Scientific Realism Volume I* (Cambridge: Cambridge University Press, 1978), p. 80.

Again, both Williams (p. 123) and Campbell (p. 130) claim that the objects of perception and of evaluation are tropes. Our senses are selectively sensitive because on any given occasion some, but not all, of an object's properties are perceived (we see a cat's shape, but not its mass). Likewise, different features of an object's properties may be evaluated differently (a medicine may be effective but its smell may be vile). Again, however, these claims are consistent with taking tropes to be substances having universals. Related points apply to Williams's further claims (p. 124) that mental events and the objects of knowledge are tropes.

Williams (pp. 114–15) explains the sense in which tropes are fundamental entities in terms of a part–whole relation. According to Williams, tropes are abstract entities. He opposes the terms 'abstract' and 'gross', wherehe understands 'abstract' to mean 'partial, incomplete, or fragmentary' (p. 122). To take his example, Heraplem (a lollipop head) is a gross part of lollipop No. 1. The colour-cum-shape of Heraplem is a 'finer' or 'more abstract' part of this lollipop, and Harlac (the colour trope of this lollipop) is a yet 'finer' and yet more 'abstract' part of the lollipop. Accordingly, Williams proposes that

entities like our fine parts or abstract components are the primary constituents of this or any possible world, the very alphabet of being (p. 115).

In this sense, then, Williams takes tropes to be fundamental entities. There are, however, at least two respects in which his definition of the notion of a trope is unsatisfactory.

First, it is not clear which parts of a given object are tropes and which are not. Williams says (p. 114) that Paraplete (the stick of lollipop No. 1) is a gross part of this lollipop, and so not a trope, whereas Harlac (the colour of this lollipop) is a 'fine or diffuse' part, and so is a trope. But Williams apparently takes the distinction between the abstract and the concrete (in his sense of those terms) to form a continuum. Thus, Paraplete is less concrete than Paraplete-cum-Heraplem, and Harlac is less abstract than the part which consists solely in its left-hand side. But then it is unclear what the rationale is for saying that certain parts are tropes, and that certain other parts are not. It is unclear how 'fine' or 'abstract' a part must be for it to qualify as a trope. Williams provides no principled answer to these questions.

Second, Williams takes the parts of a lollipop to include its colour-cum-shape and its colour. But, at least on the face of it, the parts of a lollipop are not these, but physical pieces each of which has a colour, shape, taste, and so on. And if there are parts of the lollipop which themselves lack parts, then these are also physical parts of the lollipop, with whatever physical properties belong to the smallest parts of matter. But again these parts are not the colour of the lollipop nor its shape. Accordingly, it seems that Williams's project of defining tropes as the 'finest' or 'most abstract' parts of objects does not give him the results which he wants.[5]

In what follows I will not attempt to improve on Williams's definition of the notion of a trope. But I will return to the question of what it means to say that tropes are fundamental entities.

3. THE CASE FOR TROPES

In chapter X, Campbell states what he takes to be three merits of trope theory (pp. 126–7). Since, however, there are two different interpretations of what tropes are, I will argue that where these are genuine merits of trope theory, they are shared with the theory of universals.

First, Campbell claims that the distinction between the abstract and the concrete cross-cuts the distinction between the particular and the universal. Accordingly, he states that 'it is at least a formal possibility' that some particulars should be abstract, and that some properties should be particulars (p. 126). But if the 'formal possibility' that tropes exist is a merit of trope theory, then it also seems to be a 'formal possibility' that there are substances (entities which are concrete and particular) and universals (entities which are abstract and universal). So this merit is shared with the theory of universals. Now Campbell might dispute this, since he thinks that the notion of a universal—the notion of an entity which can be identical between numerically distinct particulars—is a scandalous and obscure notion (p. 125). This, however, suggests that the mere fact that the distinction between the abstract and the concrete cross-cuts the distinction between the particular and the universal does not entail that it is a formal possibility that there are universals. But if so, it is not clear why this fact should nevertheless entail that it is a formal possibility that there are tropes.

Campbell introduces the second alleged merit of trope theory by pointing out that tropes are both abstract and particular (p. 125). Campbell's sense of the term 'abstract' differs from Williams's. According to Campbell, an entity is abstract if it can be 'brought before the mind only by a process of selection' (p. 126, *AP*, p. 3).[6] He then argues that 'the simplest

---

[5] For related criticism of the claim that tropes are parts of the objects which they are tropes of, see Peter Simons, 'Particulars in Particular Clothing: Three Trope Theories of Substance', *Philosophy and Phenomenological Research*, 54 (1994), pp. 563–4.

[6] Note that Williams (p. 122) rejects this as a reading of the sense in which tropes are abstract.

thesis' is that tropes are both abstract and particular, rather than 'the compound or intersection of two distinct categories' namely, substances and universals (pp. 126–7). He concludes that the simplest thesis is that tropes are fundamental entities which are both abstract and particular.

Campbell's definition of the term 'abstract' is unsatisfactory. There is a trivial sense in which any entity can be 'brought before the mind' (i.e. thought about) only if it is selectively attended to. For instance, to think about Bill Clinton's cat, you need to attend to one particular cat out of all the many cats there are, and you need to attend to the cat, not to its owner. Waiving this, the contrast which Campbell draws between taking a trope to be both abstract and particular, and taking it to be a substance having a universal, is a false one. Recall the second interpretation of what a trope is. On this interpretation, a trope is a complex entity which can be understood as a substance having a universal. Thus, a trope involves a universal, and so in that respect is abstract. But it also involves the substance having that universal, and so in that respect is particular. Therefore, even if the simplest thesis is to take tropes to be both particular and abstract, this thesis is compatible with taking tropes to be substances having universals. So the claim that tropes are both abstract and particular does not entail that they are fundamental entities, and that they are not substances having universals.

The third merit of trope theory which Campbell cites is as follows. A property, such as *being red*, recurs between distinct particulars. Moreover, Campbell claims, 'only particulars can be many in the way required for recurrence' (p. 127). He concludes that 'it must be the colour as a particular that is involved in the recurrence' (p. 127).

Now a property recurs between distinct particulars if and only if it is a universal which many substances have. So then it seems that the theory of universals accommodates both premises of Campbell's argument: a universal recurs between particulars, and the particulars which it recurs between are substances. But then Campbell's conclusion that the property *being red* is a particular does not follow. Indeed, as Campbell has stated it, his first premise is incompatible with trope theory. For a property recurs between distinct particulars if and only if it is a universal. But since a trope is a particular, it cannot recur. Therefore, so far from stating a merit of trope theory, Campbell's third argument undermines trope theory.

In *AP* Campbell offers three general considerations in support of trope theory (pp. 6–17). First, he argues that trope theory is superior to the theory of universals. Positing universals and substances faces a series of difficulties. How can one and the same entity—a universal—recur between distinct particulars, and thereby be wholly present at different spatial locations at the same time? What is a substance when stripped of its universals? And how are substances and universals related? Some philosophers posit a relation of *instantiation* to link them, but this seems even more obscure than the entities it relates. By contrast, since his version of trope theory does not posit substances or universals, Campbell believes that it avoids all of these difficulties.

Second, both Williams and Campbell contend that all other categories of entity can be accounted for in terms of the category of tropes.[7] For instance, Williams (p. 117) and Campbell (*AP*, pp. 43–5) claim that apparently shared properties and relations, such as the *furriness* of two rabbits, can be accounted for in terms of exactly resembling tropes. Again, they claim that the concrete particulars around us, such as rabbits and tables, can be accounted for in terms of different tropes with the same spatio-temporal location. Thus, they take rabbits and tables to be 'bundles' of tropes (Campbell, *AP*, pp. 20–1, 42, 58–9).

Campbell's third argument draws on Occam's Razor (*AP*, p. 17). We should not accept two or more categories of entity as fundamental if we need to accept only one as fundamental. Campbell then claims that instead of accepting as fundamental the categories of universals and substances, we need accept only the category of tropes as fundamental. Therefore, he concludes, the theory of universals should be rejected and trope theory accepted.

To assess these arguments, I will examine three theses advanced by Williams and Campbell. First, there is the general thesis that trope theory provides accounts of all other categories of entity. Second, there is the thesis that apparently shared properties and relations can be accounted for in terms of exactly resembling tropes. Third, there is the thesis that concrete particulars can be accounted for in terms of tropes with the same spatio-temporal location. I will examine these theses over the next four sections.

4. TROPES AND THEIR ACCOUNTS

In what sense does trope theory provide accounts of every other category of entity? What sort of accounts are these?[8] Williams describes tropes as

---

[7] 'Any possible world, and hence, of course, this one, is completely constituted by its tropes and their connections of location and similarity, and any others there may be' (Williams, p. 116).

[8] Williams and Campbell explicitly talk in terms of how tropes 'account' for other entities. See for example Williams (p. 123) and Campbell (*AP*, p. 24).

the primary constituents of this or any possible world, the very alphabet of being. They not only are actual but are the only actualities, in just this sense, that whereas entities of all other categories are literally composed of them, they are not in general composed of any other sort of entity (p. 115).

And again he says that

any possible word, and hence, of course, this one is completely constituted by its tropes and their connections of locations and similarity, and any others there may be (p. 116).

Similarly, Campbell says that

metaphysics . . . aspires, among other things, to give an account of the fundamental constituents of any reality and an exposition of how these constituents mesh to give us the reality in question . . .
    To offer a description of the basic constituents in a real situation, and of the relations between them, is to furnish an *ontological assay* of that situation. The ontological assay of any real situation uncovers its ontic structure (*AP*, p. 1).

Unfortunately, Williams and Campbell do not develop these claims further, but we might understand them as follows. Consider any entity E (some 'real situation') belonging to any given category. An account of E (an 'ontological assay') is a description of E's fundamental constituents (its 'ontic structure'). The fundamental constituents of every entity are its tropes. So an account of E is a description of what tropes exist, and of how these tropes are related to each other and to E, if and only if E exists.

On this reading, Williams and Campbell are making the following five claims:

(1) there are entities belonging to different categories;
(2) tropes belong to a single category of entities;
(3) tropes are 'primary' or 'fundamental' or 'basic constituents';
(4) tropes are the only fundamental constituents; and
(5) tropes constitute entities of all other categories.

Let us consider these claims in turn.

Intuitively, the categories provide an exclusive and exhaustive classification of all possible entities. Campbell and Williams take tropes, substances, and universals to belong to distinct categories. Now they hold that the distinction between the abstract and the concrete cross-cuts the distinction between the universal and the particular. This yields a four-fold classification which takes tropes, substances, and universals to belong to distinct categories. For instance, tropes are abstract particulars, whereas substances are (a species of) concrete particulars. So, if this classification were to establish what categories there are, it would explain why tropes, substances, and universals belong to distinct categories.[9]

_____
[9] This is clearest in pp. 125–7 of chapter X. See also *AP*, pp. 2–4.

It is not clear, however, whether Williams and Campbell do take these four categories to be the only categories. For instance, Williams says that

the trope ... provides the one rubric which is hospitable to a hundred sorts of entity which neither philosophy, science, nor common sense can forgo (p. 123).

Likewise, Campbell (*AP*, pp. 22–4) says that there are various 'structures' which trope theory can account for, and he cites events, causes, and real and Cambridge changes as examples. But Williams and Campbell do not define what they mean by a 'sort' or by a 'structure' respectively. Nor do they say how sorts or structures are related to categories.

Turning to claim (3), Williams and Campbell variously describe tropes as being 'primary' or 'fundamental' or 'basic constituents'. I take these to be synonyms. The claim here appears to be that an entity is fundamental if and only if it has no constituents. We might then say that a category is fundamental if all the entities belonging to it are fundamental, and that a category is not fundamental if some of the entities belonging to it are not fundamental. But although this might help clarify what the term 'fundamental' means, it raises the pressing question of what the term 'constituent' means.

Claim (4) is apparently the claim that every entity of every category (besides that of the category of tropes) is constituted by tropes, but that no trope is constituted by entities belonging to any category other than the category of tropes. Note that the claim that tropes are fundamental constituents (claim (3)) does not entail that tropes are the only fundamental constituents (claim (4)). Someone might accept both tropes but also the entities belonging to another category as fundamental constituents. For instance, C. B. Martin accepts both tropes and substances as fundamental.[10] Hence the claim that tropes are the only fundamental constituents is a further, independent claim. Moreover, as before, the claim that tropes are the only fundamental constituents is clear only in so far as the notion of 'constituent' is itself clear.

The claim, then, that tropes 'constitute' entities of all other categories crucially needs clarification. In §2 we saw that Williams took this constitution relation to be a part–whole relation. But we also saw the difficulties facing him in taking this to be the same relation as the part–whole relation which holds between a physical object and its physical parts. By contrast, Campbell does not say what he means by a 'constituent'. He merely states that 'the question of the constitution of a single individual is, of course, quite distinct from the relationship between complex wholes and their simple parts' (p. 131). So neither Williams nor Campbell

[10] C. B. Martin, 'Substance Substantiated', *Australasian Journal of Philosophy*, 58 (1980), 3–10.

provides a satisfactory general definition of what it is for a trope to be a constituent of something.

Nevertheless, at least for some cases they provide specific accounts of how the entities belonging to various categories are supposed to be constituted by tropes. For instance, they offer an account of how properties which are apparently shared by distinct objects, such as *being 5kg-in-mass* or *being red*, are constituted by tropes. Again, they offer an account of how concrete particulars, such as cats and cabbages, are constituted by tropes. As we will see in §5, Williams and Campbell say that a trope *F* is a constituent of the apparently shared property *being 5kg-in-mass* if and only if *F* exactly resembles every *5kg-in-mass* trope. Accordingly, they can say that the apparently shared property *being 5kg-in-mass* is exhaustively constituted (my phrase) by all and only the members of the class of *5kg-in-mass* tropes closed under exact resemblance. Again, as we shall see in §6, Williams and Campbell say that a trope *F* is a constituent of an ordinary particular *a* if and only if *F* has the same location in space and time as *a*. Accordingly, they can say that an ordinary particular such as *a* is exhaustively constituted by all and only those tropes which are at the same location in space and time as *a*.

In these ways Williams and Campbell provide specific accounts of how both apparently shared properties and ordinary particulars are constituted by tropes. In the following three sections I will see how adequate these accounts are.

5. TROPES AND RESEMBLANCE

Suppose that two rabbits are both 5kg in mass. According to trope theory, each of these rabbits has a *5kg-in-mass* trope. It might seem that these rabbits have something in common, namely, a shared property of *being 5kg-in-mass*. But according to trope theory these rabbits share the property of *being 5kg-in-mass* only in the sense that their *5kg-in-mass* tropes exactly resemble each other. The apparently shared property *being 5kg-in-mass* can be accounted for in terms of tropes. The field of tropes can be partitioned into classes closed under exact resemblance. Consider then the class of *5kg-in-mass* tropes closed under exact resemblance. All and only *5kg-in-mass* tropes are members of this class. It is then open for the trope theorist to say that the apparently shared property *being 5kg-in-mass* is not a universal. It is the class of *5kg-in-mass* tropes closed under exact resemblance. The trope theorist can say that the sense in which rabbits and cabbages have the apparently shared property of *being 5kg-in-mass* is just that these objects have tropes which are members of this class.[11]

[11] Williams, p. 118; Campbell, pp. 133–6 and *AP*, pp. 30–2, 43–5.

How successful is this account? Russell argued against theories that rejected universals but accepted the *resemblance* relation (see chapter II). He argued that *resemblance* must be admitted as a universal, on pain of a vicious regress of resemblance-instances. Adapted against trope theory, his argument might run as follows.

Consider three concrete particulars which are the same shade of red. They will exactly resemble each other in colour. Trope theory attempts to provide an account of this. According to it, each of these concrete particulars has a red trope—call these tropes F, G, and H—and these concrete particulars exactly resemble each other in colour because F, G, and H exactly resemble each other in colour. But it seems that this account is incomplete. It seems that the account should further claim that resemblance tropes hold between F, G, and H. That is, it seems that there are resemblance tropes holding between the members of the pairs F and G, G and H, and F and H. The *prima facie* case for this is that just as trope theory accounted for the resemblances between the above concrete particulars in terms of tropes, so too it seems that it should account for the resemblances between F, G, and H in terms of tropes.

Let us call the resemblance tropes in question R_1, R_2, and R_3. Each of these resemblance tropes is an *exactly-resembles-in-colour* trope holding between two *red* tropes. So each of these resemblance tropes in turn exactly resembles each other. Therefore, certain resemblance tropes hold between these tropes. That is, there are (further) resemblance tropes holding between the pairs R_1 and R_2, R_2 and R_3, and R_1 and R_3. Call these new resemblance tropes R_4, R_5, and R_6. Now, each of these resemblance tropes is an exact resemblance trope holding between two *exactly-resembles-in-colour* tropes. Specifically, each of these tropes is a trope of *exact-resemblance-between-two-exactly-resembles-in-colour* tropes. Therefore, each of these new tropes exactly resembles each other. Consequently, there must be yet further resemblance tropes, ones holding between the pairs formed by R_4, R_5, and R_6. Again, these resemblance tropes will exactly resemble each other, and we are launched on a regress.

Now trope theory sought to provide an account of resemblances between particulars solely in terms of tropes. In the example given, trope theory attempted to account for the resemblances between three red concrete particulars in terms of the red tropes F, G, and H. But this account is incomplete if it fails to account for the resemblances between these tropes themselves. So it seems that trope theory should account for the resemblances between F, G, and H in terms of the relational tropes R_1, R_2, and R_3. But these new latter tropes in turn resemble each other, and so Russell's argument is restored one level up. Thus, the trope theorist's account remains incomplete, and so he has not established his claim that an account of resemblances between particulars can be given solely in terms of tropes. The trope theorist might then attempt to provide an account of the resemblances between R_1, R_2, and R_3 in terms of further tropes. Yet the same type of result occurs: introducing new resemblance tropes introduces new tropes which resemble each other, and an account needs to be given in turn of these resemblances. This result recurs at every stage at which the trope theorist applies his account. At every stage his account will entail that there are resemblances between tropes which have not been accounted for. It follows that at every stage the account offered fails to show that resemblances between particulars can be accounted for solely in terms of tropes. It is this failure which drives the regress and makes it vicious. Moreover, if the trope theorist's account fails, the resemblance relation cannot be a trope, but must be a universal: something shared between resembling particulars.

To counter this argument, the two most promising strategies for the trope theorist seem to be the following. First, he might resist the inference from 'F and G resemble each other' to 'there exists a resemblance between F and G'. Second, he might grant that Russell has shown there is a regress, but deny that it is vicious. Now either of these may be the right response for the trope theorist to make, but this would need to be brought out. For with respect to the first strategy, the trope theorist is prepared to infer from 'F and G are concurrent' to 'there exists a concurrence relation between F and G'. So an argument is needed to show why this pattern of inference is acceptable in the case of concurrence, but not in the case of resemblance. And with respect to the second strategy, it needs to be shown why the resemblance regress is not vicious—it needs to be shown what features it has, or lacks, which make it a virtuous regress. In what follows I will consider various responses to Russell's regress argument which follow one or other of these strategies.

Both H. H. Price,[12] and Campbell (*AP*, p. 36) maintain that the theory of universals faces a similar regress. For suppose a, b, and c are substances which are *red*. These substances will resemble each other and so instantiate a further universal, namely, *resembling-in-respect-to-red*. But the instances of this universal in turn resemble each other, and so again there is a regress. But why should the realist about universals suppose that in addition to the universal *being red* there is a further one, namely *resembling-in-respect-to-red*? According to the realist about universals, for substances a, b, and c to resemble each other in respect to red just is for a, b, and c to be *red*. No further universal is called for. We have simply

---

[12] H. H. Price, *Thinking and Experience* (London: Hutchinson, 1953), pp. 23–4.

redescribed the original universal. So the regress never even starts and there is no parallel of Russell's argument here.

Price also claims that Russell's argument begs the question by taking *resemblance* to be a universal. This charge is puzzling. The argument poses a dilemma: namely, that either *resemblance* is a universal, or there is a regress of particularized *resemblances*. It is not clear how this begs the question. In fact Price seems to address this dilemma and to choose the second limb, only he further claims that there are orders of resemblance (p. 25). Russell's argument, however, can grant that particularized *resemblances* form a hierarchy of orders. But this just marks distinctions between each stage of the regress. By itself it does not show that the regress is virtuous.

Campbell claims that the original regress is not vicious because it proceeds in a direction of 'greater and greater formality and less and less substance' (*AP*, pp. 35–6). But it is not clear how literally these notions are to be construed. Moreover, by itself this claim does not show that the regress is virtuous. Each stage of a vicious regress can equally be characterized as being 'more formal' and 'less substantial' than its predecessors. But if so, the inference from the claim that a given regress has these characteristics to the claim that it is a virtuous regress is invalid.

It might be replied that in a genuinely vicious regress the very same (type of) entity reappears at each stage of the regress. But at each stage of the resemblance regress the resemblances have an increasingly abstract character. So it is not the case that the very same entity appears at each stage of this regress, and therefore it is not vicious. There remains, however, the question of what this abstract character is and of when we should say that the entities in a regress have such an 'increasingly abstract character'. Furthermore, it is arguable that on Campbell's own account of resemblance, the resemblances in the regress do not assume such an increasingly abstract character. Consider this passage:

The only difference (apart from irrelevancies like place or time) between an exactly resembling pair of reds and an exactly resembling pair of greens is that the first pair are reds and that the second greens. The *resemblings* do not have any added distinguishing character (*AP*, p. 72).

Now if there is no added distinguishing character between resemblances at the same stage of the regress, it seems natural to say that there is no added distinguishing character between resemblances at *different* stages of the regress. It seems that the resemblance relations that occur at each stage differ from those at other stages only in their *relata* and that these relations do not have any 'added distinguishing character'. It follows that these resemblances do not become increasingly abstract as we ascend the regress. So Campbell's inference is blocked. Indeed, according to the above, it is the case that the very same (type of) *relatum* occurs at each stage of the resemblance regress.

Campbell also argues that because each of the successive stages in the regress supervenes on its predecessor, none of them constitute ontic additions. According to his conception of supervenience, 'supervenient "additions" to ontology are "pseudo-additions"' (*AP*, p. 37).[13] They involve no new ontic commitment. Campbell's reason for supposing that the regress is only a case of supervenience is that it has a certain 'pattern of dependence'. Namely, given the first stage, 'the later terms in the regress arise by a smooth piece of logical reflection'; they follow by 'an automatic inevitability'; and they are 'what they are entirely because the earlier ones are as *they* are' (*AP*, p. 37). But again these points equally apply to the stages of a vicious regress. There is a 'pattern of dependence' in a vicious regress as there is in any regress. Thus, when we 'logically reflect' on a vicious regress, we find that its later terms must follow from the earlier ones; it is because of what the earlier stages in such a regress are that the later stages are what they are; and these stages also follow with 'automatic inevitability'. So Campbell's claims again fail to distinguish a virtuous regress from a vicious one. Therefore, he has not countered the charge that Russell's regress is vicious.

Campbell's last reason for supposing that a *resemblance* relation supervenes on its relata is that it is an internal relation (*AP*, pp. 37, 58). That is, it is a relation that necessarily holds given just the existence of its relata. But this does not show that *resemblance* supervenes on its relata in the sense of being no ontic addition to them. For *resemblance* could be an ontic addition that is necessarily incurred given just the existence of its *relata*. Consider a parallel. There is a necessary connection between murderers and murders such that, necessarily, if murderers exist so too do murders. But this does not show that a murder is not an ontic addition to the existence of a murderer.

Furthermore, it is true that, necessarily, if two concrete particulars each have a red trope, then these concrete particulars exactly resemble each other. But it does not follow that there is no resemblance relation between them. Likewise, it is true that, necessarily, if an *exactly-resembles-with-respect-to-red* relation holds between two concrete particulars, then each of them is red. Yet it does not follow that they do not each have a red trope. But if the latter inference is rejected (as the trope theorist must reject it), then by parity of reasoning the former inference should also be rejected.

I conclude that Russell's regress argument stands: a universal of *resemblance* has to be admitted and it cannot be accounted for in terms of tropes. Since a category can be accounted for in terms of tropes if and only if every entity which belongs to that category can be accounted for in terms of tropes, it follows that the category of universals cannot be accounted for in terms of tropes. Therefore, the trope theorist has to admit it as a fundamental category.

The next issue is whether ordinary objects—concrete particulars—can be accounted for in terms of bundles of concurrent tropes.

6. TROPES AND ORDINARY OBJECTS

Both trope theory and the theory of universals need to provide some account of what concrete particulars, such as rabbits and tables, are, and of how they have properties and relations (or, as trope theory would have it, particularized properties and relations).

Within the theory of universals, the two chief accounts of particulars are the bundle theory of universals and the substance–attribute theory of universals. On the former theory, particulars are taken to be 'bundles' of universals. On the latter theory, particulars are taken to be substances, where substances are particulars which can have universals. On the first theory, particulars are not fundamental entities; on the second theory, they are. Take these theories in turn.

On the bundle theory, a particular is a complex or 'bundle' of universals.[14] The bundle is formed by a *concurrence* relation holding between the members of each pair of universals in the bundle. Since this theory has been effectively criticized by others,[15] I will turn directly to the substance–attribute theory of universals.

The substance–attribute theory of universals involves two fundamental categories of entities: substances and universals. On this theory, a concrete particular has a property if and only if there is a substance, there is a universal property, and that substance has that property. Campbell, however, thinks that the notion of a substance faces some serious problems (*AP*, pp. 6–11). Here are three of them. First, either a substance is a particular which itself has properties, or it is a particular which itself lacks

[14] See for example Bertrand Russell, *An Inquiry into Meaning and Truth* (London: George Allen & Unwin, 1940), chapter 6, and *Human Knowledge: its Scope and Limits* (London: George Allen & Unwin, 1948), part II, chapter 3, and part IV, chapter 8.

[15] Armstrong, *Nominalism and Realism*, chapter 9; Campbell, pp. 131–2, and *AP*, pp. 18–20.

properties. By the first limb, a substance is a bare particular. But then, Campbell objects,

> the problem with bare particulars is that they have no properties. But if they have no properties they must be absolutely indistinguishable from one another. So how is it possible for there to be more than one of them? (*AP*, p. 7).

By the second limb, a substance is a complex entity which can be understood in terms of a particular having various universals. But then the above dilemma recurs: either such a particular itself has properties or it does not. It seems that we have not advanced our understanding.

The second problem is that it seems possible that two distinct ordinary objects should have exactly the same universals: the same mass, size, shape, colouring, and so forth. According to the substance–attribute theory of universals, these objects are distinct if and only if there are two distinct substances here. But Campbell objects that

> the substance is the particularizer; its role is to give the object in which it occurs a particular reality, as a definite object. But it is not enough to be *a* definite object. Something more is required. This object must be not just some particular or other . . .; it is this very one and no other. So we need not only a particularizer, but an *individuator* as well. Substrata particularize, but they do not seem able to individuate, precisely because they are indistinguishable from one another (*AP*, p. 7).

His third objection is that substances and the universals which they have must be somehow related. So it seems that there must be a relation of *instantiation* between substances and their universals. But it remains mysterious what this relation is and how it can fulfil this role.

Does trope theory escape these various difficulties? It needs to provide some account of concrete particulars, such as rabbits, tables, and the like, in terms of tropes. As with the theory of universals, such an account might be given by a bundle theory or by a substance–attribute theory. Williams (pp. 115–6) and Campbell (§2; *AP*, §2) endorse a bundle theory of tropes, whereas C. B. Martin and Michael C. LaBossiere endorse a substance–attribute theory of tropes.[16]

A theory which admits both substances and tropes, however, faces similar objections to those facing a theory of substances and universals. The notion of a substance remains obscure. An *instantiation* relation would be needed to connect tropes to the substances they are tropes of. And any theory which took both substances and tropes to be fundamental entities would be less ontologically economical than a theory which took only tropes to be fundamental entities.[17]

---

[16] Martin, 'Substance Substantiated', especially pp. 5–9; Michael C. LaBossiere, 'Substances and Substrata', *Australasian Journal of Philosophy*, 72 (1994), 360–9, especially pp. 367–9.

[17] See Campbell, *AP*, pp. 69–70, and Simons, 'Particulars in Particular Clothing', §5, for

Nevertheless, the bundle theory of tropes faces questions of its own. First, are tropes any less obscure than substances? Second, can concrete particulars be accounted for in terms of bundles of concurrent tropes? I will consider the first of these questions in the remainder of this section, and consider the second question in the next section.[18]

We saw above two problems which Campbell raises about substances. But similar ones also face tropes. First, consider a class of exactly resembling tropes, such as the class of *red* tropes. We can then raise the following dilemma. A *red* trope is a particularized property which either lacks a particularized property or has a particularized property. By the first limb, a *red* trope lacks a particularized property. But then Campbell's criticism of bare particulars should also apply to the members of the class of *red* tropes, namely that

if they have no properties they must be absolutely indistinguishable from one another. So how is it possible for there to be more than one of them? (*AP*, p. 7).

By the second limb of the dilemma, trope theory claims that a *red* trope is a complex entity which can be understood in terms of a particularized property having a particularized property. But then the above dilemma recurs with respect to this additional particularized property. Either it has or it lacks a particularized property. So it seems that we have not advanced our understanding.

Furthermore, we cannot say that a given trope is the one it is because it occupies a certain space-time location. More than one trope can occupy the same spatio-temporal location, and it even seems possible for a pair of exactly resembling tropes to occupy the same spatio-temporal location.[19] For instance, a proton has two up quarks, each with charge $+2e/3$. On the assumption that quarks occupy a single space-time point, these quarks exactly resemble each other, and have the same spatio-temporal location.[20] Thus, Campbell's claim that tropes are 'identified and distinguished from one another by location' seems mistaken (p. 136).

Trope theory also faces a problem similar to the second problem which Campbell raised against substance. It seems possible for there to be two distinct concrete particulars, such that, for every trope of each of the particulars, the other particular has a trope which exactly resembles that trope. But, as Campbell himself requires, it also has to be shown that each of these concrete particulars is the very one that it is and no other. Now

these and other objections, and Martin, 'Substance Substantiated', pp. 5–9, for a defence of the substance–attribute theory of tropes.

[18] See also Simons, 'Particulars in Particular Clothing', §4.

[19] See Campbell (*AP*, pp. 66–8), who regards this situation as an 'idle possibility'. Perhaps so, but it raises the question of what distinguishes non-identical tropes.

[20] Simons, 'Particulars in Particular Clothing', pp. 572–3, footnote 32.

Campbell claimed that because substances are indistinguishable from one
another, they cannot individuate concrete particulars. Yet since the tropes
in our example are indistinguishable from each other, they cannot
individuate these particulars either.

Campbell might reply that these difficulties can be met by taking tropes
to differ primitively from each other.[21] Perhaps so, but then the same
suggestion can be made with respect to substances. So it seems that tropes
are no better placed than substances at least with respect to meeting the
above difficulties. This conclusion is further strengthened in the next
section where I assess whether the bundle theory of tropes needs *instantiation* tropes.

7. THE INFILTRATION OF INSTANTIATION

To begin with, consider the theory of universals. Suppose that there are
substances, such as the sun and the sky, and universals such as *being yellow*
and *being blue*. At our world the sky is blue and the sun is yellow. But at
another possible world the sky is yellow and the sun is blue. This needs
explaining. The sky's being blue cannot merely be a matter of there being
a substance, the sky, and a property, *being blue*. By the above, both of these
entities exist at a world at which the sky is not blue. Moreover, it needs
explaining how substances have certain universals rather than certain
others. How is it that different worlds can contain the same substances and
universals, yet differ in which substances have which universals? What is it
about our world that explains how it is that a given substance has the
universals it does, rather than certain others?

To meet these puzzles, some realists about universals have posited an
instantiation relation linking substances with their universals. On this view,
the sky is blue if and only if the sky stands in the *instantiation* relation to
the property *being blue*. At the world in which the sky is not blue, the sky
does not stand in this relation to the property *being blue*. *Instantiation* is
also a *sui generis* relation. Unlike other relations, it is supposed to hold
between its *relata* without requiring a (further) relation of *instantiation*.
The realist about universals may either take this relation not to be further
explicable,[22] or he may acknowledge that much difficult work needs to be
done in clarifying it.

The bundle theory of tropes seems free of these difficulties. It does not
posit substances and universals. It posits only tropes standing in *con-*

---

[21] Campbell now takes this course: see *AP*, p. 69.
[22] See for instance J. Cook Wilson, *Statement and Inference* (Oxford: Oxford University
Press, 1926), §148.

currence relations (a species of relational trope).[23] So it seems that trope theory can eschew the instantiation relation. Consider, however, a concrete particular *a*, and two tropes, *F* and *G*, which are members of the bundle which constitutes *a*. What it is for *F* and *G* to belong to the same bundle and not to distinct ones? Or even to none at all? Both *F* and *G* could exist without belonging to the same bundle. Conversely, all the other tropes in the bundle could exist without *F* or *G* existing. And, according to Campbell and Williams, tropes do not even need to be in bundles to exist.[24]

To explain how tropes form bundles, trope theory invokes concurrence relations. *F* and *G* are concurrent if and only if they occupy the same spatio-temporal location.[25] Likewise, these tropes will be concurrent with every one of the other tropes which constitute *a*. Thereby, they constitute a unitary bundle, a single concrete particular. But what is it for *F* and *G* to be concurrent? It cannot be just for *F*, *G*, and a *concurrence* relation *C* to exist. All of these entities might exist without its being the case that *F* stands in *C* to *G*. Moreover, even if another *concurrence* relation *C'* is introduced, and it is claimed that *F*, *G*, and *C* stand in *C'* to each other, the original problem recurs. *F*, *G*, *C*, and *C'* could all exist at a world without *F*, *G*, and *C* standing in *C'* to each other. *C'* might relate some other *n*-tuple of tropes instead.[26] Therefore, for *F* to be concurrent with *G*, it seems that *F* and *G* must instantiate *C*. Therefore, trope theory needs *instantiation* relations (special relational tropes) after all.

It might be replied that *F* and *G* can be tagged with space-time co-ordinates, and that if the space-time co-ordinate of *F* is the same as that of *G*, it follows that *F* and *G* are concurrent. But the original problem faces us at the first step of this account. What is it for *F* and *G* to have the space-time co-ordinates that they do? We cannot arbitrarily tag these tropes with space-time co-ordinates since it is not generally up to us where they are located at any given time. Nor are these co-ordinates constituents of these tropes: otherwise tropes would be complex entities with both a property, or a relation, and a space-time co-ordinate, and this is a view which Campbell has grounds to reject (*AP*, pp. 68–9). So it seems that *F* and *G* must have their spatio-temporal location by being concurrent with space-time tropes. But then neither *F* nor *G* need have the space-time location that it does: these tropes can exist independently of any other tropes (*AP*, pp., 3, 21, 59). Therefore, *F*'s being at place-time *xyzt* cannot

---

[23] Campbell uses the term 'compresence'. I will follow Williams's terminology.

[24] See especially Campbell, pp. 127–8.

[25] Williams, pp. 115–16, 117.

[26] This is a version of Bradley's regress argument against relations. See F. H. Bradley, *Appearance and Reality*, 2nd edn (Oxford: Clarendon Press, 1897), 27–8.

simply be a matter of there existing F, a space-time trope *xyzt*, and a *concurrence* relation C. For all of these entities could exist at a world at which F did not bear C to *xyzt*. It follows that the existence of trope F and the space-time trope *xyzt* does not establish F's spatio-temporal location.[27] So it still seems that trope theory cannot dispense with *instantiation* tropes. F's being concurrent with trope *xyzt* requires F and this *space-time* trope *xyzt* together to stand in an *instantiation* trope to this *concurrence* relation.

For these reasons, then, trope theory needs to posit *instantiation* relations to account for the spatio-temporal locations of tropes, and thus for tropes to be concurrent with each other and thereby form 'trope-bundles'. This generalizes since the *instantiation* relation will also have to be posited in the case of all other so-called external relations, such as causal relations. (A relation R is an external relation if and only if it is not necessarily the case that, where R holds between x and y, if x and y exist, then R holds between them.) Thus a causal relation is an external relation because it is not necessarily the case that, where a causal relation K holds between a pair of tropes F and G, then if F and G exist, then they are causally related by K.

In short, both the realist about universals and the trope theorist need to posit an *instantiation* relation (or *instantiation* tropes), which they share the task of elucidating.

8. CONCLUSION

The notion of a trope as merely a particularized property or relation is compatible with taking tropes to be substances having universals. Thus, certain arguments for the existence of tropes can be construed equally as arguments to the effect that there are substances having universals. A stronger interpretation of the notion of a trope is that a trope is a particularized property or relation, where a trope is taken to be a fundamental entity. This is Williams's and Campbell's official interpretation of trope theory. They further claim that entities belonging to all other categories of entities can be accounted for in terms of tropes.

Trope theory, however, faces a version of Russell's regress. So universals have to be admitted as a fundamental category of entity, on pain of a vicious regress of *resemblance* tropes. It also follows that trope theory cannot account for every other category of entity. Furthermore, trope

---

[27] Williams would apparently agree: 'Location is external in the sense that a trope *per se* does not entail or necessitate or determine its location with respect to any other trope ...' (p. 116).

theory cannot dispense with *instantiation* tropes. Consequently, it faces the same difficulties here as the theory of universals. In this respect trope theory neither holds any advantage over, nor enjoys any greater simplicity, than the theory of universals. Therefore, for these reasons, Williams and Campbell's case for tropes is blunted.[28]

[28] An earlier version of this paper was published in 1994 in *The Proceedings of the Aristotelian Society*, volume 96. I am very grateful to David Armstrong, Keith Campbell, Rosanna Keefe, Peter Lipton, Fraser Macbride, Joseph Melia, Hugh Mellor, Alex Oliver, and Jamie Whyte for helpful comments. I would also like to thank Professor Mellor and Dr Oliver for the opportunity to develop the original paper for the present volume, and for their excellent editorial advice.

XII

PROPERTIES

D. M. ARMSTRONG

In the present climate of metaphysics nothing is more important, I think, than the recognition of properties and relations as fundamental constituents of reality. Once properties and relations are admitted, further questions can be raised. Should we, as our languages seem to urge us, admit alongside properties and relations, things, particulars, which have the properties and between which relations hold? Or should we instead try to construct particulars out of properties and relations, or even out of properties alone, or relations alone? Again, should we take properties and relations as universals, that is, should we take it that different particulars can have the very same property, in the full strict sense of the word 'same', and that different pairs, triples . . . *n*-tuples . . . can be related by the very same relation? Or should we instead hold that properties and relations are particulars (abstract particulars, tropes, moments) so that each particular has its own properties that no other particular can have, and pairs, etc. of particulars each their own relations? A third issue: should we allow that properties and relations themselves can be propertied and stand in relations? Or should we instead with Brian Skyrms allow nothing but a first level of properties and relations?[1]

These issues, and others, about properties and relations are of the greatest interest. And because an answer to one of the questions does not in any obvious way pre-empt the answer to any of the others, we have here a sort of metaphysician's paradise in which philosophers can wander, arguing. But before these issues can be joined there must be established the fundamental point: that there are in reality properties and relations. In this paper, I will largely confine myself to properties.

First published in *Language, Truth and Ontology*, edited by K. Mulligan (Dordrecht: Kluwer, 1992), 14–27. Reprinted by permission of Kluwer Academic Publishers and the author.
[1] Brian Skyrms, 'Tractarian Nominalism', *Philosophical Studies*, 40 (1981), 199–206.

1. WHY WE SHOULD ADMIT PROPERTIES

The great deniers of properties and relations are of two sorts: those who put their faith in *predicates* and those who appeal to *sets* (classes). Some seem to take their comfort from both at once. The resort to predicates was, I suppose, given encouragement by the great Linguistic Turn, with its hope of solving philosophical problems by semantic ascent. This turn gained us some important insights at the cost of a fundamental misdirection of philosophical energy. The appeal to sets was one effect of the immense development of set theory in this century. This raised the hope of resolving all sorts of philosophical problems by a series of set-theoretical technical fixes.

To appreciate the utter implausibility of the attempt to evade properties by means of predicates it is perhaps sufficient to consider a case where a thing's property changes. A cold thing becomes hot. For one who puts his or her faith in predicates this is a matter first of the predicate 'cold', or its semantic equivalent, *applying to* or *being true of* the object, and, second, the predicate 'hot' becoming applicable after 'cold' loses applicability. Properties in the object are but metaphysical shadows cast on that object by the predicates.

But what have predicates to do with the temperature of the object? The change in the object could have occurred even if the predicates had never existed. Furthermore, the change is something intrinsic to the object, and has nothing to do with the way the object stands to language.

I think that one has to be pretty far gone in what might be called Linguistic Idealism to find predicates much of a substitute for properties. But sets are a somewhat more serious matter. After all, to substitute classes for genuine properties is at least to remain a realist, even if a reductivist realist, about properties. Even so, an account of properties in terms of classes is still full of difficulties.

First, there is what might be called the 'Promiscuity problem'—a fairly close relative of the grue problem. Sets abound, and only a very few of them are of the slightest interest. Most of the uninteresting ones are uninteresting because they are utterly heterogeneous, that is, the members of the set have nothing in common. In particular, for most sets there is no common property, F, such that the set is the set of *all the Fs*. The result is that mere sets are insufficient to give an account of properties: at best having a property is a matter of membership of a set *of a certain sort*.

Indeed, not only are most sets too poor to support properties, others, it seems are too prosperous, and support more than one property. This is the problem for a class account of properties that all philosophers are conversant with. It is the coextension problem, the problem of the renates and the cordates, the creatures with kidneys and the creatures with hearts.

Returning to the Promiscuity problem, which I judge to be a much more serious fundamental problem, there are various ways that an account of properties in terms of class might move under pressure. One solution, pioneered by Anthony Quinton, is to introduce a new, fundamental, and so not further analyzable, notion of a *natural* class.[2] Some classes are natural, most are not. The natural ones admit of degrees of naturalness, but no analysis of naturalness is possible.

Of the difficulties that such an account faces, I shall here call attention to but one. (A problem concerning relations will be mentioned when the resemblance theory is discussed.) It is similar to the difficulty urged a moment ago against an account of properties in terms of predicates. It was said that when a thing changes temperature, it is the thing itself that changes. The change in the applicability of certain predicates is, fairly obviously, subsequent and secondary. In the same way, consider the natural class consisting of all and only the objects having temperature T. Let a be a member of this class. What have the *other* members of the class, or at any rate the other members that are wholly distinct from a, to do with a's temperature? After all there would appear to be a possible world in which these other members do not exist, or where they exist but lack temperature T.

Somewhat more attractive than a Natural Class theory is a Resemblance account. According to one version of this view, talk about properties of a particular has as its ontological ground a suitable relation of resemblance holding between the particular in question and suitable paradigms. It might seem that such a view falls victim to the argument just advanced against Predicate and Class accounts. What have the paradigms to do with the *being* of the properties of things that suitably resemble the paradigms? I used to think that this was a good argument against a Resemblance analysis as well as Predicate and Class accounts. But I have recently come to think that the consideration that resemblance is an *internal* relation, based upon the nature of its terms, will block the argument in the case of a Resemblance theory.[3] Details must be left aside here.

But it is worth noticing that the Resemblance theory, like a Class theory (and a Natural Class theory), is unable to distinguish between different but coextensive properties. In a paradigm version, for instance, it would

[2] Anthony Quinton, 'Properties and Classes', *Proceedings of the Aristotelian Society*, 58 (1957–8), 33–58; *The Nature of Things* (London: Routledge & Kegan Paul, 1973).

[3] See my *Universals: An Opinionated Introduction* (Boulder, Colorado: Westview Press, 1989), chapter 3, §11.

not be possible to set up different paradigms for the different properties. In any case, the detail required to work out a Resemblance theory is considerable, and trouble may lurk in the elaborate constructions required. There is also trouble concerning relations. The problem is that when *a* has *R* to *b*, and *c* has 'the same' *R* to *d*, the resemblance has to hold between the way *a* stands to *b*, on the one hand, and the way *c* stands to *d*, on the other. This formulation already involves the notion of relation in the phrase 'stands to'. How to eliminate this? It seems that the Resemblance theory will have to use the same device that a Class theory uses, and identify the terms that resemble with the ordered sets $\langle a,b \rangle$ and $\langle c,d \rangle$. This still involves the relational notion of *order*, and if that is to be eliminated the device of Wiener or Kuratowski will have to be employed and each ordered pair identified with unordered classes of classes. This has a consequence that is also a consequence for a class theory: different classes of classes will each serve as *a*'s having *R* to *b*, and, much worse, the same class of classes can be used for different relations between *a* and *b*. Such arbitrariness strongly suggests that the classes in question do no more than represent, map, the state of affairs of *a*'s having *R* to *b*. The classes are not *identical* with the state of affairs, which is what is needed for metaphysical analysis.

A final criticism that I will make of the Resemblance theory leads us directly to the postulation of properties. I begin by noticing that a traditional argument against the Resemblance analysis is that the resemblance relation is not a two-termed but a three-termed affair. If *a* resembles *b*, in general, they resemble in certain *respects*, and fail to resemble in other *respects*. But respects are uncomfortably close to properties, which the Resemblance theory proposes to do without.

I do not think that this traditional objection is at all conclusive as it stands. The Resemblance theorist can argue that the metaphysically fundamental relation of resemblance is two-termed (though admitting of degrees like the relations of *being distant from* or *more massive than*). It can then be argued that respects and resemblance in respects supervene upon the network of two-term resemblances which are fundamental. But the Resemblance theorist remains in some embarrassment when he comes to explain the formal properties of his fundamental relation. He has to say that the two-termed relation is non-transitive. There is an exception: the limiting case of exact resemblance. But in general: if *a* resembles *b* to degree *D* and *b* resembles *c* to the same degree, the degree to which *a* resembles *c* can take any value. Why is this? The Resemblance theory, it seems, must take it as a primitive, not to be further analysed, fact. A Property theory, however, can *derive* this non-transitivity. It is a matter of *a* resembling *b* in respect of a certain set of properties, *b* resembling *c* in respect of a *different* set of properties. This can naturally be expected to produce a different degree of resemblance between the pairs $\langle a,b \rangle$ and $\langle a,c \rangle$. The transitivity of exact resemblance is also explained, since in such a case the properties of *a*, *b*, and *c* are the same. Explanatory power is a virtue, and lack of explanation a defect, in metaphysics as much as science.

The above argument led us from resemblance to properties. But I believe that the explanatory power of a theory which gives real existence to properties (and relations) is seen most clearly in connection with *causation* and *natural law*. Suppose that the water in the kettle is heated by the fire. We surely want to deny that it is the whole fire, qua token, that causes the heating of the water. The fire, first of all, must be in the right *relations* to the kettle, say underneath, and the kettle must in turn *contain* the water. Still more importantly, the fire must be *hot*. Consider how this is explained by an account in terms of predicates. The predicate 'underneath' applies to the pair of the fire and the kettle, the predicate 'hot' to the fire and, eventually, to the water. But when we have said that these predicates apply, we have surely not said enough. The situation cries out for explanation. It is surely something definite *about* these three things that allows the predicates to apply. Must there not be something quite specific about the things which allows, indeed ensures, that these predicates apply? The predicates require *ontological correlates*. The predicate theory does have correlates indeed, but they are no more than the objects themselves, and so are far too coarse.

It is little better to appeal to classes, even natural classes. What has this fire's heating this water in this kettle, here and now, to do with the fire's membership of the class of hot things? A satisfactory correlate must be found 'within' the fire. A sophisticated Resemblance theory can, I think, appeal to the *natures* of the resembling things, natures from which the resemblances flow. The natures are suitably internal, but are as coarse as the things themselves (indeed, should perhaps be identified with the things themselves).

As with causes, so with laws. I am not speaking of law-*statements* but of the ontological correlates of true law-statements, that in the world which makes true law-statements true. Suppose it be a truth that gravitational force between bodies is equal to the product of their masses divided by the square of their distance. This appears to be a certain connection between the properties of massive things. One can try to translate the corresponding law-statements into statements of universal quantification where the subject-terms are nothing but first-order particulars. But although statements about first-order particulars may follow from law-statements, the latter as is well known, say something more, a more that is plausibly a link between properties. And even if one denies this, perhaps because one thinks that properties are not universals but particulars, it still seems that the ontological correlates of true law-statements must involve properties. How else can one pick out the uniformities which the law-statements entail?

Why has there been such hostility to properties (and relations) among so many contemporary leaders of analytic philosophy? Is it just the Ockhamist spirit? Do without properties and relations if you can! Or is it the influence of Quine, with his doctrine that the predicate of a true statement carries no ontological implications? (Together with his nasty remarks about 'McX', the upholder of universals.)[4] All these things, maybe, and others. But I think that upholders of properties and relations also have something to answer for. As so often happens, in philosophy and elsewhere, an excellent case has been ignored because its advocates overdid things and made exaggerated claims. Simply put, they found far too many properties.

What has happened is that for each distinct predicate, upholders of properties have been inclined to postulate, corresponding to it, a distinct property. Synonymous predicates, 'father' and 'male parent', were generally thought to apply in virtue of just one property. But for non-synonymous predicates, each its own property. To self-contradictory predicates, perhaps, no property corresponds. But for each of the rest, a property of its own.

As a very beginning one might eliminate from this monstrous regiment of properties all those where the corresponding predicate fails to apply, is not true of, anything. After all, the argument for properties that I advanced was for something in particulars which would allow the application of predicates. No application, no property. There is a tendency, whose rationale I do not really understand, to think of properties as necessary beings. A necessary being, if it is possible, exists, and so, if properties are necessary beings, all non-self-contradictory properties exist. But if, as I think we should, we take properties to be contingent beings, then it seems reasonable to deny that there are uninstantiated properties.

This is not to deny that it may be convenient from time to time to talk about, to make ostensible reference to, uninstantiated properties. No body is perfectly elastic, so there is no property of *being perfectly elastic*. But it may be useful to compare more or less elastic bodies in the degree to which they approach the unreachable perfect elasticity. A useful fiction, however, is still a fiction.

[4] [See 'On What There Is', chapter V of this volume.]

If predicates actually apply to, are actually true of, things, then, of course, it is perfectly legitimate to introduce *a sense* in which the things automatically have a property corresponding to just that predicate. Indeed, this is a very useful sense, a point that I have in the past tended to overlook. To make use of Carnap's phrases, the *material mode* is much less fatiguing to the imagination and the intellect than is the *formal mode*. Such properties, however, cut no ontological ice. The properties that are of ontological interest and which we are concerned with here, are those constituents of objects, of particulars, which serve as the ground in the objects for the application of predicates. And concerning these properties, the true properties I am inclined to say, there is no reason to think that to each distinct predicate that has application corresponds its own distinct property in the object. Indeed, there is much reason to think the opposite.

Instead of approaching the matter of such properties directly, it may be helpful to think in the first place in terms of 'good' or 'bad' predicates, where good and bad are to be assessed in terms of our purely theoretical interests: the sort of predicates that the spectator of all time and eternity might find attractive. And here, I think, we are led on to Plato's marvellous image of carving the beast (the great beast of reality) at the joints. The carving may be more or less precise. But as the carving is the more and more precise, so we reach predicates that are of greater and greater theoretical value, predicates more and more fit to appear in the formulations of an exact science. At the limit, monadic predicates apply in virtue of strict properties. An upholder of universals will conceive of these properties as strictly identical in their different instances. A believer in particularized properties, in tropes, will deny identity but allow the symmetrical and transitive relation of exact similarity. It is properties thus conceived that serve as the ontological foundation for the application of predicates, most predicates at any rate, to first-order particulars.

How do we determine what these ontological properties are? The answer, in part, is the same as the answer to the question 'How do kangaroos make love?'. With difficulty. In the epistemic state of nature, the only predicates to which we can give much trust are those suggested by ordinary experience and ordinary life. We cannot but take it that these predicates carve out properties that approximate to some of the joints to some extent. In that state of nature, we cannot but think that blue is better than grue. But in the present age we take ourselves to have advanced beyond the epistemic state of nature, and to have sciences that we speak of as 'mature'. There we will find the predicates that constitute our most educated guess about what are the true properties and relations.

Property-realism, whether the properties be taken as universals or particulars, should be an *a posteriori*, a scientific, realism.

If we combine an *a posteriori* or scientific realism about properties (and relations) with the speculative but attractive thesis of physicalism, then we shall look to physics, the most mature science of all, for *our best predicates so far*. Physics (perhaps it will have to be a cosmological physics as well as the physics of the very small) shows promise of giving an explanatory account of the workings of the whole space-time realm, and thus, perhaps, the whole of being. And it shows promise of doing this in terms of a quite restricted range of fundamental properties and relations. These properties and relations are for the most part quantitative in nature, and the laws that govern them are functional in nature. I will just note that quantities and functions seem to me to involve rather deep problems for the property-realist. (Happily, though, the problems for the alternative positions, such as Predicate and Class Nominalism, seem to be far worse.)

Keith Campbell has suggested, in his new book *Abstract Particulars*, which puts forward a trope metaphysics, that a metaphysics of this physicalist sort is not particularly economical with properties.[5] For suppose that some fundamental quantity such as length is really continuous. We will then be faced with the necessity to postulate continuum-many length-properties corresponding to each different length taken as a type. Some lengths may not be instantiated, but that will not bring the number down.

Continuum-many properties is a lot of properties, to be sure. But let us remember a remark that Mr Reagan made when he was Governor of California. Speaking of the Sequoia tree, he said 'seen one, seen them all.' If you have seen one length, then given only some mathematics, which is topic-neutral, you can grasp the notion of lengths of any length. The class of length-types is a unitary thing, and in taking lengths to be fundamental properties, if you do so, you are making a quite economical postulation. And it may be that a relatively small number of quantities such as length are the only fundamental quantities that physics requires us to postulate.

2. UNIVERSALS VS. TROPES

So much in defense of properties, although much more could be said. In the second part of my paper I will take up an issue *within* the theory of properties, an issue that has enjoyed quite a lot of recent discussion. It is the question whether we should take properties to be universals or particulars. There are those who admit both universal and particular properties

[5] Keith Campbell, *Abstract Particulars* (Oxford: Blackwell, 1990), p. 13.

into their ontology. Perhaps Aristotle and even Plato were among them. But I think that this position sins against economy. If you have universals, you can do without the particularized properties, and *vice-versa*. So for me, and I think for most contemporary metaphysicians, the question is which should we choose.

I was brought up by my teacher, John Anderson, to reject the Particularist position. (He used to criticize G. F. Stout's view.) I still favor the Universalist view, but recently I come to think that tropes have more to be said for them than I have allowed previously. In particular, I now see more clearly how tropes can serve as substitutes for universals in many respects.

A Trope theory is best combined with a resemblance theory, and developed as a sophisticated Resemblance Nominalism. Of particular importance here is the notion of *exact resemblance*. If we work with ordinary particulars, then, with the possible exception of such things as fundamental particles, exact resemblance is a theoretical ideal. We all remember Leibniz's unfortunate courtiers searching vainly for identical leaves in the garden. But if we move to the much thinner *tropes*, then exact resemblances may be achievable. Two tropes that are constituents of different things might resemble exactly in mass, in length, in charge, and so on. The plausible examples are again found at fundamental levels. Thus, it is at present believed that the charge on each electron is exactly the same. 'Exactly the same' appears to assume *identity* of charge in different electrons. But it can be rendered in the language of tropes by saying instead that the different charge-tropes associated with the different electrons are all exactly similar. The interesting thing about exact similarity is that it is symmetrical *and transitive*. (Less than exact similarly is not transitive, even for tropes.) As a result, the relation of exact similarity is an equivalence relation, partitioning the field of tropes into equivalence classes. Tropes will then do much the same work as universals. Suppose that a believer in universals and a believer in tropes have co-ordinated their views in the following way. For each universal property postulated, the trope theorist postulates a class of exactly similar tropes, with universals and tropes properties of the very same class of things. For each class of exactly similar tropes postulated, the Realist postulates a class of thing which all have the same property, with tropes and universals properties of the very same class of things. What inferiority is there in the Trope theory?

I used to think that the Universals theory had an important advantage here. Where we have what the trope theorist thinks of as exact similarity of tropes, we do not scruple to speak of *sameness* of property. Even a trope theorist will allow that by the lights of our present physics electrons have *exactly the same* charge. But 'same' means identical does it not? Yet the trope theory denies identity.

However, I have become convinced that in our ordinary usage 'same' does not always mean identical. There is what Bishop Butler so brilliantly characterized as a 'loose and popular' sense of the word 'same'.[6] Butler was thinking about the replacement over time of particles in an object such as a human body. We say the *same* body but we don't really mean it. It is only a loose and popular identity. By itself, even if we accept it, Butler's point is rather frustrating. What rules are we going by when we use 'same' in the loose and popular way? Here I am indebted to a Sydney student, Peter Anstey. He suggested that we are prepared to use 'same' in this relaxed way only if the things said to be the same are both members of a relevant equivalence class. Though different, the things said to be the same must both be members of the same class, where 'same class' is, of course, taken in the *strict* sense.

If one takes *portions of the lives of organisms* as a field, then it seems that they fall into equivalence classes, where the members of any one class constitute the totality of the life of a single organism (fission, fusion, and so on being neglected). It is of course difficult to spell out just what the equivalence relation is: 'identity over time' is a puzzling subject. But, if Anstey is right, it must be in virtue of this equivalence relation that we assert 'identity', and assert it even though we believe that *strict* identity is not involved. (A further suggestion by Anstey. Is this relevant to the topic of 'relevant identity'? When *a* and *b* are 'the same *F*' but not 'the same *G*', is this because the identity is loose and popular, and two different equivalence relations are involved?)

This is, alas, good news for the tropes. When we say that two electrons have the very same charge, then according to the Trope theory *strictly* the tropes involved are not identical. But the two tropes are both members of a relevant equivalence class, where the equivalence relation is exact similarity, and so can be said to be 'the same' in a loose and popular sense.

Unfortunately, this is not all the good news for the Trope theory. A very important topic in the theory of properties (and relations) is that of their *resemblance*. Particulars resemble: that is clear enough. But so do properties. The colors all resemble each other, so do the shapes, the masses, the lengths. One property can resemble another more than it does a third. Redness is more like orange than it is like yellow. A kilo is more like a pound than it is like an ounce.

[6] Joseph Butler (1736), 'Of Personal Identity' in *Personal Identity*, edited by John Perry (Berkeley: University of California Press, 1975), 99–105.

We may think of the whole field of properties as arranged in a multi-dimensional order. This order appears to be largely objective, and is to be interpreted as a resemblance-order. For properties to stand near to each other in the order is for them to resemble each other quite closely.

If these properties are universals, then it will be natural to construe these resemblances between properties in accordance with the old slogan 'all resemblance is partial identity'. That is how I construe it myself. Resembling universals have common constituents, with either one of the properties containing all the constituents of the other universals and more besides, or else a mere overlap in constituents. I say 'constituents' rather than 'part' because I think that this partial identity is not the simple sort of partial identity envisaged by the mereological calculus, the calculus of whole and part. (A point that confused me for many years.) I cannot go further into the matter here. To do so would involve getting into a huge new topic: the theory of facts or states of affairs.[7]

But however all this may be, an upholder of tropes can deal with the resemblance of properties in a way that parallels the treatment of the topic by an upholder of universals. We have seen the potential to set up a one–one correlation between properties taken as universals, on the one side, and equivalence classes of exactly similar tropes, on the other. To make the matter vivid, select just one trope from each of these equivalence classes and range each of these tropes opposite to its corresponding universal. This structure of tropes will exactly reflect the multi-dimensional resemblance structure of the universals.

How resemblance is interpreted will presumably differ in the two structures. The Trope theory is not under pressure to interpret resemblance between tropes as partial identity, a move that is indeed against the spirit of trope theory, although that option would be open. (Similarly, it is an option for the Universals theory to treat resemblance between *universals* as primitive and unanalyzable, although that goes against the spirit of a Universals theory.) A Trope theory, with exact resemblance already treated as a primitive, will presumably embrace the view that, in fundamental cases at least, lesser degrees of resemblance between tropes are also primitive and unanalyzable. But the point I want principally to make here is that the Trope theory is in as good a position as the Universals theory to deal with the difficult topic of resemblance of properties. The friends of the tropes can say to the friends of the universals: 'Anything you can do, I can do better, or at least equally well'.

But I finish now by saying I do not believe in the tropes. First, there is the question, already touched upon, of the Axioms of Resemblance. The

---

[7] See my *Universals: An Opinionated Introduction.*

trope theorist requires such axioms. *First*, there is symmetry. If *a* resembles *b* to degree *D*, then *b* resembles *a* to degree *D*. *Second*, there is failure of transitivity. If *a* resembles *b* to degree *D*, and *b* resembles *c* to degree *D*, then it is not normally the case that *a* resembles *c* to degree *D*. This holds for tropes as much as for ordinary particulars. However, *third*, transitivity is restored for a special case. If *a* exactly resembles *b*, and *b* exactly resembles *c*, then *a* exactly resembles *c*. This transitivity is a particular case of a more general principle: if *a* resembles *b* to degree *D* and *b* exactly resembles *c*, then *a* resembles *c* to degree *D*. Resemblance to degree *D* is preserved under the substitution of exact resemblers.

For the trope theorist these necessities are *brute* necessities, fundamental necessities that cannot be explained further. The Universals theory need carry no such ontological baggage. The symmetry of resemblance is simply the symmetry of identity. The transitivity of exact resemblance is the transitivity of identity. The non-transitivity of ordinary resemblance is the non-transitivity of partial identity. The Axioms of Resemblance are but particular cases of the axioms that govern identity.

Explanation is a virtue in metaphysics, as elsewhere. I submit that this startlingly easy deduction of the properties of resemblance from the entirely uncontroversial properties of identity is a major advantage of the Universals theory. It enables one to see the intuitive force behind the old, inconclusive, criticism brought against Resemblance Nominalisms that resemblance is resemblance *in identical respects*.

My second reason for rejecting the Trope theory is more controversial, depending as it does on views that would be contested by many. It is that I think that universals are required to get a satisfactory account of laws of nature.

I note again that by laws of nature I mean not true law statements, but that entity, state of affairs, in the world that makes true law statements true. I believe that the contemporary orthodoxy on laws of nature—that basically they are mere regularities in the four-dimensional scenery—is in a similar position to that enjoyed by the regimes in power in Eastern Europe until a few months ago, if 'enjoyed' is the right word. No doubt the end to Regularity theories of law will not come so suddenly, though, because inside their own subject philosophers are great conservatives.

Regularity theories of laws face the grue problem. That, I think, can only be got over by introducing properties, sparse properties, into one's ontology. However, the properties could, I think, be tropes as well as being universals, so there is no advantage to universals here. More to the present point, even with properties given, Regularity theories make laws into *molecular* states of affairs. These tokens of a certain phenomenon

behave in a certain way, so do these, so do all instances of the phenomenon. There is here no *inner connection* between, say, cause and effect in
the individual tokens that fall under the causal law. This conclusion can, I
think, be enforced by noting with Reichenbach and others that only some
cosmic regularities are manifestations of law; by the difficulty in seeing
how such a molecular state of affairs could 'sustain counterfactuals'; and
by the incredible shifts that are necessary to accommodate probabilistic
laws within a regularity approach.

Only a higher-order fact about the universals involved in the individual
positive instances falling under the law can, as far as I can see, provide the
atomic state of affairs that will solve these difficulties. If *being an F* ensures
or makes probable to some degree that the F, or something related to it,
is a G, with F and G universals, then I think that an internal connection is
provided. More controversially, I think it can also be seen that such
a connection automatically, analytically, and yet non-trivially provides for
a regularity or statistical distribution to flow from the connection. Indeed,
I think that, although postulating such a connection does not cure wooden
legs or halt tooth decay, it does go a great way to help us with the problem
of induction.[8]

So: my idea is that a Universals theory can provide us with a satisfactory
account of laws of nature, while a Trope theory cannot. It is a controversial
and complex argument, which cannot be assessed in any hurry. But even
without this, the Trope theory still needs its Axioms of Resemblance, and
that is a clear-cut disadvantage. I know of no such compensating disadvantage for the view that properties are universals.

[8] For all this see my *What is a Law of Nature?* (Cambridge: Cambridge University Press,
1983).

XIII

MODAL REALISM AT WORK: PROPERTIES

DAVID LEWIS

We have frequent need, in one connection or other, to quantify over properties. If we believe in possible worlds and individuals, and if we believe in set-theoretic constructions out of things we believe in, then we have entities suited to play the role of properties.

The simplest plan is to take a property just as the set of all its instances— *all* of them, this- and other-worldly alike. Thus the property of being a donkey comes out as the set of all donkeys, the donkeys of other worlds along with the donkeys of ours.

The usual objection to taking properties as sets is that different properties may happen to be coextensive. All and only the creatures with hearts are creatures with kidneys; all and only the talking donkeys are flying pigs, since there are none of either. But the property of having a heart is different from the property of having a kidney, since there could have been an animal with a heart but no kidneys. Likewise the property of being a talking donkey is different from the property of being a flying pig. If we take properties as sets, so it is said, there is no distinguishing different but accidentally coextensive properties.

But according to modal realism, these 'accidentally coextensive' properties are not coextensive at all. They only appear so when we ignore their other-worldly instances. If we consider all the instances, then it never can happen that two properties are coextensive but might not have been. It is contingent whether two properties have the same this-worldly instances. But it is not contingent whether they have the same instances *simpliciter*.

It is a mistake to say that if a property were a set, then it would have its instances—its members—essentially, and that therefore it never could be contingent whether something has or lacks it. Consider the property of being a talking donkey, which I say is the set of all talking donkeys throughout the worlds. The full membership of this set does not vary from

This is an abridgement of section 1.5 of David Lewis, *On the Plurality of Worlds* (Oxford: Blackwell Publishers, 1986). Reprinted by permission of the publisher and author.

world to world. What does vary from world to world is the subset we get by restricting ourselves to the world in question. That is how the number of instances is contingent; for instance, it is contingently true that the property has no instances. Further, it is a contingent matter whether any particular individual has the property. Take Brownie, an other-worldly talking donkey. Brownie himself is, once and for all, a member of the set; hence, once and for all, an instance of the property. But it is contingent whether Brownie talks; Brownie has counterparts who do and counterparts who don't. In just the same way, it is contingent whether Brownie belongs to the set: Brownie has counterparts who do and counterparts who don't. That is how it is contingent whether Brownie has the property.

As it is for properties, so it is for relations. An instance of a dyadic relation is an ordered pair of related things; then we may take the relation again to be the set of its instances—all of them, this- and other-worldly alike. Again, it is no problem that different relations may happen to be coextensive; for this is only to say that the this-worldly parts of the set are the same, and there is more to a set than its this-worldly part. Again, a pair may stand in a relation contingently, if it has counterpart pairs that do and counterpart pairs that don't. In the same way, a triadic relation can be taken as a set of ordered triples, and so on. Also we can include relations of variable degree, since there is no reason why pairs and triples, for instance, cannot both belong to a single set.

Often it is said that things have some of their properties relative to this or that. Thirst is not a property you have or lack *simpliciter*; you have it at some times and lack it at others. The road has different properties in different places; here it is surfaced, there it is mud. Nine has the property of numbering the planets at our world, but not at a possible world where a planet takes the place of our asteroid belt. (I mean the solar planets at present; and I mean to take another world where there are clear counterparts of the solar system and the present time.) Relative to Ted, Fred has the property of being a father, but relative to Ed, he has the property of being a son. Relative to the number 18, the number 6 has the property of being a divisor; but not relative to 17.

A property that is instantiated in this relative way could not be the set of its instances. For when something has it relative to this but not to that, is the thing to be included in the set or not? Therefore we often see philosophers go to great lengths to provide for relative instantiation when they construct 'properties' in terms of possible worlds and individuals. A property is taken as a function from worlds to sets of things, giving for each world the things that have the property relative to that world. Or it is a function from world-time pairs to things, thus providing also for temporary properties like thirst. In the same way we could take the property of being surfaced as a function that assigns to each place the set of things surfaced there; or the property of being a son as the function that assigns to each person a set of sons; or the property of being a divisor as a function that assigns to each number the set of its divisors.

I find such constructions misguided: what is had by one thing relative to another might be better called a *relation*, not a *property*.[1] It may indeed turn out that one thing stands in a relation because another thing has a property, as when the part of the road that is at a certain place has the property of being surfaced, and that is how the whole road bears the 'surfaced at' relation to that place. Likewise it is by having temporal parts which are thirsty that a person is thirsty at various times. Of course, a disbeliever in temporal parts cannot agree; *he* thinks thirst is irreducibly relational. That is a central feature of his view and, for better or for worse, it ought to be unhidden. That is why I do not approve of the terminology of 'properties' instantiated relative to this or that—it obfuscates and belittles the distinction between relations and genuine properties, and so puts us off guard against those theories that try to tell us that there are only relations where we might have thought there were genuine properties. And that is why I offer a treatment of properties that requires things to have or lack them *simpliciter*, together with a separate but parallel treatment of relations.

Likewise I have made no place for properties that admit of degree, so that things may have more or less of the same property. Instead, there are families of plain properties: the various lengths, the various masses. And there are relations to numbers, such as the mass-in-grams relation that (a recent temporal part of) Bruce bears to a number close to 4,500.

I identify propositions with certain properties—namely, with those that are instantiated only by entire possible worlds. Then if properties generally are the sets of their instances, a proposition is a set of possible worlds. A proposition is said to *hold* at a world, or to be *true* at a world. The proposition is the same thing as the property of being a world where that proposition holds; and that is the same thing as the set of worlds where that proposition holds. A proposition holds at just those worlds that are members of it.

Everyone agrees that it won't do to take a property as the set of its this-worldly instances, because then two properties will be taken to be identical

---

[1] More precisely, what is had by X relative to Y is not a property of X. It *is* a property of the pair ⟨X,Y⟩—on my account, any relation is a property of the pairs (or triples, or whatnot) that instantiate it.

if they happen to be coextensive. Some will say that it is just as bad to take a property as the set of all its instances throughout the worlds, because then two properties will be taken to be identical if they are necessarily coextensive. The stock example concerns the properties of triangularity and of trilaterality. Necessarily, a planar figure bounded by line segments has the same number of angles as sides. So, throughout the worlds, all and only triangles are trilaterals. Yet don't we want to say that these are two different properties?

Sometimes we do, sometimes we don't. I don't see it as a matter for dispute. Here there is a rift in our talk of properties, and we simply have two different conceptions. It's not as if we have fixed once and for all, in some perfectly definite and unequivocal way, on the things we call 'the properties', so that now we are ready to enter into the debate about such questions as, for instance, whether two of them ever are necessarily coextensive. Rather, we have the word 'property', introduced by way of a varied repertory of ordinary and philosophical uses. The word has thereby become associated with a role in our commonsensical thought and in a variety of philosophical theories. To deserve the name of 'property' is to be suited to play the right theoretical role; or better, to be one of a class of entities which together are suited to play the right role collectively. But it is wrong to speak of *the* role associated with the word 'property', as if it were fully and uncontroversially settled. The conception is in considerable disarray. It comes in many versions, differing in a number of ways. The question worth asking is: which entities, if any, among those we should believe in, can occupy which versions of the property role? My answer is, in part, that sets of *possibilia* are entities we should believe in which are just right for *one* version of the property role.

There's no point in insisting that this one is the only rightful conception of the properties. Another version of the property role ties the properties more closely to the meanings of their standard names, and to the meanings of the predicates whereby they may be ascribed to things. 'Triangular' means having three angles, 'trilateral' means having three sides. These meanings differ. (Or do they? The conception of 'meaning' also is in disarray!) So on this conception of properties, we want to distinguish triangularity from trilaterality, though we never can distinguish their instances. We can put the distinction to use, for instance, in saying that one of the two properties is trivially coextensive with triangularity, whereas the other is non-trivially coextensive with triangularity.

This conception demands that properties should be *structured*. If we want to match up properties with the meanings of linguistic expressions that have syntactic structure, then we want to give the properties themselves some kind of quasi-syntactic structure. We can construct structured properties on the model of structured 'meanings'. We needn't build them from scratch; we can begin with the unstructured properties and relations we have already, the sets of this- and other-worldly instances. So these structured properties will require *possibilia* just as much as the unstructured ones did. We will need not only properties and relations of individuals; also we will make use of a higher-order unstructured relation that holds between properties and relations of individuals. It is a relation all the same—a set of pairs—and it is constructed out of *possibilia* just as much as first-order properties and relations of individuals are.

Let A be the relation of being an angle of; let S be the relation of being a side of. Suppose for simplicity that these can be left as unstructured relations; we could go to a deeper level of analysis if we like, but that would complicate the construction without showing anything new. Let T be the higher-order unstructured relation which holds between an unstructured property F of individuals and an unstructured relation G of individuals iff F is the property of being something which exactly three things bear relation G to. A certain unstructured property is the unique thing which bears T to A, and therefore it is the (unstructured) property of triangularity; it also is the unique thing which bears T to S, and therefore it is the (unstructured) property of trilaterality. Therefore let us take the structured property of triangularity as the pair $\langle T,A \rangle$, and the structured property of trilaterality as the pair $\langle T,S \rangle$. Since S and A differ, we have the desired difference between the two pairs that we took to be our two structured properties.

Likewise we can construct structured relations. And if at some deeper level of analysis, we had structured versions of the relation of being an angle of and the relation of being a side—these might be pairs $\langle A_1,A_2 \rangle$ and $\langle S_1,S_2 \rangle$ respectively, or something still more complicated—then we could build these instead of the original A and S into our structured properties, getting structured triangularity as $\langle T,\langle A_1 A_2 \rangle \rangle$ and structured trilaterality as $\langle T,\langle S_1 S_2 \rangle \rangle$.

There is no contest between structured and unstructured versions of the properties, relations and propositions. Given the combined resources of set theory and modal realism, we have both versions. (That is: we have suitable candidates to fill both versions of the roles associated with the terms 'property', 'relation', and 'proposition'.) Both versions require *possibilia*. We needn't worry about which versions better deserve the names, since previous use of the names has not been uniform enough to settle the matter.

There is another great rift in our talk of properties. Sometimes we conceive of properties as *abundant*, sometimes as *sparse*. The abundant properties may be as extrinsic, as gruesomely gerrymandered, as miscellaneously disjunctive, as you please. They pay no heed to the qualitative joints, but carve things up every which way. Sharing of them has nothing to do with similarity. Perfect duplicates share countless properties and fail to share countless others; things as different as can be imagined do exactly the same. The abundant properties far outrun the predicates of any language we could possibly possess. There is one of them for every condition we could write down, even if we could write at infinite length and even if we could name all those things that must remain nameless because they fall outside our acquaintance. In fact, the properties are as abundant as the sets themselves, because for any set whatever, there is the property of belonging to that set. It is these abundant properties, of course, that I have identified with the sets.

The sparse properties are another story. Sharing of them makes for qualitative similarity, they carve at the joints, they are intrinsic, they are highly specific, the sets of their instances are *ipso facto* not entirely miscellaneous, there are only just enough of them to characterise things completely and without redundancy.

Physics has its short list of 'fundamental physical properties': the charges and masses of particles, also their so-called 'spins' and 'colours' and 'flavours', and maybe a few more that have yet to be discovered. In other worlds where physics is different, there will be instances of different fundamental physical properties, alien to this world. And in unphysicalistic worlds, the distribution of fundamental physical properties won't give a complete qualitative characterization of things, because some of the 'fundamental' properties of things will not be in any sense physical. What physics has undertaken, whether or not ours is a world where the undertaking will succeed, is an inventory of the *sparse* properties of this-worldly things. Else the project makes no sense. It would be quixotic to take inventory of the *abundant properties*—the list would not be short, nor would we discover it by experimental and theoretical investigation.

I would not recommend that we enter into debate over whether the properties really are abundant or whether they really are sparse. We needn't choose up sides. Rather we should acknowledge that we have both conceptions, and that an adequate account of what there is ought to accommodate both.[2]

---

[2] Here I am in partial agreement with George Bealer, *Quality and Concept* (Oxford: Clarendon Press, 1982), who advocates a twofold scheme of abundant 'concepts' and sparse 'qualities'. However, he brings the abundant-versus-sparse division into line with the structured-versus-unstructured division, whereas I take the two divisions as cutting across each other.

If we have the abundant properties (as we do, given set theory and *possibilia*) then we have one of them for each of the sparse properties. So we may as well say that the sparse properties are just some—a very small minority—of the abundant properties. We need no other entities, just an inegalitarian distinction among the ones we've already got. When a property belongs to the small minority, I call it a *natural* property.[3]

Probably it would be best to say that the distinction between natural properties and others admits of degree. Some few properties are *perfectly* natural. Others, even though they may be somewhat disjunctive or extrinsic, are at least somewhat natural in a derivative way, to the extent that they can be reached by not-too-complicated chains of definability from the perfectly natural properties. The colours, as we now know, are inferior in naturalness to such perfectly natural properties as mass or charge; grue and bleen are inferior to the colours; yet even grue does not plumb the real depths of gruesomeness. If it did, we would not have been able to name it.

Relations, like properties, can be conceived as abundant or as sparse: a relation for any set of pairs (or triples, or . . .) whatever, or else a minimum basis of relations sufficient to characterise the relational aspects of likeness and difference. Again we may say that some relations are natural, or that some are more natural than others; and that the natural relations are the same sort of thing as other relations, just a distinguished minority among the sets of pairs, triples, and so on. Also propositions can be conceived as abundant or sparse, and sets of worlds may accordingly be divided into the more and less natural. This is automatic, given the division of properties plus the identification of propositions with properties of worlds.

In systematic philosophy we constantly need the distinction between the more and the less natural properties. It is out of the question to be without it. I have discussed some of its uses in 'New Work for a Theory of Universals' [chapter XIV of this volume]. Here I shall mention only one.

We distinguish *intrinsic* properties, which things have in virtue of the way they themselves are, from *extrinsic* properties, which they have in virtue of their relations or lack of relations to other things. How to draw the distinction? Some approaches fail, some fall into circularity. But if we start by distinguishing natural from unnatural properties, then the

---

[3] The name is borrowed from the familiar term 'natural kind'; the contrast is meant to be with unnatural, gerrymandered, gruesome properties. The name has proved to have a drawback: it suggests to some people that it is supposed to be *nature* that distinguishes the natural properties from the rest; and therefore that the distinction is a contingent matter, so that a property might be natural at one world but not at another. I do not mean to suggest any such thing. A property is natural or unnatural *simpliciter*, not relative to one or another world.

distinction between intrinsic and extrinsic properties is not far away. It cannot be said that all intrinsic properties are perfectly natural—a property can be unnatural by reason of disjunctiveness, as the property of being tripartite-or-liquid-or-cubical is, and still it is intrinsic if its disjuncts are. But it can plausibly be said that all perfectly natural properties are intrinsic. Then we can say that two things are *duplicates* iff (1) they have exactly the same perfectly natural properties, and (2) their parts can be put into correspondence in such a way that corresponding parts have exactly the same perfectly natural properties, and stand in the same perfectly natural relations. (Maybe the second clause is redundant. That depends on whether we acknowledge some *structural* properties—properties having to do with the way a thing is composed of parts with their own properties and relations—as perfectly natural.) Then we can go on to say that an *intrinsic* property is one that can never differ between two duplicates.

There is a corresponding distinction among relations. An *internal* relation is one that supervenes on the intrinsic natures of its *relata*: if X_1 and Y_1 stand in the relation but X_2 and Y_2 do not, then there must be a difference in intrinsic nature either between the Xs or else between the Ys. If X_1 and X_2 are duplicates (or identical), and so are Y_1 and Y_2, then the pairs $\langle X_1, Y_1 \rangle$ and $\langle X_2, Y_2 \rangle$ stand in exactly the same internal relations. Relations of similarity or difference in intrinsic respects are internal.

Some other relations, notably relations of spatiotemporal distance, are not internal; they do not supervene on the natures of the *relata*. If X_1 and X_2 are duplicates (or identical), and so are Y_1 and Y_2, it may yet happen that the pairs $\langle X_1, Y_1 \rangle$ and $\langle X_2, Y_2 \rangle$ stand in different relations of distance. Consider a (classical) hydrogen atom, which consists of an electron orbiting a proton at a certain distance. If we take a duplicate of the electron and a duplicate of the proton, then they needn't exhibit the same distance — they may not comprise an atom, they may be in different galaxies or different worlds.

However there is a different way in which relations of distance do supervene on intrinsic character. If, instead of taking a duplicate of the electron and a duplicate of the proton, we take a duplicate of the whole atom, then it will exhibit the same electron-proton distance as the original atom. Although distance fails to supervene on the intrinsic natures of the *relata* taken separately, it does supervene on the intrinsic nature of the composite of the *relata* taken together—in this case, the composite hydrogen atom.

There are other relations for which not even that much is true, for instance the relation of having the same owner. It involves more than the *relata* taken either separately or together, since it also drags in the owner and however much of the rest of the world it takes for there to be the institution of ownership. Thus we don't just have the internal relations versus all the rest; we have a three-way classification. I shall say that a relation is *external* iff it does not supervene on the natures of the *relata* taken separately, but it does supervene on the nature of the composite of the *relata* taken together. A relation of intrinsic similarity is internal; a relation of distance is external; but the relation of having the same owner is neither internal nor external.

I distinguish *duplication* from *indiscernibility*. Two things are *duplicates* iff they have the same intrinsic qualitative character; and that is a matter of the perfectly natural (hence *ex officio* intrinsic) properties of those things and their parts, and of the perfectly natural external relations of their parts. Two things are *indiscernible* iff they have the same intrinsic and extrinsic qualitative character. Extrinsic qualitative character, wherein duplicates may differ, consists of extrinsic properties that are, though not perfectly natural, still somewhat natural in virtue of their definability from perfectly natural properties and relations. Indiscernibles share all their somewhat natural properties. They do not, of course, share all their properties without exception—not if we admit, for any set, a property of belonging to that set, as we automatically do if we identify properties with sets.

To illustrate, contrast two kinds of eternal recurrence. Some worlds exhibit *one-way* eternal recurrence: there is a beginning of time and then there is a first epoch, a second epoch just like the first, and a third, and so *ad infinitum*. Then corresponding inhabitants of the different epochs are duplicates—they differ in no intrinsic respect—but they are not indiscernible. They differ in their extrinsic qualitative character in that one inhabits the first epoch, another inhabits the seventeenth, and so on. Other worlds exhibit *two-way* eternal recurrence: there is no last epoch and no first, the epochs are ordered like the integers rather than the natural numbers. Then the corresponding inhabitants of different epochs are not only duplicates but indiscernibles. But still they don't share all their properties, because for any two of them there are sets which contain one without the other.

Many philosophers are sceptical about the distinction between natural and gruesome properties. They think it illegitimate, unless it can somehow be drawn in terms that do not presuppose it. It is impossible to do that, I think, because we presuppose it constantly. Shall we say that natural properties are the ones that figure in laws of nature?—Not if we are going to use naturalness of properties when we draw the line between laws of nature and accidental regularities. Shall we say that they are the ones that figure in the content of thought?—Not if we are going to say that avoidance of gratuitous gruesomeness is part of what constitutes the correctness of an ascription of content. Shall we say that they are the ones whose instances are united by resemblance?—Not if we are going to say that resemblance is the sharing of natural properties. Unless we are prepared to forgo some of the uses of the distinction between natural and unnatural properties, we shall have no easy way to define it without circularity. That is no reason to reject the distinction. Rather, that is a reason to accept it—as primitive, if need be.

I would willingly accept the distinction as primitive, if that were the only way to gain the use of it elsewhere in our analyses. The contribution to unity and economy of theory would be well worth the cost. But I think there are two attractive alternatives: theories which, for some price both in ontology and in primitives, give us resources to analyse the distinction without forgoing any of its applications. I have two such theories in mind. One is a sparse theory of immanent universals, more or less as presented in D. M. Armstrong's *Universals and Scientific Realism*. The other is a theory of tropes, more or less as in D. C. Williams's 'On the Elements of Being', but made sparse in a way that imitates Armstrong's theory.[4] In the contest between these three alternatives—primitive naturalness, universals, or tropes—I think the honours are roughly even, and I remain undecided.

The two theories go as follows. To each perfectly natural property there corresponds a universal, or else a set of tropes. Wherever the property is instantiated, there the corresponding universal, or one of the corresponding tropes, is present. Let us assume that unit positive charge is a perfectly natural property, which is instantiated by momentary stages of various particles. For short: charge is instantiated by particles. Wherever there is a charged particle, there the universal of charge, or else one of the tropes of charge, is present. It is located there, just as the particle itself is. Indeed, it is part of the particle. It is not a spatiotemporal part: the universal or trope occupies the whole of the spatiotemporal region, point-

---

[4] D. M. Armstrong, *Universals and Scientific Realism* (Cambridge: Cambridge University Press, 1978); D. C. Williams, 'On the Elements of Being', *Review of Metaphysics*, 7 (1953), 3–18 [chapter IX of this volume] and 171–92. A theory of universals similar to Armstrong's is the principal system of Nelson Goodman, *The Structure of Appearance* (Cambridge, Mass.: Harvard University Press, 1951), provided we take it to apply not only to appearance, but to things generally. Other presentations of trope theory—under a variety of names, and with various differences of doctrine—include G. F. Stout, 'Are the Characteristics of Particular Things Universal or Particular?' *Aristotelian Society Supplementary Volume*, 3 (1923), 114–22; Keith Campbell, 'The Metaphysic of Abstract Particulars' [chapter X of this volume]; and Mark Johnston, *Particulars and Persistence* (Ph.D. dissertation, Princeton University, 1983).

sized or larger, that the particle itself occupies. Besides the universal or trope of charge, other universals or tropes also will be present as further non-spatiotemporal parts of the same particle. For instance, there will be a universal or trope of mass.

The difference between universals and tropes comes when we consider two instances of the same perfectly natural property—for instance, two particles each having unit positive charge. Each one contains a non-spatiotemporal part corresponding to charge. But if this non-spatiotemporal part is a universal, then it is the same universal for both particles. One and the same universal recurs; it is multiply located; it is wholly present in both particles, a shared common part whereby the two particles overlap. Being alike by sharing a universal is 'having something in common' in an absolutely literal sense. If the non-spatiotemporal part whereby a charged particle is charged is a trope, on the other hand, then there are different tropes for different charged particles. There is no recurrence, no sharing of a multiply located non-spatiotemporal part. Instead, we say that the charge-trope of one particle and the charge-trope of another are *duplicate* tropes, in a way that a charge-trope and a mass-trope, say, are not.

If there are universals, we can say that the particle is composed partly of its several universals, but not entirely; because another particle exactly like it would have the very same universals, and yet the two particles would not be the same. We can say that the particle consists of its universals together with something else, something non-recurrent, that gives it its particularity. Then we need a primitive notion to say how that something gets united with its universals. I shall call this union 'instantiation'. (I trust there will be no confusion with the 'instantiation' of a property-taken-as-a-set by its members.) We can either say that the universal is instantiated by the whole of a particular; or that it is instantiated by the part that gives the particularity, the residue which is left if we take an ordinary particular and subtract its universals.

(It cannot be said, unfortunately, that a universal is instantiated by just anything that has it as a part. For one thing, the relation of part to whole is transitive; so if a universal of charge is a part of a particle which is part of an atom, then the universal in turn is part of the atom; but it is the particle, not the atom, which instantiates the universal. And so on up; the universal is part of everything, however big, that the particle is part of. Further, suppose there are disunified wholes composed of miscellaneous parts, as indeed I believe. These might include universals which they do not instantiate.)

If there are tropes, we might say that the particle is composed entirely of its tropes; there is no problem with a second particle exactly like it, since that second particle is composed not of the same tropes but of duplicate tropes. Then we need a primitive notion—'instantiation' in yet another sense—to say how the tropes that comprise the particle are united. It is an advantage of tropes over universals that we need no special thing to confer particularity—that is, non-recurrence—since the tropes are particular already. The companion drawback is that we need the primitive notion of duplicate tropes, whereas with universals we just say that it is one and the same universal throughout the charged particles.[5]

A theory of universals might attempt to analyse all similarity in terms of shared universals. (Whether it can succeed depends on what can be said about similarity between universals themselves; see Armstrong, *Universals and Scientific Realism*, chapters 22 and 23.) A theory of tropes must be less ambitious. It cannot analyse all similarity, because duplication of tropes is itself a primitive notion of similarity. But duplication of tropes is much better behaved than other relations of similarity that we might contemplate taking as primitive. The similarity of particles is a messy business: particles can be alike in one respect and not in another, for instance when they are alike in mass but opposite in charge. A theory that starts with similarity-in-some-respect and attempts to recover the respects of comparisons by analysis will run into serious trouble. (See Armstrong, chapter 5; and Goodman, *The Structure of Appearance*, chapter V.) It's simpler with tropes: two charge tropes are alike or not, and that's that. If you will not countenance primitive similarity in any form, then trope theory is not for you. But if you will, then duplication of tropes is an especially satisfactory form for primitive similarity to take.

A universal unifies the set of all and only those particulars that instantiate it. A maximal set of duplicate tropes—that is, a set of tropes that are duplicates of one another but not of any other trope not included in the set—likewise unifies the set of all and only those particulars which instantiate some trope in the set. If we accept a theory of universals or of tropes, we can define a perfectly natural property (of particulars) as any set that is thus unified.

This may seem roundabout. If indeed we accept a theory of universals, why not give up the plan of identifying properties with sets of their instances, and say that the universal itself is the property? Or if we accept

---

[5] A universal recurs; a trope has duplicates. We could also imagine an intermediate thing that sometimes recurs and sometimes has duplicates. A trope theorist who also believes in strict identity over time might say that charge recurs along the world-line of one persisting particle, but is duplicated between one persisting particle and another. Campbell, 'The Metaphysic of Abstract Particulars', and Johnston, *Particulars and Persistence*, favour this sort of theory.

a theory of tropes, why not say that the set of duplicate tropes is the property? Surely these things, if they exist, are fine candidates for the role of properties—and no *possibilia* are needed.

Yes and no. In the first place, we would still need *possibilia* if we wanted to acknowledge uninstantiated properties alien to this world. Universals and tropes are present in their instances, and so must have instances if they are to be present at all. If uninstantiated properties are universals, they are other-worldly universals. If they are sets of tropes, they are sets of other-worldly tropes.

In the second place, universals or sets of duplicate tropes would be fine for the role of *sparse* properties, but the sparse properties are not enough. There may be no urgent need to quantify over all of the very abundant and very gruesome properties that modal realism has on offer as sets of *possibilia*. But certainly we want to go well beyond the perfectly natural properties. When we speak of the various properties that a believer ascribes to himself and the things around him, or when we say that Fred hasn't many virtues, or when we say that sound taxonomy will take account of the biochemical as well as the anatomical properties of organisms, then we quantify over properties that are neither flagrantly gruesome nor perfectly natural. We would not wish to repudiate all properties that are in any way disjunctive or negative or extrinsic. However, universals or tropes are credible only if they are sparse. It is quite easy to believe that a point particle divides into a few non-spatiotemporal parts in such a way that one of them gives the particle its charge, another gives it its mass, and so on. But it is just absurd to think that a thing has (recurring or non-recurring) non-spatiotemporal parts for *all* its countless abundant properties! And it is little better to think that a thing has a different non-spatiotemporal part for each one of its properties that we might ever mention or quantify over. The most noteworthy property of this bed is that George Washington slept in it—surely this is true on some legitimate conception of properties—but it is quite unbelievable that *this* property corresponds to some special non-spatiotemporal part of the bed! This is not one of the perfectly natural properties that might correspond to a universal or a trope; rather it is a property that gains a degree of derivative naturalness, because it is definable in a not-too-complicated way from the perfectly natural properties. The universals or sets of duplicate tropes would not be good candidates to serve as the abundant properties, or even the not-too-abundant-and-not-too-sparse properties. They make a useful adjunct to a broader theory of properties, not a replacement for it.

(A note on terminology. Sometimes 'universal' becomes just another rough synonym for 'property'. The two words are used loosely and interchangeably, equally infected with indecision between rival versions of the definitive theoretical role. On that usage, any candidates whatever for the role of properties, abundant or sparse, could equally deserve the name of universals. But I do not use the two words loosely and interchangeably. Instead, I reserve the word 'universal' strictly for the things, if such there be, that are wholly present as non-spatiotemporal parts in each of the things that instantiate some perfectly natural property.)

Just as monadic universals or tropes might serve to single out the perfectly natural properties, so polyadic universals or tropes might serve to single out the perfectly natural relations. Indeed, if we buy into universals or tropes just in order to avoid taking naturalness as primitive, it seems that we had better be able to cover the relations as well as the properties.[6] Suppose we have a dyadic universal or trope corresponding to the relation of being a certain minute distance apart; and suppose a proton and an electron are that distance apart, and together comprise an atom. Then the dyadic universal or trope is present as a non-spatiotemporal part of the atom. It has the same divided location that the atom itself has. But in a different way; unlike the atom, the universal or trope is not itself divided. It doesn't have one part in the proton and another in the electron. If we accept this theory, we just have to accept that an undivided thing can have a divided location. It is part of the atom; but no part of it is part of the proton or part of the electron. If we accept this theory, we must say that the proton and the electron do not exhaust the atom.[7] All this is

---

[6] There just might be another way to define naturalness of relations: by a very short list, fixed once and for all. It seems a little strange to discuss naturalness of relations in a general way when we have only one really clear example: the spatiotemporal relations. Maybe a few more: maybe part-whole and identity. Maybe set membership. Maybe, if we're unlucky, an irreducible relation of causal or lawful connection. But it's still a short list. If we tried to define the natural properties once and for all by a short list—there are the mass properties, the charge properties, the quark colours and flavours, . . .—we ought to suspect that we had left off not only the this-worldly natural properties we have yet to discover, but also the nameless alien natural properties that are found at other worlds. It seems a bit less clear that we need to leave room for alien natural relations. What if the few natural relations of this-worldly things are the only ones to be found at any world? I regard this hypothesis as far-fetched, but not altogether absurd.

[7] I said that an external relation, although it does not supervene on the intrinsic natures of its *relata* separately, does supervene on the intrinsic nature of the composite of its *relata*—for instance, the electron-proton distance supervenes on the intrinsic nature of the whole atom. To make this work under a theory of universals or tropes, 'composite' must be understood in a special way. The *relata* are just the electron and the proton, but their composite has to be augmented to include also their distance-universal or distance-trope, and any other dyadic universals or tropes that may connect the electron and the proton. (See D. C. Williams, 'Necessary Facts', *Review of Metaphysics*, 16 (1963), 603–5.) Might we throw in too much, and falsely certify the relation of having the same owner as external because we had thrown in a corresponding universal or trope? No fear!—The alleged universal or trope would be spurious, so a sparse theory will deny its existence. Just as we can safely say that all perfectly natural

disturbingly peculiar, much more so than the monadic case, but if the price is right we could learn to tolerate it.

The atom has the structural property of consisting of a proton and an electron a certain distance apart. Is there a structural universal or a structural trope to correspond to this property? If so, that too is present as a non-spatiotemporal part of the atom. We might think that if sparseness is wanted, then this extra thing is superfluous. We already have the monadic universals or tropes of the two particles, and the dyadic universal or trope of distance between them. The presence of these already settles the atom's structure—so what would a structural universal or trope add? But just as the atom itself is not some extra thing over and above its proton and its electron and their distance, so we might say that the atom's structural universal or trope is no extra thing. It is somehow composed of the simpler universals or tropes, and so is nothing over and above them; so we needn't complain of its redundancy. It is not entirely clear how the composition of structural universals would work and so I think it doubtful whether a theory of universals ought to admit them.[8] Structural tropes, on the other hand, seem unproblematic.

properties are *ex officio* intrinsic, so we can say that all perfectly natural relations are external, and those will be the only relations to which there correspond dyadic universals or tropes.

[8] See my 'Against Structural Universals', *Australasian Journal of Philosophy*, 64 (1986), 25–46; and Armstrong, *Universals and Scientific Realism*, volume II, pp. 69–70.

XIV

NEW WORK FOR A THEORY OF UNIVERSALS

DAVID LEWIS

INTRODUCTION

D. M. Armstrong offers a theory of universals as the only adequate answer to a 'compulsory question' for systematic philosophy: the problem of One over Many.[1] I find this line of argument unpersuasive. But I think there is more to be said for Armstrong's theory than he himself has said. For as I bear it in mind considering various topics in philosophy, I notice time and again that it offers solutions to my problems. Whatever we may think of the problem of One over Many, universals can earn their living doing other much-needed work.

I do not say that they are indispensable. The services they render could be matched using resources that are Nominalistic in letter, if perhaps not in spirit.[2] But neither do I hold any presumption against universals, to the effect that they are to be accepted only if we have no alternative. I therefore suspend judgement about universals themselves. I only insist that, one way or another, their work must be done.

I shall investigate the benefits of adding universals to my own usual ontology. That ontology, though Nominalistic, is in other respects generous. It consists of *possibilia*—particular, individual things, some of which comprise our actual world and others of which are unactualized[3]—

Reprinted from the *Australasian Journal of Philosophy*, 61/4 (December 1983), 343–77.

[1] D. M. Armstrong, *Universals and Scientific Realism* (Cambridge: Cambridge University Press, 1978), henceforth cited as *Universals*; see also his 'Against "Ostrich" Nominalism: A Reply to Michael Devitt' [chapter VIII of this volume].

[2] In this paper, I follow Armstrong's traditional terminology: 'universals' are repeatable entities, wholly present wherever a particular instantiates them; 'Nominalism' is the rejection of such entities. In the conflicting modern terminology of Harvard, classes count as 'universals' and 'Nominalism' is predominantly the rejection of classes. Confusion of the terminologies can result in grave misunderstanding; see W. V. Quine, 'Soft Impeachment Disowned', *Pacific Philosophical Quarterly*, 61 (1980), 450–51.

[3] Among 'things' I mean to include all the gerrymandered wholes and parts admitted by the most permissive sort of mereology. Further, I include such physical objects as spatiotemporal regions and force fields, unless an eliminative reduction of them should prove desirable.

together with the iterative hierarchy of classes built up from them. Thus I already have at my disposal a theory of properties as classes of *possibilia*. Properties, so understood, are not much like universals. Nor can they, unaided, take over the work of universals. Nevertheless they will figure importantly in what follows, since for me they are part of the environment in which universals might operate.

The friend of universals may wonder whether they would be better employed not as an addition to my ontology of *possibilia* and classes, but rather as a replacement for parts of it. A fair question, and an urgent one; nevertheless not a question considered in this paper.

In the next section, I shall sketch Armstrong's theory of universals, contrasting universals with properties understood as classes of *possibilia*. Then I shall say why I am unconvinced by the One over Many argument. Then I shall turn to my principal topic: how universals could help me in connection with such topics as duplication, supervenience, and divergent worlds; a minimal form of materialism; laws and causation; and the content of language and thought. Perhaps the list could be extended.

UNIVERSALS AND PROPERTIES

Language offers us several more or less interchangeable words: 'universal'; 'property', 'quality', 'attribute', 'feature', and 'characteristic'; 'type', 'kind', and 'sort'; and perhaps others. And philosophy offers us several conceptions of the entities that such words refer to. My purpose is not to fix on one of these conceptions; but rather to distinguish two (at opposite extremes) and contemplate helping myself to both. Therefore some regimentation of language is called for; I apologise for any inconvenience caused. Let me reserve the word 'universal' for those entities, if such there be, that mostly conform to Armstrong's account. And let me reserve the word 'property' for classes—any classes, but I have foremost in mind classes of things. To have a property is to be a member of the class.[4]

Why call them 'properties' as well as 'classes'?—Just to underline the fact that they need not be classes of *actual* things. The property of being a donkey, for instance, is the class of *all* the donkeys. This property belongs

Further, I include such nonphysical objects as gods and spooks, though not—I hope—as parts of the same world as us. Worlds themselves need no special treatment. They are things—big ones, for the most part.

[4] My conception of properties resembles the doctrine of Class Nominalism considered in *Universals*, I, pp. 28–43. But, strictly speaking, a Class Nominalist would be someone who claims to solve the One over Many problem simply by means of properties taken as classes, and that is far from my intention.

to—this class contains—not only the actual donkeys of this world we live in, but also all the unactualised, otherworldly donkeys.

Likewise I reserve the word 'relation' for arbitrary classes of ordered pairs, triples, ... Thus a relation among things is a property of 'tuples of things. Again, there is no restriction to actual things. Corresponding roughly to the division between properties and relations of things, we have the division between 'monadic' and 'polyadic' universals.

Universals and properties differ in two principal ways. The first difference concerns their instantiation. A universal is supposed to be wholly present wherever it is instantiated. It is a constituent part (though not a spatiotemporal part) of each particular that has it. A property, by contrast, is spread around. The property of being a donkey is partly present wherever there is a donkey, in this or any other world. Far from the property being part of the donkey, it is closer to the truth to say that the donkey is part of the property. But the precise truth, rather, is that the donkey is a member of the property.

Thus universals would unify reality (*Cf. Universals*, I, p. 109) in a way that properties do not. Things that share a universal have not just joined a single class. They literally have something in common. They are not entirely distinct. They overlap.

By occurring repeatedly, universals defy intuitive principles. But that is no damaging objection, since plainly the intuitions were made for particulars. For instance, call two entities *copresent* if both are wholly present at one position in space and time. We might intuit offhand that copresence is transitive. But it is not so, obviously, for universals. Suppose for the sake of argument that there are universals: round, silver, golden. Silver and round are copresent, for here is a silver coin; golden and round are copresent, for there is a gold coin; but silver and golden are not copresent. Likewise, if we add universals to an ontology of *possibilia*, for the relation of being part of the same possible world.[5] I and some otherworldly dragon are not worldmates; but I am a worldmate of the universal golden, and so is the dragon. Presumably I need a mixed case involving both universals and particulars. For why should any two universals ever fail to be world-

---

[5] If universals are to do the new work I have in store for them, they must be capable of repeated occurrence not only within a world but also across worlds. They would then be an exception to my usual principle—meant for particulars, of course—that nothing is wholly present as part of two different worlds. But I see no harm in that. If two worlds are said to overlap by having a coin in common, and this coin is supposed to be wholly round in one world and wholly octagonal in the other, I stubbornly ask what shape it is, and insist that shape is not a relation to worlds. (See my 'Individuation by Acquaintance and by Stipulation', *Philosophical Review*, 92 (1983), 3–32.) I do not see any parallel objections if worlds are said to overlap by sharing a universal. What contingent, nonrelational property of the universal could we put in place of shape of the coin in raising the problem? I cannot think of any.

mates? Lacking such failures, the worldmate relation among universals alone is trivially transitive.

The second difference between universals and properties concerns their abundance. This is the difference that qualifies them for different work, and thereby gives rise to my interest in having universals and properties both.

A distinctive feature of Armstrong's theory is that universals are sparse. There are the universals that there must be to ground the objective resemblances and the causal powers of things, and there is no reason to believe in any more. All of the following alleged universals would be rejected:

not golden,	first examined before 2000 A.D.
golden or wooden,	being identical,
metallic,	being alike in some respect,
self-identical,	being exactly alike,
owned by Fred,	being part of,
belonging to class C,	owning,
grue,	being paired with by some pair in R

(where C and R are utterly miscellaneous classes). The guiding idea, roughly, is that the world's universals should comprise a minimal basis for characterising the world completely. Universals that do not contribute at all to this end are unwelcome, and so are universals that contribute only redundantly. A satisfactory inventory of universals is a non-linguistic counterpart of a primitive vocabulary for a language capable of describing the world exhaustively.

(That is rough: Armstrong does not dismiss redundant universals out of hand, as the spirit of his theory might seem to demand. Conjunctive universals—as it might be, golden-and-round—are accepted, though redundant; so are analysable structural universals. The reason is that if the world were infinitely complex, there might be no way to cut down to a minimal basis. The only alternative to redundancy might be inadequacy, and if so we had better tolerate redundancy. But the redundancy is mitigated by the fact that complex universals consist of their simpler—if perhaps not absolutely simple—constituents. They are not distinct entities. See *Universals*, II, pp. 30–42 and 67–71.)

It is quite otherwise with properties. Any class of things, be it ever so gerrymandered and miscellaneous and indescribable in thought and language, and be it ever so superfluous in characterizing the world, is nevertheless a property. So there are properties in immense abundance. (If the number of things, actual and otherwise, is beth-2, an estimate I regard as more likely low than high, then the number of properties of things is beth-3. And that is a big infinity indeed, except to students of the outer reaches of set theory.) There are so many properties that those specifiable in English, or in the brain's language of synaptic interconnections and neural spikes, could be only an infinitesimal minority.

Because properties are so abundant, they are undiscriminating. Any two things share infinitely many properties, and fail to share infinitely many others. That is so whether the two things are perfect duplicates or utterly dissimilar. Thus properties do nothing to capture facts of resemblance. That is work more suited to the sparse universals. Likewise, properties do nothing to capture the causal powers of things. Almost all properties are causally irrelevant, and there is nothing to make the relevant ones stand out from the crowd. Properties carve reality at the joints—and everywhere else as well. If it's distinctions we want, too much structure is no better than none.

It would be otherwise if we had not only the countless throng of all properties, but also an élite minority of special properties. Call these the *natural* properties.[6] If we had properties and universals both, the universals could serve to pick out the natural properties. Afterwards the universals could retire if they liked, and leave their jobs to the natural properties. Natural properties would be the ones whose sharing makes for resemblance, and the ones relevant to causal powers. Most simply, we could call a property *perfectly* natural if its members are all and only those things that share some one universal. But also we would have other less-than-perfectly natural properties, made so by families of suitable related universals.[7] Thus we might have an imperfectly natural property of being metallic, even if we had no such single universal as metallic, in virtue of a close-knit family of genuine universals one or another of which is instantiated by any metallic thing. These imperfectly natural properties would be natural to varying degrees.

Let us say that an *adequate* theory of properties is one that recognises an objective difference between natural and unnatural properties; preferably,

---

[6] See *Universals*, I, pp. 38–41; Anthony Quinton, 'Properties and Classes', *Proceedings of the Aristotelian Society*, 48 (1957), 33–58; and W. V. Quine, 'Natural Kinds', in his *Ontological Relativity* (New York: Columbia University Press, 1969). See also George Bealer, *Quality and Concept* (Oxford: Oxford University Press, 1982), especially pp. 9–10 and 177–87. Like me, Bealer favours an inegalitarian twofold conception of properties: there are abundant 'concepts' and sparse 'qualities', and the latter are the ones that 'determine the logical, causal, and phenomenal order of reality' (p. 10). Despite this point of agreement, however, Bealer's views and mine differ in many ways.

[7] Here I assume that some solution to the problem of resemblance of universals is possible, perhaps along the lines suggested by Armstrong in *Universals*, II, pp. 48–52 and 101–31; and that such a solution could be carried over into a theory of resemblance of perfectly natural properties, even if we take naturalness of properties as primitive.

a difference that admits of degree. A combined theory of properties and universals is one sort of adequate theory of properties.

But not the only sort. A Nominalistic theory of properties could achieve adequacy by other means. Instead of employing universals it could draw primitive distinctions among particulars. Most simply, a Nominalist could take it as a primitive fact that some classes of things are perfectly natural properties; others are less-than-perfectly natural to various degrees; and most are not at all natural. Such a Nominalist takes 'natural' as a primitive predicate, and offers no analysis of what he means in predicating it of classes. His intention is to select the very same classes as natural properties that the user of universals would select. But he regards the universals as idle machinery, fictitiously superimposed on the primitive objective difference between the natural properties and the others.[8]

Alternatively, a Nominalist in pursuit of adequacy might prefer to rest with primitive objective resemblance among things. (He might not think that 'natural' was a very natural primitive, perhaps because it is to be predicated of classes.) Then he could undertake to define natural properties in terms of the mutual resemblance of their members and the failure of resemblance between their members and their non-members. Unfortunately, the project meets with well-known technical difficulties. These can be solved, but at a daunting price in complexity and artificiality of our primitive. We cannot get by with the familiar dyadic 'resembles'. Instead we need a predicate of resemblance that is both contrastive and variably polyadic. Something like

$x_1, x_2, \ldots$ resemble one another and do not likewise resemble any of $y_1, y_2, \ldots$

(where the strings of variables may be infinite, even uncountable) must be taken as understood without further analysis.[9] If adequate Nominalism

---

[8] This is the Moderate Class Nominalism considered in *Universals*, I, pp. 38–41. It is akin to the views of Quinton, 'Properties and Classes'; but plus the unactualised members of the natural classes, and minus any hint that 'natural' could receive a psychologistic analysis.

[9] Such a theory is a form of Resemblance Nominalism, in Armstrong's classification, but it is unlike the form that he principally considers. See *Universals*, I, pp. 44–63. For discussions of the problem of defining natural classes in terms of resemblance, and of the trickery that proves useful in solving this problem, see Nelson Goodman, *The Structure of Appearance* (Cambridge, Mass.: Harvard University Press, 1951), chapters 4–6; W. V. Quine, 'Natural Kinds'; and Adam Morton, 'Complex Individuals and Multigrade Relations', *Noûs*, 9 (1975), 309–18.

To get from primitive resemblance to perfectly natural properties, I have in mind a definition as follows. We begin with R as our contrastive and variably polyadic primitive. We want it to turn out that $x_1, x_2, \ldots Ry_1, y_2, \ldots$ iff some perfectly natural property is shared by all of $x_1, x_2, \ldots$ but by none of $y_1, y_2, \ldots$ We want to define N, another variably polyadic predicate, so that it will turn out that $Nx_1, x_2, \ldots$ iff $x_1, x_2, \ldots$ are all and only the members of some perfectly natural property. Again we must allow for, and expect, the case where there are infinitely many x's. We define $Nx_1, x_2, \ldots$ as:

requires us to choose between this and a primitive predicate of classes, we might well wonder whether the game is worth the candle. I only say we might wonder; I know of no consideration that seems to me decisive.

At this point, you may see very well why it could be a good idea to believe in universals as well as properties; but you may see no point in having properties as well as universals. But properties have work of their own, and universals are ill-suited to do the work of properties.

It is properties that we need, sometimes natural and sometimes not, to provide an adequate supply of semantic values for linguistic expressions. Consider such sentences as these:

(1) Red resembles orange more than it resembles blue.
(2) Red is a colour.
(3) Humility is a virtue.
(4) Redness is a sign of ripeness.

Prima facie, these sentences contain names that cannot be taken to denote particular, individual things. What is the semantic role of these words? If we are to do compositional semantics in the way that is best developed, we need entities to assign as semantic values to these words, entities that will encode their semantic roles. Perhaps sometimes we might find paraphrases that will absolve us from the need to subject the original sentence to semantic analysis. That is the case with (1), for instance.[10] But even if

$\exists y_1, y_2, \ldots \forall z(z, x_1, x_2, \ldots Ry_1, y_2, \ldots \equiv z=x_1 \lor z=x_2 \lor \ldots)$.

Then we finish the job by defining a perfectly natural property as a class such that, if $x_1, x_2, \ldots$ are all and only its members, then $Nx_1, x_2, \ldots$.

We might have taken N as primitive instead of R. But would that have been significantly different, given the interdefinability of the two? On the other hand, taking N as primitive also seems not significantly different from taking perfect naturalness of classes as primitive. It is only a difference between speaking in the plural of individuals and speaking in the singular of their classes, and that seems no real difference. Is plural talk a disguised form of class talk? Or *vice versa*? (See the discussion in *Universals*, I, pp. 32–4; also Max Black, 'The Elusiveness of Sets', *Review of Metaphysics*, 24 (1971), 614–36; Eric Stenius, 'Sets', *Synthese*, 27 (1974), 161–88; and Kurt Gödel, 'Russell's Mathematical Logic', *The Philosophy of Bertrand Russell*, edited by P. A. Schilpp (Cambridge: Cambridge University Press, 1944). At any rate, it is not at all clear to me that Moderate Class Nominalism and Resemblance Nominalism in its present form are two different theories, as opposed to a single theory presented in different styles.

[10] In virtue of the close resemblance of red and orange, it is possible for a red thing to resemble an orange one very closely; it is not possible for a red thing to resemble a blue one quite so closely. Given our ontology of *possibilia*, all possibilities are realised. So we could paraphrase (1) by

(1′) Some red thing resembles some orange thing more than any red thing resembles any blue thing

so long as it is understood that the things in question needn't be part of our world, or of any one world. Or if we did not wish to speak of unactualised things, but we were willing to take ordinary-language modal idioms as primitive, we could instead give the paraphrase:

such paraphrases sometimes exist—even if they *always* exist, which seems unlikely—they work piecemeal and frustrate any systematic approach to semantics.

Armstrong takes it that such sentences provide a subsidiary argument for universals, independent of his main argument from the One over Many problem. (*Universals*, I, pp. 58–63; also 'Against "Ostrich" Nominalism'.[11]) I quite agree that we have here an argument for something. But not for universals as opposed to properties. Properties can serve as the requisite semantic values. Indeed, properties are much better suited to the job than universals are. That is plain even from the examples considered. It is unlikely that there are any such genuine universals as the colours (especially determinable colours, like red, rather than determinate shades), or ripeness, or humility. Armstrong agrees (*Universals*, I, p. 61) that he cannot take (1)–(4) as straightforwardly making reference to universals. He must first subject them to paraphrase. Even if there always is a paraphrase that does refer to, or quantify over, genuine universals, still the need for paraphrase is a threat to systematic semantics. The problem arises exactly because universals are sparse. There is no corresponding objection if we take the requisite semantic values as properties.

Other sentences make my point more dramatically.

(5) Grueness does not make for resemblance among all its instances.
(6) What is common to all who suffer pain is being in some or another state that occupies the pain role, presumably not the same state in all cases.

The point is not that these sentences are true—though they are—but that they require semantic analysis. (It is irrelevant that they are not ordinary language.) A universal of grueness would be anathema; as would a universal such that, necessarily, one has it if he is in some state or other that occupies the pain role in his case.[12] But the corresponding properties are no problem.

(1'') A red thing can resemble an orange thing more closely than a red thing can resemble a blue thing.

It is necessary to use the ordinary-language idioms, or some adequate formalisation of them, rather than standard modal logic. You cannot express (1'') in modal logic (excluding an enriched modal logic that would defeat the point of the paraphrase by quantifying over degrees of resemblance or whatnot) because you cannot express cross-world relations, and in particular cannot express the needed cross-world comparison of similarity.

[11] He derives the argument, and a second semantic argument to be considered shortly, from Arthur Pap, 'Nominalism, Empiricism and Universals: I', *Philosophical Quarterly*, 9 (1959), 330–40, and Frank Jackson, 'Statements about Universals' [chapter VI of this volume.]

[12] Or better, in the case of creatures of his kind. See my 'Mad Pain and Martian Pain', in *Readings in Philosophy of Psychology*, I, edited by Ned Block (Cambridge, Mass.: Harvard University Press, 1980), 216–22.

Indeed, we have a comprehension schema applying to any predicate phrase whatever, however complicated. (Let it even be infinitely long; let it even include imaginary names for entities we haven't really named.) Let x range over things, P over properties (classes) of things. Then:

$$\exists_{\mathrm{r}} P \square \forall x \ (x \text{ has } P \equiv \phi x).$$

We could appropriately call this 'the property of ϕ-ing' in those cases where the predicate phrase is short enough to form a gerund, and take this property to be the semantic value of the gerund. Contrast this with the very different relationship of universals and predicates set forth in *Universals*, II, pp. 7–59.

Consider also those sentences which *prima facie* involve second-order quantification. From *Universals*, I, p. 62, and 'Against "Ostrich" Nominalism' we have these.

> (7) He has the same virtues as his father.
> (8) The dresses were of the same colour.
> (9) There are undiscovered fundamental physical properties.
> (10) Acquired characteristics are never inherited.
> (11) Some zoological species are cross-fertile.

Prima facie, we are quantifying either over properties or over universals. Again, paraphrases might defeat the presumption, but in a piecemeal way that threatens systematic semantics. In each case, properties could serve as the values of the variables of quantification. Only in case (9) could universals serve equally well. To treat the other cases, not to mention

> (12) Some characteristics, such as the colours, are more disjunctive than they seem.

as quantifications over universals, we would again have to resort to some preliminary paraphrase. (Armstrong again agrees: *Universals*, I, p. 63.) This second semantic argument, like the first, adduces work for which properties are better qualified than universals.

Which is not to deny that a partnership might do better still. Let it be granted that we are dealing with quantifications over properties. Still, these quantifications—like most of our quantifications—may be tacitly or explicitly restricted. In particular, they usually are restricted to natural properties. Not to perfectly natural properties that correspond to single universals, except in special cases like (9), but to properties that are at least somewhat more natural than the great majority of the utterly miscellaneous. That is so for all our examples, even (12). Then even though we quantify over properties, we still need either universals or the resources of an adequate Nominalism in order to say which of the properties we mostly quantify over.

I also think that it is properties that we need in characterising the content of our intentional attitudes. I believe, or I desire, that I live in one of the worlds in a certain class, rather than any world outside that class. This class of worlds is a property had by worlds. I believe, or I desire, that my world has that property. (The class of worlds also may be called a *proposition*, in one of the legitimate senses of that word, and my 'propositional attitude' of belief or desire has this proposition as its 'object'.) More generally, subsuming the previous case, I believe or I desire that I myself belong to a certain class of *possibilia*. I ascribe a certain property to myself, or I want to have it. Or I might ascribe a property to something else, or even to myself, under a relation of acquaintance I bear to that thing.[13] Surely the properties that give the content of attitudes in these ways cannot be relied on to be perfectly natural, hence cannot be replaced by universals. It is interesting to ask whether there is any lower limit to their naturalness (see the final section of this paper), but surely no very exacting standard is possible. Here again properties are right for the job, universals are not.

ONE OVER MANY

Armstrong's main argument for universals is the 'One over Many'. It is because I find this argument unconvincing that I am investigating alternative reasons to accept a theory of universals.

Here is a concise statement of the argument, taken by condensation from 'Against "Ostrich" Nominalism' (p. 102). A very similar statement could have been drawn from the opening pages of *Universals*.

I would wish to start by saying that many different particulars can all have what appears to be the same nature and draw the conclusion that, as a result, there is a *prima facie* case for postulating universals. We are continually talking about different things having the same property or quality, being of the same sort or kind, having the same nature, and so on. Philosophers draw the distinction between sameness of token and sameness of type. But they are only making explicit a distinction which ordinary language (and so, ordinary thought) perfectly recognises. I suggest that the fact of sameness of type is a Moorean fact: one of the many facts which even philosophers should not deny, whatever philosophical account or analysis they give of such facts. Any comprehensive philosophy must try to give some account of Moorean facts. They constitute the compulsory questions in the philosophical examination paper.

[13] See my 'Attitudes *De Dicto* and *De Se*', *Philosophical Review*, 88 (1979), 513–43; and 'Individuation by Acquaintance and by Stipulation'.

From this point of departure, Armstrong makes his case by criticising rival attempts to answer the compulsory question, and by rejecting views that decline to answer it at all.

Still more concisely, the One over Many problem is presented as the problem of giving some account of Moorean facts of apparent sameness of type. Thus understood, I agree that the question is compulsory; I agree that Armstrong's postulation of shared universals answers it; but I think that an adequate Nominalism also answers it.

An effort at systematic philosophy must indeed give an account of any purported fact. There are three ways to give an account. (1) 'I deny it'—this earns a failing mark if the fact is really Moorean. (2) 'I analyse it thus' —this is Armstrong's response to the facts of apparent sameness of type. Or (3) 'I accept it as primitive'. Not every *account* is an *analysis*! A system that takes certain Moorean facts as primitive, as unanalysed, cannot be accused of failing to make a place for them. It neither shirks the compulsory question nor answers it by denial. It does give an account.

An adequate Nominalism, of course, is a theory that takes Moorean facts of apparent sameness of type as primitive. It predicates mutual resemblance of the things which are apparently of the same type; or it predicates naturalness of some property that they all share, *i.e.* that has them all as members; and it declines to analyse these predications any further. That is why the problem of One over Many, rightly understood, does not provide more than a *prima facie* reason to postulate universals. Universals afford one solution, but there are others.

I fear that the problem does not remain rightly understood. Early in *Universals* it undergoes an unfortunate double transformation. In the course of a few pages (*Universals*, I, pp. 11–16) the legitimate demand for an account of Moorean facts of apparent sameness of type turns into a demand for an analysis of predication in general. The *analysandum* becomes the schema '*a* has the property *F*'. The turning point takes only two sentences (p. 12):

How is [the Nominalist] to account for the apparent (if usually partial) identity of numerically different particulars? How can two different things both be white or both be on a table?

And very soon (pp. 16–17) those who 'refuse to countenance universals but who at the same time see no need for any reductive analyses [of the schema of predication]', those according to whom 'there are no universals but the proposition that *a* is *F* is perfectly all right as it is', stand accused of dodging the compulsory question.

When the demand for an account—for a place in one's system—turned into a demand for an analysis, then I say that the question ceased to be compulsory. And when the *analysandum* switched, from Moorean facts of apparent sameness of type to predication generally, then I say that the question ceased to be answerable at all. The transformed problem of One over Many deserves our neglect. The ostrich that will not look at it is a wise bird indeed.

Despite his words, I do not think that Armstrong really means to demand, either from Nominalists or from himself, a *fully* general analysis of predication. For none is so ready as he to insist that not just any shared predicate makes for even apparent sameness of type. (That is what gives his theory its distinctive interest and merit.) It would be better to put the transformed problem thus: one way or another, all predication is to be analysed. Some predications are to be analysed away in terms of others. Here we have one-off analyses for specific predicates—as it might be, for 'grue'. But all those predications that remain, after the one-off analyses are finished, are to be analysed wholesale by means of a general analysis of the schema '*a* has property *F*'.

There is to be no unanalysed predication. Time and again, Armstrong wields this requirement against rival theories. One theory after another falls victim to the 'relation regress': in the course of analysing other predications, the theory has resort to a new predicate that cannot, on pain of circularity, be analysed along with the rest. So falls Class Nominalism (including the version with primitive naturalness that I deem adequate): it employs predications of class membership, which predications it cannot without circularity analyse in terms of class membership. So falls Resemblance Nominalism: it fails to analyse predications of resemblance. So fall various other, less deserving Nominalisms. And so fall rival forms of Realism, for instance Transcendent, Platonic Realism: this time, predications of participation evade analysis. Specific theories meet other, specific objections; suffice it to say that I think these inconclusive against the two Nominalisms that I call adequate. But the clincher, the one argument that recurs throughout the many refutations, is the relation regress. And this amounts to the objection that the theory under attack does not achieve its presumed aim of doing away with all unanalysed predication and therefore fails to solve the transformed problem of One over Many.

Doing away with all unanalysed predication is an unattainable aim, and so an unreasonable aim. No theory is to be faulted for failing to achieve it. For how could there be a theory that names entities, or quantifies over them, in the course of its sentences, and yet altogether avoids primitive predication? Artificial tricks aside,[14] the thing cannot be done.

[14] Let *S* be the syntactic category of sentences, let *N* be the category of names, and for any categories *x* and *y*, let *x/y* be the category of expressions that attach to *y*-expressions to make *x*-

What's true is that a theory may be faulted for its overabundant primitive predications, or for unduly mysterious ones, or for unduly complicated ones. These are not fatal faults, however. They are to be counted against a theory, along with its faults of overly generous ontology or of disagreement with less-than-Moorean commonsensical opinions. Rival philosophical theories have their prices, which we seek to measure. But it's all too clear that for philosophers, at least, there ain't no such thing as a free lunch.

How does Armstrong himself do without primitive predication?—He doesn't. Consider the predicate 'instantiates' (or 'has'), as in 'particular *a* instantiates universal *F*' or 'this electron has unit charge'. No one-off analysis applies to this specific predicate. 'Such identity in nature [as results from the having of one universal in many particulars] is literally inexplicable, in the sense that it cannot be further explained.' (*Universals*, I, p. 109.) Neither do predications of 'instantiates' fall under Armstrong's general analysis of (otherwise unanalysed) predication. His is a non-*relational* Realism: he declines, with good reason, to postulate a dyadic universal of instantiation to bind particulars to their universals. (And if he did, it would only postpone the need for primitive predication.) So let all who have felt the bite of Armstrong's relation regress rise up and cry '*Tu quoque!*' and let us mark well that Armstrong is prepared to give *one* predicate 'what has been said to be the privilege of the harlot: power without responsibility. The predicate is informative, it makes a vital contribution to telling us what is the case, the world is different if it is different, yet ontologically it is supposed not to commit us. Nice work: if you can get it.' (Compare Armstrong on Quine's treatment of predication, 'Against "Ostrich" Nominalism', pp. 104–5.)

Let us dump the project of getting rid of primitive predication, and return to the sensible—though not compulsory—project of analysing Moorean facts of apparent sameness of type. Now does the relation regress serve Armstrong better? I think not. It does make better sense within the more sensible project, but it still bites Armstrong and his rivals with equal force. Let the Nominalist say 'These donkeys resemble each other, so likewise do those stars, and there analysis ends.' Let the Platonist say 'This statue participates in the Form of beauty, likewise that lecture participates in the Form of truth, and there analysis ends.' Let Armstrong

---

expressions. Predicates, then, are category S/N. (Or $(S/N)/N$ for two-place predicates, and so on.) To embed names (or variables in the category of names) into sentences without primitive predication, take any category Q which is neither S nor N, nor S/N, and let there be primitives of categories Q/N and S/Q. Or take Q_1 and Q_2, different from S and N and S/N and each other, and let the primitives be of categories Q_1/N, Q_2/Q_1, and S/Q_2. Or ... I cannot see how this trickery could be a genuine alternative to, rather than a disguise for, primitive predication.

say 'This electron instantiates unit charge, likewise that proton instantiates tripartiteness, and there analysis ends.' It is possible to complain in each case that a fact of sameness of type has gone unanalysed, the types being respectively resemblance, participation, and instantiation. But it is far from evident that the alleged facts are Moorean, and still less evident that the first two are more Moorean than the third. None of them are remotely the equals of the genuine Moorean fact that, in some sense, different lumps of gold are the same in kind.

Michael Devitt has denounced the One over Many problem as a mirage better left unseen.[15] I have found Devitt's discussion instructive and I agree with much of what he says. But Devitt has joined Armstrong in transforming the One over Many problem. He takes it to be the problem of analysing the schema

a and *b* have the same property (are of the same type), *F*-ness

otherwise than by means of a one-off analysis for some specific *F*. To that problem it is fair to answer as he does that

a is *F*; *b* is *f*

is analysis enough, once we give over the aim of doing without primitive predication. But Devitt has set himself too easy a problem. If we attend to the modest, untransformed One over Many problem, which is no mirage, we will ask about a different *analysandum*:

a and *b* have some common property (are somehow of the same type)

in which it is not said what *a* and *b* have in common. This less definite *analysandum* is not covered by what Devitt has said. If we take a clearly Moorean case, he owes us an account: either an analysis or an overt resort to primitive predication of resemblance.

DUPLICATION, SUPERVENIENCE, AND DIVERGENT WORLDS

Henceforth I shall speak only of my need for the distinction between natural and unnatural, or more and less natural, properties. It is to be understood that the work I have in store for an adequately discriminatory theory of properties might be new work for a theory of universals, or it might instead be work for the resources of an adequate Nominalism.

---

[15] '"Ostrich Nominalism" or "Mirage Realism"?' [chapter VII of this volume]. Devitt speaks on behalf of Quine as well as himself; Quine indicates agreement with Devitt in 'Soft Impeachment Disowned'.

I begin with the problem of analysing duplication. We are familiar with cases of approximate duplication, *e.g.* when we use copying machines. And we understand that if these machines were more perfect than they are, the copies they made would be perfect duplicates of the original. Copy and original would be alike in size and shape and chemical composition of the ink marks and the paper, alike in temperature and magnetic alignment and electrostatic charge, alike even in the exact arrangement of their electrons and quarks. Such duplicates would be exactly alike, we say. They would match perfectly, they would be qualitatively identical, they would be indiscernible.

But they would not have exactly the same properties, in my sense of the word. As in the case of any two things, countless class boundaries would divide them. Intrinsically, leaving out their relations to the rest of the world, they would be just alike. But they would occupy different spatio-temporal positions; and they might have different owners, be first examined in different centuries, and so on.

So if we wish to analyse duplication in terms of shared properties, it seems that we must first distinguish the *intrinsic* (or 'internal') properties from the *extrinsic* (or 'external' or 'relational') properties. Then we may say that two things are duplicates iff they have precisely the same intrinsic properties, however much their extrinsic properties might differ. But our new problem of dividing the properties into intrinsic and extrinsic is no easier than our original problem of analysing duplication. In fact, the two problems are joined in a tight little circle of interdefinability. Duplication is a matter of sharing intrinsic properties; intrinsic properties are just those properties that never differ between duplicates. Property *P* is intrinsic iff, for any two duplicate things, not necessarily from the same world, either both have *P* or neither does. *P* is extrinsic iff there is some such pair of duplicates of which one has *P* and the other lacks *P*.[16]

---

[16] Given duplication, we can also subdivide the extrinsic properties, distinguishing pure cases from various mixtures of extrinsic and intrinsic. Partition the things, of this and other worlds, into equivalence classes under the relation of duplication. A property may divide an equivalence class, may include it, or may exclude it. A property *P* is extrinsic, as we said, if it divides at least some of the classes. We have four subcases. (1) *P* divides every class; then we may call *P purely extrinsic.* (2) *P* divides some classes, includes some, and excludes none; then *P* is the disjunction of an intrinsic property and a purely extrinsic property. (3) *P* divides some, excludes some, and includes none; then *P* is the conjunction of an intrinsic property and a purely extrinsic property. (4) *P* divides some, includes some, and excludes some; then *P* is the conjunction of an intrinsic property and an impurely extrinsic property of the sort considered in the second case, or equivalently is the disjunction of an intrinsic property and an impurely extrinsic property of the sort considered in the third case.

We can also classify relations as intrinsic or extrinsic, but in two different ways. Take a dyadic relation, i.e. a class of ordered pairs. Call the relation *intrinsic to its relata* iff, whenever *a* and *a'* are duplicates (or identical) and *b* and *b'* are duplicates (or identical), then both or neither of the pairs $\langle a,b \rangle$ and $\langle a',b' \rangle$ stand in the relation. Call the relation *intrinsic to its pairs* iff,

If we relied on our physical theory to be accurate and exhaustive, we might think to define duplication in physical terms. We believe that duplicates must be alike in the arrangement of their electrons and quarks —why not put this forward as a definition? But such a 'definition' is no analysis. It presupposes the physics of our actual world; however physics is contingent and known *a posteriori*. The definition does not apply to duplication at possible worlds where physics is different, or to duplication between worlds that differ in their physics. Nor does it capture what those ignorant of physics mean when they speak—as they do—of duplication.

The proper course, I suggest, is to analyse duplication in terms of shared properties; but to begin not with the intrinsic properties but rather with natural properties. Two things are qualitative duplicates if they have exactly the same perfectly natural properties.[17]

Physics is relevant because it aspires to give an inventory of natural properties—not a complete inventory, perhaps, but a complete enough inventory to account for duplication among actual things. If physics succeeds in this, then duplication within our world amounts to sameness of physical description. But the natural properties themselves are what matter, not the theory that tells us what they are. If Materialism were false and physics an utter failure, as is the case at some deplorable worlds, there would still be duplication in virtue of shared natural properties.

On my analysis, all perfectly natural properties come out intrinsic. That seems right. The converse is not true. Intrinsic properties may be disjunctive and miscellaneous and unnatural, so long as they never differ between duplicates. The perfectly natural properties comprise a basis for the intrinsic properties; but arbitrary Boolean compounds of them, how-

whenever the pairs ⟨*a*,*b*⟩ and ⟨*a'*,*b'*⟩ themselves are duplicates, then both or neither of them stand in the relation. In the second case, a stronger requirement is imposed on the pairs. For instance, they might fail to be duplicate pairs because the distance between *a* and *b* differs from the distance between *a'* and *b'*, even though *a* and *a'* are duplicates and *b* and *b'* are duplicates. In traditional terminology, 'internal relations' are intrinsic to their *relata*; 'external relations' are intrinsic to their pairs but not to their *relata*; and relations extrinsic even to their pairs, such as the relation of belonging to the same owner, get left out of the classification altogether.

Our definition of intrinsic properties in terms of duplication closely resembles the definition of 'differential properties' given by Michael Slote in 'Some Thoughts on Goodman's Riddle', *Analysis*, 27 (1967), 128–32, and in *Reason and Scepticism* (London: George Allen & Unwin, 1970). But where I quantify over *possibilia*, Slote applies modality to ordinary, presumably actualist, quantifiers. That makes a difference. An extrinsic property might differ between duplicates, but only when the duplicates inhabit different worlds; then Slote would count the property as differential. An example is the property of being a sphere that inhabits a world where there are pigs or a cube that inhabits a world without pigs.

See my 'Extrinsic properties', *Philosophical Studies*, 44 (1983), 197–200, for further discussion of the circle from duplication to intrinsicness and back.

[17] Likewise ⟨*a*,*b*⟩ and ⟨*a'*,*b'*⟩ are duplicate pairs iff *a* and *a'* have exactly the same perfectly natural properties, and so do *b* and *b'*, and also the perfectly natural relations between *a* and *b* are exactly the same as those between *a'* and *b'*.

ever unnatural, are still intrinsic. Hence if we adopt the sort of adequate Nominalism that draws a primitive distinction between natural and unnatural properties, that is not the same thing as drawing a primitive distinction between intrinsic and extrinsic properties. The former distinction yields the latter, but not *vice versa*.

Likewise, if we adopt the sort of adequate Nominalism that begins with a suitable relation of partial resemblance, that is not the same thing as taking duplication itself as primitive. Again, the former yields the latter, but not *vice versa*.

If instead we reject Nominalism, and we take the perfectly natural properties to be those that correspond to universals (in the sense that the members of the property are exactly those things that instantiate the universal), then all the properties that correspond to universals are intrinsic. So are all the Boolean compounds—disjunctions, negations, etc.—of properties that correspond to universals. The universals themselves are intrinsic *ex officio*, so to speak.

But here I must confess that the theory of universals for which I offer new work cannot be exactly Armstrong's theory. For it must reject extrinsic universals; whereas Armstrong admits them, although not as irreducible. (See *Universals*, II, pp. 78–9.) I think he would be better off without them, given his own aims. (1) They subvert the desired connection between sharing of universals and Moorean facts of partial or total sameness of nature. Admittedly, there is such a thing as resemblance in extrinsic respects: things can be alike in the roles they play *vis-à-vis* other things, or in the origins they spring from. But such resemblances are not what we mean when we say of two things that they are of the same kind, or have the same nature. (2) They subvert the desired immanence of universals: if something instantiates an extrinsic universal, that is not a fact just about that thing. (3) They are not needed for Armstrong's theory of laws of nature; any supposed law connecting extrinsic universals of things can be equivalently replaced by a law connecting intrinsic structures of larger systems that have those things as parts.

Thus I am content to say that if there are universals, intrinsic duplicates are things having exactly the same universals. We need not say '. . . exactly the same *intrinsic* univerals' because we should not believe in any other kind.

Not only is duplication of interest in its own right; it also is needed in dealing with other topics in metaphysics. Hence such topics create a derived need for natural properties. I shall consider two topics where I find need to speak of duplication: supervenience and divergent worlds.

* * *

First, supervenience. A supervenience thesis is a denial of independent variation. Given an ontology of *possibilia*, we can formulate such theses in terms of differences between possible individuals or worlds. To say that so-and-so supervenes on such-and-such is to say that there can be no difference in respect to so-and-so without difference in respect of such-and-such. Beauty of statues supervenes on their shape, size, and colour, for instance, if no two statues, in the same or different worlds, ever differ in beauty without also differing in shape or size or colour.[18]

A supervenience thesis is, in a broad sense, reductionist. But it is a stripped-down form of reductionism, unencumbered by dubious denials of existence, claims of ontological priority, or claims of translatability. One might wish to say that in some sense the beauty of statues is nothing over and above the shape and size and colour that beholders appreciate, but without denying that there is such a thing as beauty, without claiming that beauty exists only in some less-than-fundamental way, and without undertaking to paraphrase ascriptions of beauty in terms of shape etc. A supervenience thesis seems to capture what the cautious reductionist wishes to say.

Even if reductionists ought to be less cautious and aim for translation, still it is a good idea to attend to the question of supervenience. For if supervenience fails, then no scheme of translation can be correct and we needn't go on Chisholming away in search of one. If supervenience succeeds, on the other hand, then some correct scheme must exist; the remaining question is whether there exists a correct scheme that is less than infinitely complex. If beauty is supervenient on shape etc., the worst that can happen is that an ascription of beauty is equivalent to an uncountably infinite disjunction of maximally specific descriptions of shape etc., which descriptions might themselves involve infinite conjunctions.

Interesting supervenience theses usually involve the notion of qualitative duplication that we have just considered. Thus we may ask what does or doesn't supervene on the qualitative character of the entire world, throughout all of history. Suppose that two possible worlds are perfect qualitative duplicates—must they then also have exactly the same distributions of objective probability, the same laws of nature, the same counterfactuals and causal relations? Must their inhabitants have the same *de re* modal properties? If so, it makes sense to pursue such projects as a frequency analysis of probability, a regularity analysis of laws of nature, or a comparative similarity analysis of causal counterfactuals and *de re* modality. If not, such projects are doomed from the start, and we needn't

---

[18] For a general discussion of supervenience, see Jaegwon Kim, 'Supervenience and Nomological Incommensurables', *American Philosophical Quarterly*, 15 (1978), 149–56.

look at the details of the attempts. But we cannot even raise these questions of supervenience unless we can speak of duplicate worlds. And to do that, I have suggested, we need natural properties.

(Note that if possible worlds obey a principle of identity of qualitative indiscernibles, then all these supervenience theses hold automatically. If no two worlds are duplicates, then *a fortiori* no two are duplicates that differ in their probabilities, laws, . . ., or anything else.)

We might also ask whether qualitative character supervenes on anything less. For instance, we might ask whether global qualitative character supervenes on local qualitative character. Say that two worlds are *local duplicates* iff they are divisible into corresponding small parts in such a way that (1) corresponding parts of the two worlds are duplicates, and (2) the correspondence preserves spatiotemporal relations. (The exact meaning depends, of course, on what we mean by 'small'.) If two worlds are local duplicates, then must they be duplicates *simpliciter*? Or could they differ in ways that do not prevent local duplication—*e.g.* in external relations, other than the spatiotemporal relations themselves, between separated things? Again, we must make sense of duplication—this time, both in the large and in the small—even to ask the question.[19]

*　*　*

Next, divergent worlds. I shall say that two possible worlds *diverge* iff they are not duplicates but they do have duplicate initial temporal segments. Thus our world and another might match perfectly up through the year 1945, and go their separate ways thereafter.

Note that we need no identity of times across worlds. Our world through our 1945 duplicates an initial segment of the other world; that otherworldly segment ends with a year that indeed resembles our 1945, but it is part of otherworldly time, not part of our time. Also, we need no separation of time and space that contravenes Relativity—we have initial temporal segments, of this or another world, if we have spatiotemporal regions bounded by spacelike surfaces that cut the world in two.

I distinguish *divergence* of worlds from *branching* of worlds. In branching, instead of duplicate segments, one and the same initial segment is allegedly shared as a common part by the two overlapping worlds. Branching is problematic in ways that divergence is not. First, because an inhabit-

---

[19] Such a thesis of supervenience of the global on the local resembles the 'holographic hypothesis' considered and rejected by Saul Kripke in 'Identity Through Time', presented at the 1979 conference of the American Philosophical Association, Eastern Division, and elsewhere.

ant of the shared segment cannot speak unequivocally of *the* world he lives in. What if he says there will be a sea fight tomorrow, meaning of course to speak of the future of his own world, and one of the two worlds he lives in has a sea fight the next day and the other doesn't? Second, because overlap of worlds interferes with the most salient principle of demarcation for worlds, *viz.* that two possible individuals are part of the same world iff they are linked by some chain of external relations, *e.g.* of spatiotemporal relations. (I know of no other example.) Neither of these difficulties seems insuperable, but both are better avoided. That makes it reasonable to prefer a theory of nonoverlapping divergent worlds to a theory of branching worlds. Then we need to be able to speak of qualitative duplication of world-segments, which we can do in terms of shared natural properties.

Divergent (or branching) worlds are of use in defining Determinism. The usual definitions are not very satisfactory. If we say that every event has a cause, we overlook probabilistic causation under Indeterminism. If we speak of what could be predicted by a superhuman calculator with unlimited knowledge of history and the laws of nature, we overlook obstacles that might prevent prediction even under Determinism, or else we try to make nonvacuous sense of counterfactuals about what our predictor could do if he had some quite impossible combination of powers and limitations.

A better approach is as follows. First, a system of laws of nature is Deterministic iff no two divergent worlds both conform perfectly to the laws of that system. Second, a world is Deterministic iff its laws comprise a Deterministic system. Third, Determinism is the thesis that our world is Deterministic.[20]

(Alternative versions of Determinism can be defined in similar fashion. For instance, we could strengthen the first step by prohibiting convergence as well as divergence of law-abiding worlds. Or we could even require that no two law-abiding worlds have duplicate momentary slices without being duplicates throughout their histories. Or we could define a weaker sort of Determinism: we could call a world *fortuitously* Deterministic, even if its laws do not comprise a Deterministic system, iff no world both diverges from it and conforms to its laws. The laws and early history of such a world

---

[20] This approach is due, in essence, to Richard Montague, 'Deterministic Theories', in *Decisions, Values and Groups*, II (London: Pergamon Press, 1962), and in his *Formal Philosophy* (New Haven: Yale University Press, 1974). But Montague did not speak as I have done of duplication of initial segments of worlds in virtue of the sharing of certain élite properties. Instead, he used sameness of description in a certain vocabulary, which vocabulary was left as an unspecified parameter of his analysis. For he wrote as a logician obliged to remain neutral on questions of metaphysics.

suffice to determine later history, but only because the situations in which the laws fall short of Determinism never arise. We might equivalently define fortuitous Determinism as follows: for any historical fact F and any initial segment S of the world, there are a true proposition H about the history of S and a true proposition L about the laws of nature, such that H and L together strictly imply F.[21] Does this definition bypass our need to speak of duplication of initial segments? Not so, for we must ask what it means to say that H is about the history of S. I take that to mean that H holds at both or neither of any two worlds that both begin with segments that are duplicates of S.)

Divergent worlds are important also in connection with the sort of counterfactual conditional that figures in patterns of causal dependence. Such counterfactuals tend to be temporally asymmetric, and this is what gives rise to the asymmetry of causation itself. Counterfactuals of this sort do not 'backtrack': it is not to be said that if the present were different a different past would have led up to it, but rather that if the present were different, the same past would have had a different outcome. Given a hypothesised difference at a certain time, the events of future times normally would be very different indeed, but the events of past times (except perhaps for the very near past) would be no different. Thus actuality and its counterfactual alternatives are divergent worlds, with duplicate initial segments.[22]

MINIMAL MATERIALISM

There is a difficulty that arises if we attempt to formulate certain reductionist views, for instance Materialism, as supervenience theses. A solution to this difficulty employs natural properties not only by way of duplication but in a more direct way also.

Roughly speaking, Materialism is the thesis that physics—something not too different from present-day physics, though presumably somewhat improved—is a comprehensive theory of the world, complete as well as

[21] A closely related definition appears in Peter van Inwagen, 'The Incompatibility of Free Will and Determinism', *Philosophical Studies*, 27 (1975), 185–99.

[22] See my 'Counterfactual Dependence and Time's Arrow', *Noûs*, 13 (1979), 455–76; Jonathan Bennett's review of my *Counterfactuals*, *Canadian Journal of Philosophy*, 4 (1974), 381–402; P. B. Downing, 'Subjunctive Conditionals, Time Order, and Causation', *Proceedings of the Aristotelian Society*, 59 (1959), 125–40; Allan Gibbard and William Harper, 'Counterfactuals and Two Kinds of Expected Utility', in *Foundations and Applications of Decision Theory*, edited by C. A. Hooker *et al.* (Dordrecht: Reidel, 1978), and in *Ifs*, edited by W. L. Harper *et al.* (Dordrecht: Reidel, 1981); and Frank Jackson, 'A Causal Theory of Counterfactuals', *Australasian Journal of Philosophy*, 55 (1977), 3–21.

correct. The world is as physics says it is, and there's no more to say. World history written in physical language is all of world history. That is rough speaking indeed; our goal will be to give a better formulation. But before I try to say more precisely what Materialism is, let me say what it is not. (1) Materialism is not a thesis of finite translatibility of all our language into the language of physics. (2) Materialism is not to be identified with any one Materialist theory of mind. It is a thesis that motivates a variety of theories of mind: versions of Behaviourism, Functionalism, the mind-body identity theory, even the theory that mind is all a mistake. (3) Materialism is not just the theory that there are no things except those recognised by physics. To be sure, Materialists don't believe in spirits, or other such nonphysical things. But antimaterialists may not believe in spirits either—their complaint needn't be that physics omits some of the things that there are. They may complain instead that physics overlooks some of the ways there are for physical things to differ; for instance, they may think that physical people could differ in what their experience is like. (4) That suggests that Materialism is, at least in part, the thesis that there are no natural properties instantiated at our world except those recognised by physics. That is better, but I think still not right. Couldn't there be a natural property X (in the nature of the case, it is hard to name an example!) which is shared by the physical brains in worlds like ours and the immaterial spirits that inhabit other worlds? Or by thisworldly quarks and certain otherworldly particles that cannot exist under our physics? Physics could quite properly make no mention of a natural property of this sort. It is enough to recognise the special case applicable to our world, X-cum-physicality, brainhood or quarkhood as it might be. Then if by physical properties we mean those properties that are mentioned in the language of physics, a Materialist ought not to hold that all natural properties instantiated in our world are physical properties.

At this point, it ought to seem advisable to formulate Materialism as a supervenience thesis: no difference without physical difference. Or, contraposing: physical duplicates are duplicates *simpliciter*. *A fortiori*, no mental difference without physical difference; physical duplicates are mental duplicates. The thesis might best be taken as applying to whole possible worlds, in order to bypass such questions as whether mental life is to some extent extrinsic to the subject. So we have this first of several attempted formulations of Materialism:

> *M1.* Any two possible worlds that are exactly alike in all respects recognised by physics are qualitative duplicates.

But this will not do. In making Materialism into a thesis about how just any two worlds can and cannot differ, *M1* puts Materialism forward as a necessary truth. That is not what Materialists intend. Materialism is meant to be a contingent thesis, a merit of our world that not all other worlds share. Two worlds could indeed differ without differing physically, if at least one of them is a world where Materialism is false. For instance, our Materialistic world differs from a nonmaterialistic world that is physically just like ours but that also contains physically epiphenomenal spirits.

There is a noncontingent supervenience thesis nearby that might appeal to Materialists:

> *M2.* There is no difference, *a fortiori* no mental difference, without some nonmental difference. Any two worlds alike in all non-mental respects are duplicates, and in particular do not differ in respect of the mental lives of their inhabitants.

This seems to capture our thought that the mental is a pattern in a medium, obtaining in virtue of local features of the medium (neuron firings) and perhaps also very global features (laws of nature) that are too small or too big to be mental themselves. But *M2* is not Materialism. It is both less and more. Less, obviously, because it never says that the medium is physical. More, because it denies the very possibility of what I shall call *Panpsychistic* Materialism.

It is often noted that psychophysical identity is a two-way street: if all mental properties are physical, then some physical properties are mental. But perhaps not just some but *all* physical properties might be mental as well; and indeed every property of anything might be at once physical and mental. Suppose there are indeed worlds where this is so. If so, presumably there are many such worlds, not all duplicates, differing *inter alia* in the mental lives of their inhabitants. But all differences between such worlds are mental (as well as physical), so none are nonmental. These worlds will be vacuously alike in all nonmental respects, for lack of any nonmental respects to differ in. Then *M2* fails. And not just at the troublemaking worlds; *M2* is noncontingent, so if it fails at any worlds, it fails at all—even decent Materialistic worlds like ours. Maybe Panpsychistic Materialism is indeed impossible—how do you square it with a broadly functional analysis of mind?—but a thesis that says so is more than just Materialism.

A third try. This much is at least true:

> *M3.* No two Materialistic worlds differ without differing physically; any two Materialistic worlds that are exactly alike physically are duplicates.

But *M3* is not a formulation of Materialism, for the distinction between Materialistic and other worlds appears within *M3*. All we learn is that the Materialistic worlds comprise a class within which there is no difference without physical difference. But there are many such classes. In fact any world, however spirit-ridden, belongs to such a class.

A fourth try. Perhaps we should confine our attention to nomologically possible worlds, thus:

> *M4.* Among worlds that conform to the actual laws of nature, no two differ without differing physically; any two such worlds that are exactly alike physically are duplicates.

But again we have something that is both less and more than Materialism. Less, because *M4* could hold at a world where Materialism is false but where spiritual phenomena are correlated with physical phenomena according to strict laws. More, because *M4* fails to hold at a Materialistic, spirit-free world if the laws of that world do not preclude the existence of epiphenomenal spirits. Our world might be such a world, a world where spirits are absent but not outlawed.[23]

So far, a supervenience formulation of Materialism seems elusive. But I think we can succeed if we join the idea of supervenience with the idea that a nonmaterialistic world would have something extra, something that a Materialistic world lacks. It might have spirits; or it might have physical things that differ in nonphysical ways, for instance in what their experience is like. In either case there are extra natural properties, properties instantiated in the nonmaterialistic world but nowhere to be found in the Materialistic world. Let us say that a property is *alien* to a world iff (1) it is not instantiated by any inhabitant of that world, and (2) it is not analysable as a conjunction of, or as a structural property constructed out of, natural properties all of which are instantiated by inhabitants of that world. (I need the second clause because I am following Armstrong, *mutatis mutandis*, in declining to rule out perfectly natural properties that are conjunctive or structurally complex. See *Universals*, II, pp. 30–42 and 67–71. It would be wrong to count as alien a complex property analysable in terms of nonalien constituents.) If our world is Materialistic, then it is safe to say that some of the natural properties instantiated in any nonmaterialistic world are properties alien to our world. Now we can proceed at last to formulate Materialism as a restricted and contingent supervenience thesis:

---

[23] This objection against *M4* as a formulation of 'the ontological primacy of the microphysical' appears in Terence Horgan, 'Supervenience and Microphysics', *Pacific Philosophical Quarterly*, 63 (1982), 29–43.

> *M5.* Among worlds where no natural properties alien to our world
> are instantiated, no two differ without differing physically; any
> two such worlds that are exactly alike physically are duplicates.[24]

*   *   *

We took materialism to uphold the comprehensiveness of 'something not
too different from present-day physics, though presumably somewhat
improved'. That was deliberately vague. Materialist metaphysicians want
to side with physics, but not to take sides within physics. Within physics,
more precise claims of completeness and correctness may be at issue.
Physics (ignoring latter-day failures of nerve) is the science that aspires to
comprehensiveness, and particular physical theories may be put forward
as fulfilling that aspiration. If so, we must again ask what it means to claim
comprehensiveness. And again, the answer may be given by a supervenience formulation: no difference without physical difference as conceived by such-and-such grand theory. But again it must be understood as
a restricted and contingent supervenience thesis, applying only among
worlds devoid of alien natural properties.

Thus the business of physics is not just to discover laws and causal
explanations. In putting forward as comprehensive theories that recognise
only a limited range of natural properties, physics proposes inventories of
the natural properties instantiated in our world. Not complete inventories,
perhaps. But complete enough to account for all the duplications and
differences that could arise in the absence of alien natural properties.
Of course, the discovery of natural properties is inseparable from the
discovery of laws. For an excellent reason to think that some hitherto
unsuspected natural properties are instantiated—properties deserving of
recognition by physics, the quark colours as they might be—is that without
them, no satisfactory system of laws can be found.

This is reminiscent of the distinctive *a posteriori*, scientific character of
Armstrong's Realism (*Universals*, I, pp. 8–9, and *passim*). But in the setting
of an ontology of *possibilia*, the distinction between discovering what
universals or natural properties there actually are and discovering which

---

[24] This formulation resembles one proposed by Horgan in 'Supervenience and Microphysics'. The principal difference is as follows. Horgan would count as alien (my term, not his)
any property cited in the fundamental laws of otherworldly microphysics that is not also
explicitly cited in the fundamental laws of thisworldly microphysics. Whether the property is
instantiated in either world doesn't enter into it. But must an alien property figure in laws of
otherworldly *physics*? Must it figure in any otherworldly laws at all? It seems that a Materialistic world might differ without differing physically from a world where there are properties
alien in my sense but not in Horgan's—perhaps a world where laws are in short supply.

ones are actually instantiated fades away. And the latter question is *a posteriori* on any theory. What remains, and remains important, is that physics discovers properties. And not just any properties—natural properties. The discovery is, for instance, that neutrinos are not all alike. That is not the discovery that different ones have different properties in my sense, belong to different classes. We knew that much *a priori*. Rather, it is the surprising discovery that some *natural* property differentiates some neutrinos from others. That discovery has in fact been made; I should like to read an account of it by some philosopher who is not prepared to adopt a discriminatory attitude toward properties and who thinks that all things are equally similar and dissimilar to one another.

LAWS AND CAUSATION

The observation that physics discovers natural properties in the course of discovering laws may serve to introduce our next topic: the analysis of what it is to be a law of nature. I agree with Armstrong that we need universals, or at least natural properties, in explaining what lawhood is, though I disagree with his account of how this is so.

Armstrong's theory, in its simplest form,[25] holds that what makes certain regularities lawful are second-order states of affairs $N(F,G)$ in which the two ordinary, first-order universals F and G are related by a certain dyadic second-order universal N. It is a contingent matter which universals are thus related by the lawmaker N. But it is necessary—and necessary *simpliciter*, not just nomologically necessary—that if $N(F,G)$ obtains, then F and G are constantly conjoined. There is a necessary connection between the second-order state of affairs $N(F,G)$ and the first-order lawful regularity $\forall x(Fx \supset Gx)$; and likewise between the conjunctive state of affairs $N(F,G)$ & Fa and its necessary consequence Ga.

A parallel theory could be set up with natural properties in place of Armstrong's first- and second-order universals. It would have many of the attractive features that Armstrong claims on behalf of his theory, but at least one merit would be lost. For Armstrong, the lawful necessitation of Ga by Fa is a purely local matter: it involves only a, the universals F and G that are present in a, and the second-order lawmaking universal that is

[25] *Universals*, II, pp. 148–57. A more developed form of the theory appears in D. M. Armstrong, *What is a Law of Nature?* (Cambridge: Cambridge University Press, 1983). Similar theories have been proposed in Fred I. Dretske, 'Laws of Nature', *Philosophy of Science*, 44 (1977), 248–68, and in Michael Tooley, 'The Nature of Laws', *Canadian Journal of Philosophy*, 4 (1977), 667–98.

present in turn in (or between) these two universals. If we replace the universals by properties, however natural, that locality is lost. For properties are classes with their membership spread around the worlds, and are not wholly present in *a*. But I do not think this is a conclusive objection, for our intuitions of locality often seem to lead us astray. The selective regularity theory I shall shortly advocate also sacrifices locality, as does any regularity theory of law.

What leads me (with some regret) to reject Armstrong's theory, whether with universals or with natural properties, is that I find its necessary connections unintelligible. Whatever N may be, I cannot see how it could be absolutely impossible to have $N(F,G)$ and Fa without Ga. (Unless N just *is* constant conjunction, or constant conjunction plus something else, in which case Armstrong's theory turns into a form of the regularity theory he rejects.) The mystery is somewhat hidden by Armstrong's terminology. He uses 'necessitates' as a name for the lawmaking universal N; and who would be surprised to hear that if F 'necessitates' G and a has F, then a must have G? But I say that N deserves the name of 'necessitation' only if, somehow, it really can enter into the requisite necessary connections. It can't enter into them just by bearing a name, any more than one can have mighty biceps just by being called 'Armstrong'.

I am tempted to complain in Humean fashion of alleged necessary connections between distinct existences, especially when first-order states of affairs in the past supposedly join with second-order states of affairs to necessitate first-order states of affairs in the future. That complaint is not clearly right: the sharing of universals detracts from the distinctness of the necessitating and the necessitated states of affairs. But I am not appeased. I conclude that necessary connections can be unintelligible even when they are supposed to obtain between existences that are not clearly and wholly distinct.[26]

Thus I do not endorse Armstrong's way of building universals, or alternatively natural properties, into the analysis of lawhood. Instead I favour a regularity analysis. But I need natural properties even so.

[26] Armstrong's more developed theory in *What is a Law of Nature?* complicates the picture in two ways. First, the second-order state of affairs $N(F,G)$ is itself taken to be a universal, and its presence in its instances detracts yet further from the distinctness of the necessitating and the necessitated states of affairs. Second, all laws are defeasible. It is possible after all to have $N(F,G)$ and Fa without Ga, namely if we also have $N(E\&F,H)$ and Ea, where H and G are incompatible. (The law that Fs are Gs might be *contingently* indefeasible, if no such defeating state of affairs $N(E\&F,H)$ obtains; but no law has its indefeasibility built in essentially.) It remains true that there are alleged necessary connections that I find unintelligible, but they are more complicated than before. To necessitate a state of affairs, we need not only the first- and second-order states of affairs originally considered, but also a negative existential to the effect that there are no further states of affairs of the sort that could act as defeaters.

Certainly not just any regularity is a law of nature. Some are accidental. So an adequate regularity analysis must be selective. Also, an adequate analysis must be collective. It must treat regularities not one at a time, but rather as candidates to enter into integrated systems. For a given regularity might hold either as a law or accidentally, depending on whether other regularities obtain that can fit together with it in a suitable system. (Thus I reject the idea that lawhood consists of 'lawlikeness' plus truth.) Following Mill and Ramsey,[27] I take a suitable system to be one that has the virtues we aspire to in our own theory-building, and that has them to the greatest extent possible given the way the world is. It must be entirely true; it must be closed under strict implication; it must be as simple in axiomatisation as it can be without sacrificing too much information content; and it must have as much information content as it can have without sacrificing too much simplicity. A law is any regularity that earns inclusion in the ideal system. (Or, in case of ties, in every ideal system.) The ideal system need not consist entirely of regularities; particular facts may gain entry if they contribute enough to collective simplicity and strength. (For instance, certain particular facts about the Big Bang might be strong candidates.) But only the regularities of the system are to count as laws.

We face an obvious problem. Different ways to express the same content, using different vocabulary, will differ in simplicity. The problem can be put in two ways, depending on whether we take our systems as consisting of propositions (classes of worlds) or as consisting of interpreted sentences. In the first case, the problem is that a single system has different degrees of simplicity relative to different linguistic formulations. In the second case, the problem is that equivalent systems, strictly implying the very same regularities, may differ in their simplicity. In fact, the content of any system whatever may be formulated very simply indeed. Given system S, let F be a predicate that applies to all and only things at worlds where S holds. Take F as primitive, and axiomatise S (or an equivalent thereof) by the single axiom $\forall x Fx$. If utter simplicity is so easily attained, the ideal theory may as well be as strong as possible. Simplicity and strength needn't be traded off. Then the ideal theory will include (its simple axiom will strictly imply) all truths, and *a fortiori* all regularities. Then, after all, every regularity will be a law. That must be wrong.

---

[27] John Stuart Mill, *A System of Logic* (London: Parker, 1843), book III, chapter IV, §1; F. P. Ramsey's 1928 'Universals of Law and of Fact' [chapter 7A in his *Philosophical Papers* (Cambridge: Cambridge University Press, 1990)]. Ramsey regarded this theory of law as superseded by the different theory in his 1929 'General Propositions and Causality' [chapter 7B in his *Philosophical Papers*], but I prefer his first thoughts to his second. I present a theory of lawhood along the lines of Ramsey's earlier theory in my *Counterfactuals* (Oxford: Blackwell, 1973), pp. 73–5. A revision to that discussion is needed in the probabilistic case, which I here ignore.

The remedy, of course, is not to tolerate such a perverse choice of primitive vocabulary. We should ask how candidate systems compare in simplicity when each is formulated in the simplest eligible way; or, if we count different formulations as different systems, we should dismiss the ineligible ones from candidacy. An appropriate standard of eligibility is not far to seek: let the primitive vocabulary that appears in the axioms refer only to perfectly natural properties.

Of course, it remains an unsolved and difficult problem to say what simplicity of a formulation is. But it is no longer the downright insoluble problem that it would be if there were nothing to choose between alternative primitive vocabularies.

(One might think also to replace strict implication by deducibility in some specified calculus. But this second remedy seems unnecessary given the first, and seems incapable of solving our problem by itself.)

If we adopt the remedy proposed, it will have the consequence that laws will tend to be regularities involving natural properties. Fundamental laws, those that the ideal system takes as axiomatic, must concern perfectly natural properties. Derived laws that follow fairly straightforwardly also will tend to concern fairly natural properties. Regularities concerning unnatural properties may indeed be strictly implied, and should count as derived laws if so. But they are apt to escape notice even if we someday possess a good approximation to the ideal system. For they will be hard to express in a language that has words mostly for not-too-unnatural properties, as any language must. (See the next section.) And they will be hard to derive, indeed they may not be finitely derivable at all, in our deductive calculi. Thus my account explains, as Armstrong's does in its very different way, why the scientific investigation of laws and of natural properties is a package deal; why physicists posit natural properties such as the quark colours in order to posit the laws in which those properties figure, so that laws and natural properties get discovered together.

*   *   *

If the analysis of lawhood requires natural properties, then so does the analysis of causation. It is fairly uncontroversial that causation involves laws. That is so according to both of the leading theories of causation: the deductive-nomological analysis, on which the laws are applied to the actual course of events with the cause and effect present; and the counterfactual analysis that I favour, on which the laws are applied to counterfactual situations with the cause hypothesised away. These counterfactual alternatives may need to break actual laws at the point where they diverge from actuality, but the analysis requires that they evolve thereafter in accordance with the actual laws.[28]

According to my counterfactual analysis, causation involves natural properties in a second way too. We need the kind of counterfactuals that avoid backtracking; else the analysis faces fatal counterexamples involving epiphenomenal side-effects or cases of causal preemption. As I have already noted, these counterfactuals are to be characterised in terms of divergent worlds, hence in terms of duplicate initial world-segments, hence in terms of shared natural properties.

Causation involves natural properties in yet another way. (Small wonder that I came to appreciate natural properties after working on the analysis of causation!) Causation holds between events. Unless we distinguish genuine from spurious events, we will be left with too many putative causes. You put a lump of butter on a skillet, and the butter melts. What event causes this? There is one event that we can call a moving of molecules. It occurs in the region where the skillet is, just before the butter melts. This is an event such that, necessarily, it occurs in a spatiotemporal region only if that region contains rapidly moving molecules. Surely this event is a cause of the melting of the butter.

Heat is that phenomenon, whatever it may be, that manifests itself in certain familiar characteristic ways. Let us say: heat is that which occupies the heat-role. (It won't matter whether we take the definite description plain, as I prefer, or rigidified.) In fact, but contingently, it is molecular motion that occupies the heat-role. It might have been molecular non-motion, or caloric fluid, or what you will. Now consider an alleged second event, one that we may call a having-the-occupant-of-the-heat-role. The second event occurs just when and where the first does, in the region where the hot skillet is. It occurs there in virtue of the two facts (1) that the skillet's molecules are moving rapidly, and (2) that the region in question is part of a world where molecular motion is what occupies the heat-role. But this second event differs from the first. The necessary conditions for its occurrence are different. Necessarily, it occurs in a region only if that region contains whatever phenomenon occupies the heat-role in the world of which that region is part. So in those worlds where caloric fluid occupies the heat-role and molecular motion does not, the first event occurs only in regions with molecular motion whereas the second occurs only in regions with caloric fluid.

Certainly the first event causes the melting of the butter, but shall we say that the second event does so as well? No; that seems to multiply

<hr>

[28] See my 'Causation', *Journal of Philosophy*, 70 (1973), 556–67 [reprinted in *Causation*, edited by Ernest Sosa and Michael Tooley (Oxford: Oxford University Press, 1993), 193–207].

causes beyond belief by playing a verbal trick. But if there really are two events here, I cannot see why the second has less of a claim than the first to be a cause of the melting of the butter. It is out of the question to say that the first and the second events are one and the same—then this one event would have different conditions of occurrence from itself. The best solution is to deny that the alleged second event is a genuine event at all. If it isn't, of course it can't do any causing.

Why is the first event genuine and the second spurious? Compare the properties involved: containing rapidly moving molecules versus containing whatever phenomenon occupies the heat-role. (I mean these as properties of the spatiotemporal region; other treatments of events would take instead the corresponding properties of the skillet, but my point would still apply.) The first is a fairly natural, intrinsic property. The second is highly disjunctive and extrinsic. For all sorts of different phenomena could occupy the heat-role; and whether the phenomenon going on in a region occupies the role depends not only on what goes on in the region but also on what goes on elsewhere in the same world. Thus the distinction between more and less natural properties gives me the distinction between genuine and spurious events that I need in order to disown an overabundance of causes. If a property is too unnatural, it is inefficacious in the sense that it cannot figure in the conditions of occurrence of the events that cause things.[29]

THE CONTENT OF LANGUAGE AND THOUGHT

Hilary Putnam has given an argument which he regards as a refutation of a 'radically non-epistemic' view of truth, but which I regard rather as a *reductio* against Putnam's premises.[30] In particular, it refutes his assumption that *'we* interpret our languages or nothing does' ('Models and Reality', p. 482) so that any constraint on reference must be established by

---

[29] See the discussion of impotence of dispositions in Elizabeth W. Prior, Robert Pargetter, and Frank Jackson, 'Three Theses About Dispositions', *American Philosophical Quarterly*, 19 (1982), 251–7. If a disposition is not identified with its actual basis, there is a threat of multiplication of putative causes similar to that in my example. We would not wish to say that the breaking of a struck glass is caused both by its fragility and by the frozen-in stresses that are the basis thereof; and if forced to choose, we should choose the latter. I suggest that the fragility is inefficacious because it is too unnatural a property, too disjunctive and extrinsic, to figure in the conditions of occurrence of any event.

[30] Hilary Putnam, 'Realism and Reason', in his *Meaning and the Moral Sciences* (London: Routledge & Kegan Paul, 1978), 123–40, and 'Models and Reality', *Journal of Symbolic Logic*, 45 (1980), 464–82. The reader is warned that the argument as I present it here may not be quite as Putnam intended it to be. For I have made free in reading between the lines and in restating the argument in my own way.

our own stipulation in language or thought. Gary Merrill has suggested that Putnam may be answered by appeal to a constraint that depends on an objective structure of properties and relations in the world.[31] I agree, and find here another point at which we need natural properties.

Putnam's argument, as I understand it, is as follows. First, suppose that the only constraint on interpretation of our language (or perhaps our language of thought) is given by a description theory of reference of a global and futuristic sort. An 'intended interpretation' is any interpretation that satisfies a certain body of theory: viz. the idealised descendant of our current total theory that would emerge at the end of inquiry, an ideal theory refined to perfection under the guidance of all needed observation and our best theoretical reasoning. If so, intended interpretations are surprisingly abundant. For any world can satisfy any theory (ideal or not), and can do so in countless very different ways, provided only that the world is not too small and the theory is consistent. Beyond that, it doesn't matter what the world is like or what the theory says. Hence we have radical indeterminacy of reference. And we have the coincidence that Putnam welcomes between satisfaction under all intended interpretations and 'epistemic truth'. For the ideal theory is the whole of 'epistemic truth', the intended interpretations are just those interpretations of our language that satisfy the ideal theory, and (unless the world is too small or ideal theory is inconsistent) there are some such interpretations.

I take this to refute the supposition that there are no further constraints on reference. But Putnam asks: how could there be a further constraint? How could we ever establish it? By stipulation, by saying or thinking something. But whatever we say or think will be in language (or language of thought) that suffers from radical indeterminacy of interpretation. For the saving constraint will not be there until we succeed in establishing it. So the attempted stipulation must fail. The most we can do is to contribute a new chapter to current and ideal theory, a chapter consisting of whatever we said or thought in our stipulation. And this new theory goes the way of all theory. So we cannot establish a further constraint; and 'we interpret our language or nothing does'; so there cannot be any further constraint. We cannot lift ourselves by our bootstraps, so we must still be on the ground.

Indeed we cannot lift ourselves by our bootstraps, but we are off the ground, so there must be another way to fly. Our language does have a fairly determinate interpretation (a Moorean fact!) so there must be some constraint not created ex nihilo by our stipulation.

[31] G. H. Merrill, 'The Model-Theoretic Argument Against Realism', Philosophy of Science, 47 (1980), 69–81.

What can it be? Many philosophers would suggest that it is some sort of causal constraint. If so my case is made, given my arguments in the previous section: we need natural properties to explain determinacy of interpretation. But I doubt that it really is a causal constraint, for I am inclined to think that the causal aspect of reference *is* established by what we say and think. Thus: I think of a thing as that which I am causally acquainted with in such-and-such a way, perhaps perceptually or perhaps through a channel of acquaintance that involves the naming of the thing and my picking up of the name. I refer to that thing in my thought, and derivatively in language, because it is the thing that fits this causal and egocentric description extracted from my theory of the world and of my place in the world.[32]

I would instead propose that the saving constraint concerns the referent —not the referrer, and not the causal channels between the two. It takes two to make a reference, and we will not find the constraint if we look for it always on the wrong side of the relationship. Reference consists in part of what we do in language or thought when we refer, but in part it consists in eligibility of the referent. And this eligibility to be referred to is a matter of natural properties.

That is the suggestion Merrill offers. (He offers it not as his own view, but as what opponents of Putnam ought to say; and I gratefully accept the offer.) In the simplest case, suppose that the interpretation of the logical vocabulary somehow takes care of itself, to reveal a standard first-order language whose nonlogical vocabulary consists entirely of predicates. The parts of the world comprise a domain; and sets, sets of pairs, . . ., from this domain are potential extensions for the predicates. Now suppose we have an all-or-nothing division of properties into natural and unnatural. Say that a set from the domain is *eligible* to be the extension of a one-place predicate iff its members are just those things in the domain that share some natural property; and likewise for many-place predicates and natural relations. An *eligible interpretation* is one that assigns none but eligible extensions to the predicates. A so-called 'intended' interpretation is an eligible interpretation that satisfies the ideal theory. (But the name is misleading: it is not to be said that our intentions establish the constraint requiring eligibility. That way lies the futile bootstrap-tugging that we must avoid.) Then if the natural properties are sparse, there is no reason to expect any overabundance of intended interpretations. There may even be none. Even ideal theory runs the risk of being unsatisfiable, save in 'unintended' ways. Because satisfaction is not guaranteed, we accomplish

[32] See Stephen Schiffer, 'The Basis of Reference', *Erkenntnis*, 13 (1978), 171–206.

something if we manage to achieve it by making a good fit between theory and the world. All this is as it should be.

The proposal calls for refinement. First, we need to provide for richer forms of language. In this we can be guided by familiar translations, for instance between modal language with higher-order quantification and first-order language that explicitly mentions *possibilia* and classes built up from them. Second, it will not do to take naturalness of properties as all-or-nothing. Here, above all, we need to make naturalness—and hence eligibility—a comparative matter, or a matter of degree. There are salient sharp lines, but not in the right places. There is the line between the perfectly natural properties and all the rest, but surely we have predicates for much-less-than-perfectly natural properties. There is the line between properties that are and that are not finitely analysable in terms of perfectly natural properties, but that lets in enough highly unnatural properties that it threatens not to solve our problem. We need gradations; and we need some give and take between the eligibility of referents and the other factors that make for 'intendedness', notably satisfaction of appropriate bits of theory. (Ideal theory, if we keep as much of Putnam's story as we can.) Grueness is not an absolutely ineligible referent (as witness my reference to it just now) but an interpretation that assigns it is to that extent inferior to one that assigns blueness instead. *Ceteris paribus*, the latter is the 'intended' one, just because it does better on eligibility.

Naturalness of properties makes for differences of eligibility not only among the properties themselves, but also among things. Compare Bruce with the cat-shaped chunk of miscellaneous and ever-changing matter that follows him around, always a few steps behind. The former is a highly eligible referent, the latter is not. (I haven't succeeded in referring to it, for I didn't say just which such chunk 'it' was to be.) That is because Bruce, unlike the cat-shaped chunk, has a boundary well demarcated by differences in highly natural properties. Where Bruce ends, there the density of matter, the relative abundance of the chemical elements, . . . abruptly change. Not so for the chunk. Bruce is also much more of a locus of causal chains than is the chunk; this too traces back to natural properties, by the considerations of the previous section. Thus naturalness of properties sets up distinctions among things. The reverse happens also. Once we are away from the perfectly natural properties, one thing that makes for naturalness of a property is that it is a property belonging exclusively to well-demarcated things.

* * *

You might well protest that Putnam's problem is misconceived, wherefore no need has been demonstrated for resources to solve it. Putnam seems to conceive of language entirely as a repository of theory, and not at all as a practice of social interaction. We have the language of the encyclopedia, but where is the language of the pub? Where are the communicative intentions and the mutual expectations that seem to have so much to do with what we mean? In fact, where is thought? It seems to enter the picture, if at all, only as the special case where the language to be interpreted is hard-wired, unspoken, hidden, and all too conjectural.

I think the point is well taken, but I think it doesn't matter. If the problem of intentionality is rightly posed there will still be a threat of radical indeterminacy, there will still be a need for saving constraints, there will still be a remedy analogous to Merrill's suggested answer to Putnam, and there will still be a need for natural properties.

Set language aside and consider instead the interpretation of thought. (Afterward we can hope to interpret the subject's language in terms of his beliefs and desires regarding verbal communication with others.) The subject is in various states, and could be in various others, that are causally related to each other, to the subject's behaviour, and to the nearby environment that stimulates his senses. These states fit into a functional organisation, they occupy certain causal roles. (Most likely they are states of the brain. Maybe they involve something that is language-like but hard-wired, maybe not. But the nature of the states is beside the point.) The states have their functional roles in the subject as he now is, and in the subject as he is at other times and as he might have been under other circumstances, and even in other creatures of the same kind as the subject. Given the functional roles of the states, the problem is to assign them content. Propositional content, some would say; but I would agree only if the propositions can be taken as egocentric ones, and I think an 'egocentric proposition' is simply a property. States indexed by content can be identified as a belief that this, a desire for that, a perceptual experience of seeming to confront so-and-so, an intention to do such-and-such. (But not all ordinary ascriptions of attitudes merely specify the content of the subject's states. Fred and Ted might be alike in the functional roles of their states, and hence have states with the same content in the narrowly psychological sense that is my present concern, and hence believe alike *e.g.* by each believing himself to have heard of a pretty town named 'Castlemaine'. Yet they might be acquainted via that name with different towns, as opposite ends of the earth, so that Fred and not Ted believes that Castlemaine, Victoria, is pretty.) The problem of assigning content to functionally characterised states is to be solved by means of constraining principles. Foremost among these are principles of fit. If a state is to be interpreted as an intention to raise one's hand, it had better typically cause the hand to go up. If a state (or complex of states) is to be interpreted as a system of beliefs and desires—or better, degrees of belief and desire—according to which raising one's hand would be a good means to one's ends, and if another state is to be interpreted as an intention to raise one's hand, then the former had better typically cause the latter. Likewise on the input side. A state typically caused by round things before the eyes is a good candidate for interpretation as the visual experience of confronting something round; and its typical impact on the states interpreted as systems of belief ought to be interpreted as the exogenous addition of a belief that one is confronting something round, with whatever adjustment that addition calls for.

So far, so good. But it seems clear that preposterous and perverse misinterpretations could nevertheless cohere, could manage to fit the functional roles of the states because misassignment of content at one point compensates for misassignment at another. Let us see just how this could happen, at least under an oversimplified picture of interpretation as follows. An interpretation is given by a pair of functions C and V. C is a probability distribution over the worlds, regarded as encapsulating the subject's dispositions to form beliefs under the impact of sensory evidence: if a stream of evidence specified by proposition E would put the subject into a total state S—for short, if E yields S—we interpret S to consist in part of the belief system given by the probability distribution $C(-/E)$ that comes from C by conditionalising on E. V is a function from worlds to numerical desirability scores, regarded as encapsulating the subject's basic values: if E yields S, we interpret S to consist in part of the system of desires given by the $C(-/E)$-expectations of V. Say that C and V *rationalise* behaviour B after evidence E iff the system of desires given by the $C(-/E)$-expectations of V ranks B at least as high as any alternative behaviour. Say that C and V *fit* iff, for any evidence-specifying E, E yields a state that would cause behaviour rationalised by C and V after E. That is our only constraining principle of fit. (Where did the others go?—We built them into the definitions whereby C and V encapsulate an assignment of content to various states.) Then any two interpretations that always rationalise the same behaviour after the same evidence must fit equally well. Call two worlds *equivalent* iff they are alike in respect of the subject's evidence and behaviour, and note that any decent world is equivalent *inter alia* to horrendously counterinductive worlds and to worlds where everything unobserved by the subject is horrendously nasty. Fit depends on the total of C for each equivalence class, and on the C-expectation of V within each

class, but that is all. Within a class, it makes no difference which world gets
which pair of values of C and V. We can interchange equivalent worlds *ad
lib* and preserve fit. So, given any fitting and reasonable interpretation, we
can transform it into an equally fitting perverse interpretation by swapping
equivalent worlds around so as to enhance the probabilities of counterinductive worlds, or the desirabilities of nasty worlds, or both. *Quod erat
demonstrandum.*

(My simplifications were dire: I left out the egocentricity of belief and
desire and evidence, the causal aspect of rationalised behaviour, the role
of intentions, change of basic values, limitations of logical competence,
.... But I doubt that these omissions matter to my conclusion. I conjecture
that if they were remedied, we could still transform reasonable interpretations into perverse ones in a way that preserves fit.)

If we rely on principles of fit to do the whole job, we can expect radical
indeterminacy of interpretation. We need further constraints, of the sort
called principles of (sophisticated) charity, or of 'humanity'.[33] Such principles call for interpretations according to which the subject has attitudes
that we would deem reasonable for one who has lived the life that he has
lived. (Unlike principles of crude charity, they call for imputations of error
if he has lived under deceptive conditions.) These principles select among
conflicting interpretations that equally well conform to the principles of
fit. They impose *a priori*—albeit defeasible—presumptions about what
sorts of things are apt to be believed and desired; or rather, about what
dispositions to develop beliefs and desires, what inductive biases and basic
values, someone may rightly be interpreted to have.

It is here that we need natural properties. The principles of charity will
impute a bias towards believing that things are green rather than grue,
toward having a basic desire for long life rather than for long-life-unless-
one-was-born-on-Monday-and-in-that-case-life-for-an-even-number-of-
weeks. In short, they will impute eligible content, where ineligibility
consists in severe unnaturalness of the properties the subject supposedly
believes or desires or intends himself to have. They will impute other
things as well, but it is the imputed eligibility that matters to us at present.

Thus the threat of radical indeterminacy in the assignment of content to
thought is fended off. The saving constraint concerns the content—not the
thinker, and not any channels between the two. It takes two to index states
with content, and we will not find the constraint if we look for it always on
the wrong side of the relationship. Believing this or desiring that consists
in part in the functional roles of the states whereby we believe or desire,

[33] See my 'Radical Interpretation', *Synthese*, 23 (1974), 331–44; and Richard E. Grandy,
'Reference, Meaning and Belief', *Journal of Philosophy*, 70 (1973), 439–52.

but in part it consists in the eligibility of the content. And this eligibility to be thought is a matter, in part, of natural properties.

Consider the puzzle whereby Kripke illustrates Wittgenstein's paradox that 'no course of action could be determined by a rule, because every course of action can be made out to accord with the rule'.[34] A well-educated person working arithmetic problems intends to perform addition when he sees the '+' sign. He does not intend to perform quaddition, which is just like addition for small numbers but which yields the answer 5 if any of the numbers to be quadded exceeds a certain bound. Wherefore does he intend to add and not to quadd? Whatever he says and whatever is written in his brain can be perversely (mis)interpreted as instructing him to quadd. And it is not enough to say that his brain state is the causal basis of a disposition to add. Perhaps it isn't. Perhaps if a test case arose he would abandon his intention, he would neither add nor quadd but instead would put his homework aside and complain that the problems are too hard.

The naive solution is that adding means going on in the same way as before when the numbers get big, whereas quadding means doing something different; there is nothing present in the subject that constitutes an intention to do different things in different cases; therefore he intends addition, not quaddition. We should not scoff at this naive response. It is the correct solution to the puzzle. But we must pay to regain our naiveté. Our theory of properties must have adequate resources to somehow ratify the judgement that instances of adding are all alike in a way that instances of quadding are not. The property of adding is not perfectly natural, of course, not on a par with unit charge or sphericality. And the property of quadding is not perfectly unnatural. But quadding is worse by a disjunction. So quaddition is to that extent less of a way to go on doing the same, and therefore it is to that extent less of an eligible thing to intend to do.

It's not that you couldn't possibly intend to quadd. You could. Suppose that today there is as much basis as there ever is to interpret you as intending to add and as meaning addition by your word 'addition' and quaddition by 'quaddition'; and tomorrow you say to yourself in so many words that it would be fun to tease the philosophers by taking up quaddition henceforth, and you make up your mind to do it. But you have to go out of your way. Adding and quadding aren't on a par. To intend to add, you need only have states that would fit either interpretation and leave it to charity to decree that you have the more eligible intention. To intend to quadd, you must say or think something that creates difficulties of fit for

---

[34] See Saul A. Kripke, 'Wittgenstein on Rules and Private Language: an Elementary Exposition', in *Perspectives on Wittgenstein*, edited by Irving Block (Oxford: Blackwell, 1981).

the more eligible intention and thereby defeats the presumption in its favour. You must do something that, taking principles of fit and presumptions of eligibility and other principles of charity together, tilts the balance in favour of an interpretation on which you intend to quadd. How ironic that we were worried to find nothing positive to settle the matter in favour of addition! For the lack of anything positive that points either way just *is* what it takes to favour addition. Quaddition, being less natural and eligible, needs something positive in its favour. Addition can win by default.

What is the status of the principles that constrain interpretation, in particular the charitable presumption in favour of eligible content? We must shun several misunderstandings. It is not to be said (1) that as a contingent psychological fact, the contents of our states turn out to be fairly eligible, we mostly believe and desire ourselves to have not-too-unnatural properties. Still less should it be said (2) that we should daringly presuppose this in our interpreting of one another, even if we haven't a shred of evidence for it. Nor should it be said (3) that as a contingent psychological fact we turn out to have states whose content involves some properties rather than others, and that is what makes it so that the former properties are more natural. (This would be a psychologistic theory of naturalness.) The error is the same in all three cases. It is supposed, wrongly as I think, that the problem of interpretation can be solved without bringing to it the distinction between natural and unnatural properties; so that the natural properties might or might not turn out to be the ones featured in the content of thought according to the correct solution, or so that they can afterwards be defined as the ones that are so featured. I think this is overoptimistic. We have no notion how to solve the problem of interpretation while regarding all properties as equally eligible to feature in content. For that would be to solve it without enough constraints. Only if we have an independent, objective distinction among properties, and we impose the presumption in favour of eligible content *a priori* as a constitutive constraint, does the problem of interpretation have any solution at all. If so, then any correct solution must automatically respect the presumption. There's no contingent fact of psychology here to be believed, either on evidence or daringly.

Compare our selective and collective theory of lawhood: lawhood of a regularity just consists in its fitting into an ideally high-scoring system, so it's inevitable that laws turn out to have what it takes to make for high scores. Likewise, I have suggested, contenthood just consists in getting assigned by a high-scoring interpretation, so it's inevitable that contents tend to have what it takes to make for high scores. And in both cases, I've suggested that part of what it takes is naturalness of the properties involved. The reason natural properties feature in the contents of our attitudes is that naturalness is part of what it is to feature therein. It's not that we're built to take a special interest in natural properties, or that we confer naturalness on properties when we happen to take an interest in them.[35]

[35] I am indebted to comments by Gilbert Harman, Lloyd Humberstone, Frank Jackson, Mark Johnston, Donald Morrison, Kim Sterelny, and others; and especially to discussion and correspondence with D. M. Armstrong over several years, without which I might well have believed to this day that set theory applied to *possibilia* is all the theory of properties that anyone could ever need.

XV

CAUSALITY AND PROPERTIES

SYDNEY SHOEMAKER

1

It is events, rather than objects or properties, that are usually taken by philosophers to be the terms of the causal relationship. But an event typically consists of a change in the properties or relationships of one or more objects, the latter being what Jaegwon Kim has called the 'constituent objects' of the event.[1] And when one event causes another, this will be in part because of the properties possessed by their constituent objects. Suppose, for example, that a man takes a pill and, as a result, breaks out into a rash. Here the cause and effect are, respectively, the taking of the pill and the breaking out into a rash. Why did the first event cause the second? Well, the pill was penicillin, and the man was allergic to penicillin. No doubt one could want to know more—for example, about the biochemistry of allergies in general and this one in particular. But there is a good sense in which what has been said already explains why the one event caused the other. Here the pill and the man are the constituent objects of the cause event, and the man is the constituent object of the effect event. Following Kim we can also speak of events as having 'constituent properties' and 'constituent times'. In this case the constituent property of the cause event is the relation expressed by the verb 'takes', while the constituent property of the effect event is expressed by the predicate 'breaks out into a rash'. The constituent times of the events are their times of occurrence. Specifying the constituent objects and properties of the cause and effect will tell us what these events consisted in, and together with a specification of their constituent times will serve to identify them; but it will not, typically, explain why the one brought about the other. We explain this by mentioning certain properties of their

First published in *Time and Cause*, edited by P. van Inwagen (Dordrecht: D. Reidel, 1980), 109–35. Reprinted by permission of Kluwer Academic Publishers and the author.

[1] See Jaegwon Kim, 'Causation, Nomic Subsumption, and the Concept of Event', *The Journal of Philosophy*, 70 (1973), 27–36. I should mention that it was reflection on this excellent paper that first led me to the views developed in the present one.

constituent objects. Given that the pill was penicillin, and that the man was allergic to penicillin, the taking of the pill by the man was certain, or at any rate very likely, to result in an allergic response like a rash. To take another example, suppose a branch is blown against a window and breaks it. Here the constituent objects include the branch and the window, and the causal relationship holds because of, among other things, the massiveness of the one and the fragility of the other.

It would appear from this that any account of causality as a relation between events should involve, in a central way, reference to the properties of the constituent objects of the events. But this should not encourage us to suppose that the notion of causality is to be analyzed away, in Humean fashion, in terms of some relationship between properties—for example, in terms of regularities in their instantiation. For as I shall try to show, the relevant notion of a property is itself to be explained in terms of the notion of causality in a way that has some strikingly non-Humean consequences.

2

Philosophers sometimes use the term 'property' in such a way that for every predicate F true of a thing there is a property of the thing which is designated by the corresponding expression of the form 'being F'. If 'property' is used in this broad way, every object will have innumerable properties that are unlikely to be mentioned in any causal explanation involving an event of which the object is a constituent. For example, my typewriter has the propertyof being over one hundred miles from the current heavyweight boxing champion of the world. It is not easy to think of a way in which its having this property could help to explain why an event involving it has a certain effect, and it seems artificial, at best, to speak of my typewriter's acquisition of this property as one of the causal effects of the movements of the heavyweight champion.

It is natural, however, to feel that such properties are not 'real' or 'genuine' properties. Our intuitions as to what are, and what are not, genuine properties are closely related to our intuitions as to what are, and what are not, genuine changes. A property is genuine if and only if its acquisition or loss by a thing constitutes a genuine change in that thing. One criterion for a thing's having changed is what Peter Geach calls the 'Cambridge criterion'. He formulates this as follows: 'The thing called "x" has changed if we have "$F(x)$ at time t" true and "$F(x)$ at time t'" false, for some interpretations of "*F*", "*t*", and "*t'*".[2] But as Geach points out, this gives the result that Socrates undergoes a change when he comes to be shorter than Theaetetus in virtue of the latter's growth, and even that he undergoes a change every time a fresh schoolboy comes to admire him. Such 'changes', those that intuitively are not genuine changes, Geach calls 'mere "Cambridge" changes'. For Geach, real changes are Cambridge changes, since they satisfy the Cambridge criterion, but some Cambridge changes, namely those that are *mere* Cambridge changes, fail to be real changes. Since it is mere Cambridge changes, rather than Cambridge changes in general, that are to be contrasted with real or genuine changes, I shall introduce the hyphenated expression 'mere-Cambridge' to characterize these. And I shall apply the terms 'Cambridge' and 'mere-Cambridge' to properties as well as to changes. Mere-Cambridge properties will include such properties as being 'grue' (in Nelson Goodman's sense), historical properties like being over twenty years old and having been slept in by George Washington, relational properties like being fifty miles south of a burning barn,[3] and such properties as being such that Jimmy Carter is President of the United States.

It is worth mentioning that in addition to distinguishing between real and mere-Cambridge properties and changes, we must also distinguish between real and mere-Cambridge resemblance or similarity, and between real and mere-Cambridge differences. Cambridge similarities hold in virtue of the sharing of Cambridge properties. And mere-Cambridge similarities hold in virtue of the sharing of mere-Cambridge properties: there is such a similarity between all grue things; there is one between all things fifty miles south of a burning barn; there is one between all beds slept in by George Washington; and there is one between all things such that Jimmy Carter is President of the United States. It will be recalled that the notion of similarity, or resemblance, plays a prominent role in Hume's account of causality. His first definition of *cause* in the *Treatise* is 'an object precedent and contiguous to another, and where all the objects resembling the former are plac'd in a like relation of priority and contiguity to those objects, that resemble the latter.'[4] Hume clearly regarded the notion of resemblance as quite unproblematical and in no need of

---

[2] Peter Geach, *God and the Soul* (London: Routledge & Kegan Paul, 1969), p. 71. See also Jaegwon Kim, 'Non-Causal Relations', *Noûs*, 8 (1974), 41–52, and 'Events as Property Exemplifications', in *Action and Theory* edited by M. Brand and D. Walton (Dordrecht; Reidel, 1976), 159–77.

[3] I take this example from Kim, 'Causation, Nomic Subsumption, and the Concept of Event'.

[4] David Hume, *A Treatise of Human Nature*, edited by L. A. Selby-Bigge (Oxford: Oxford University Press, 1888), book I, part III, section XIV, p. 170.

elucidation.[5] Yet it is plain that he needs a narrower notion of resemblance than that of Cambridge resemblance if his definition of causality is to have the desired content. Cambridge resemblances are too easily come by; any two objects share infinitely many Cambridge properties, and so 'resemble' one another in infinitely many ways. There are also infinitely many Cambridge differences between any two objects. What Hume needs is a notion of resemblance and difference which is such that some things resemble a given thing more than others do, and such that some things may resemble a thing exactly (without being numerically identical to it) while others resemble it hardly at all. Only 'real' or 'genuine' resemblance will serve his purposes. If it turns out, as I think it does, that in order to give a satisfactory account of the distinction between real and mere-Cambridge properties, changes, similarities, and differences we must make use of the notion of causality, the Humean project of defining causality in terms of regularity or 'constant conjunction', notions that plainly involve the notion of resemblance, is seriously undermined.

I have no wish to legislate concerning the correct use of the terms 'property', 'change', 'similar', and so forth. It would be rash to claim that the accepted use of the term 'property' is such that what I have classified as mere-Cambridge properties are not properties. But I do think that we have *a* notion of what it is to be a property which is such that this is so—in other words, which is such that not every phrase of the form 'being so and so' stands for a property which something has just in case the corresponding predicate of the form 'is so and so' is true of it, and is such that sometimes a predicate is true of a thing, not because (or only because) of any properties *it* has, but because something else, perhaps something related to it in certain ways, has certain properties. It is this narrow conception of what it is to be a property, and the correlative notions of change and similarity, that I am concerned to elucidate in this essay. (I should mention that I am concerned here only with the sorts of properties with respect to which change is possible; my account is not intended to apply to such properties of numbers as being even and being prime.)

3

John Locke held that *'Powers make a great part of our complex* Ideas *of substances.'*[6] And there is one passage in which Locke seems to suggest

---

[5] 'When any objects *resemble* each other, the resemblance will at first strike the eye, or rather the mind, and seldom requires a second examination' *Treatise*, book I, part III, section I, p. 70.

[6] John Locke, *Essay Concerning Human Understanding*, edited by Peter H. Nidditch (Oxford: Oxford University Press, 1975), book II, chapter 23, section VIII, p. 300.

that all qualities of substances are powers: he says, in explanation of his usage of the term 'quality', that 'the Power to produce any *Idea* in our mind, I call *quality* of the Subject wherein that power is'.[7] This suggests a theory of properties, namely that properties are causal powers, which is akin to the theory I shall be defending. As it happens, this is not Locke's view. If one ascribed it to him on the basis of the passage just quoted, one would have to ascribe to him the view that all qualities are what he called 'secondary qualities'—powers to produce certain mental effects ('ideas') in us. But Locke recognized the existence of powers that are not secondary qualities, namely powers (for example, the power in the sun to melt wax) to produce effects in material objects. These have been called 'tertiary qualities'. And he distinguished both of these sorts of powers from the 'primary qualities' on which they 'depend'. Nevertheless, the view which Locke's words unintentionally suggest is worth considering.

What would seem to be the same view is sometimes put by saying that all properties are dispositional properties. But as thus formulated, this view seems plainly mistaken. Surely we make a distinction between dispositional and nondispositional properties, and can mention paradigms of both sorts. Moreover, it seems plain that what dispositional properties something has, what powers it has, depends on what nondispositional properties it has—just as Locke thought that the powers of things depend on their primary qualities and those of their parts.

In fact, I believe, there are two different distinctions to be made here, and these are often conflated. One is not a distinction between kinds of *properties* at all, but rather a distinction between kinds of *predicates*. Sometimes it belongs to the meaning, or sense, of a predicate that if it is true of a thing then under certain circumstances the thing will undergo certain changes or will produce certain changes in other things. This is true of what are standardly counted as dispositional predicates, for example, 'flexible', 'soluble', 'malleable', 'magnetized', and 'poisonous'. Plainly not all predicates are of this sort. Whether color predicates are is a matter of controversy. But whatever we say about this, it seems plain that predicates like 'square', 'round' and 'made of copper' are not dispositional in this sense. There are causal powers associated with being made of copper—for example, being an electrical conductor. But presumably this association is not incorporated into the meaning of the term 'copper'.

The first distinction, then, is between different sorts of predicates and I think that the term 'dispositional' is best employed as a predicate of predicates, not of properties. A different distinction is between powers, in a sense I am about to explain, and the properties in virtue of which things

---

[7] *Essay*, book II, chapter 8, section VIII, p. 134.

have the powers they have.[8] For something to have a power, in this sense, is for it to be such that its presence in circumstances of a particular sort will have certain effects.[9] One can think of such a power as a function from circumstances to effects. Thus if something is poisonous its presence in someone's body will produce death or illness; in virtue of this, being poisonous is a power. Here it is possible for things to have the same power in virtue of having very different properties. Suppose that one poisonous substance kills by affecting the heart, while another kills by directly affecting the nervous system and brain. They produce these different effects in virtue of having very different chemical compositions. They will of course differ in their powers as well as in their properties, for one will have the power to produce certain physiological effects in the nervous system, while the other will have the power to produce quite different physiological effects in the heart. But there is one power they will share, in virtue of having these different powers, namely that of producing death if ingested by a human being. Properties here play the role, *vis-à-vis* powers, that primary qualities play in Locke; it is in virtue of a thing's properties that the thing has the powers (Locke's secondary and tertiary qualities) that it has.

There is a rough correspondence between this distinction between powers and properties and the earlier distinction between dispositional and nondispositional predicates. By and large, dispositional predicates ascribe powers while nondispositional monadic predicates ascribe properties that are not powers in the same sense.

4

On the view of properties I want to propose, while properties are typically not powers of the sort ascribed by dispositional predicates, they are related to such powers in much the way that such powers are related to the causal effects which they are powers to produce. Just as powers can be thought of as functions from circumstances to causal effects, so the properties on which powers depend can be thought of as functions from properties to

[8] What does 'in virtue of' mean here? For the moment we can say that a thing has a power in virtue of having certain properties if it is a lawlike truth that whatever has those properties has that power. On the theory I shall be defending it turns out that this is a matter of the possession of the properties entailing the possession of the power (that is, its being true in all possible worlds that whatever has the properties has the power).

[9] In speaking of 'circumstances' I have in mind the relations of the objects to other objects; instead of speaking of 'presence in circumstances of a particular sort' I could instead speak of 'possession of particular relational properties'. Being in such and such circumstances is a mere-Cambridge property of an object, not a genuine (intrinsic) property of it.

powers (or, better, as functions from sets of properties to sets of powers). One might even say that properties are second-order powers; they are powers to produce first-order powers (powers to produce certain sorts of events) if combined with certain other properties. But the formulation I shall mainly employ is this: what makes a property the property it is, what determines its identity, is its potential for contributing to the causal powers of the things that have it. This means, among other things, that if under all possible circumstances properties X and Y make the same contribution to the causal powers of the things that have them, X and Y are the same property.

To illustrate this, let us take as our example of a property the property of being 'knife-shaped'—I shall take this to be a highly determinate property which belongs to a certain knife in my kitchen and to anything else of exactly the same shape. Now if all that I know about a thing is that it has this property, I know nothing about what will result from its presence in any circumstances. What has the property of being knife-shaped could be a knife, made of steel, but it could instead be a piece of balsa wood, a piece of butter, or even an oddly shaped cloud of some invisible gas. There is no power which necessarily belongs to all and only the things having this property. But if this property is combined with the property of being knife-sized and the property of being made of steel, the object having these properties will necessarily have a number of powers. It will have the power of cutting butter, cheese, and wood, if applied to these substances with suitable pressure, and also the power of producing various sorts of sense-impressions in human beings under appropriate observational conditions, and also the power of leaving an impression of a certain shape if applied to soft wax and then withdrawn, and so on. The combination of the property of being knife-shaped with the property of being made of glass will result in a somewhat different set of powers, which will overlap with the set which results from its combination with the property of being made of steel. Likewise with its combination with the property of being made of wood, the property of being made of butter, and so on.

Let us say that an object has power P conditionally upon the possession of the properties in set Q if it has some property r such that having the properties in Q together with r is causally sufficient for having P, while having the properties in Q is not by itself causally sufficient for having P. Thus, for example, a knife-shaped object has the power of cutting wood conditionally upon being knife-sized and made of steel; for it is true of knife-shaped things, but not of things in general, that if they are knife-sized and made of steel they will have the power to cut wood. When a thing has a power conditionally upon the possession of certain properties, let us say that this amounts to its having a *conditional power*. Our knife-shaped object has the conditional power of being able to cut wood if knife-sized and made of steel. The identity condition for conditional powers is as follows: if *A* is the conditional power of having power *P* conditionally upon having the properties in set *Q*, and *B* is the conditional power of having *P'* conditionally upon having the properties in set *Q'*, then *A* is identical to *B* just in case *P* is identical to *P'* and *Q* is identical to *Q'*. Having introduced this notion of a conditional power, we can express my view by saying that properties are clusters of conditional powers. (I shall count powers *simpliciter* as a special case of conditional powers.) I have said that the identity of a property is determined by its causal potentialities, the contributions it is capable of making to the causal powers of things that have it. And the causal potentialities that are essential to a property correspond to the conditional powers that make up the cluster with which the property can be identified; for a property to have a causal potentiality is for it to be such that whatever has it has a certain conditional power.

This account is intended to capture what is correct in the view that properties just are powers, or that all properties are dispositional, while acknowledging the truth of a standard objection to that view, namely that a thing's powers or dispositions are distinct from, because 'grounded in', its intrinsic properties.[10]

Before I give my reasons for holding this view, I should mention one *prima facie* objection to it. Presumably the property of being triangular and the property of being trilateral do not differ in the contributions they make to the causal powers of the things that have them, yet it is natural to say that these, although necessarily coextensive, are different properties. It seems to me, however, that what we have good reason for regarding as distinct are not these properties, as such, but rather the concepts of triangularity and trilaterality, and the meanings of the expressions 'triangular' and 'trilateral'. If we abandon, as I think we should, the idea that properties are the meanings of predicate expressions, and if we are careful to distinguish concepts from what they are concepts of, I see no insuperable obstacle to regarding the properties themselves as identical.

---

[10] After this was written I found that Peter Achinstein has advanced a causal account of property identity which, despite a different approach, is in some ways similar to the account proposed here. See his 'The Identity of Properties', *American Philosophical Quarterly*, 11 (1974), 257–76. There are also similarities, along with important differences, between my views and those presented by D. H. Mellor in 'In Defense of Dispositions', *The Philosophical Review*, 83 (1974), 157–81, and those presented by R. Harré and E. H. Madden in *Causal Powers: A Theory of Natural Necessity* (Oxford: Blackwell, 1975).

5

My reasons for holding this theory of properties are, broadly speaking, epistemological. Only if some causal theory of properties is true, I believe, can it be explained how properties are capable of engaging our knowledge, and our language, in the way they do.

We know and recognize properties by their effects, or, more precisely, by the effects of the events which are the activations of the causal powers which things have in virtue of having the properties. This happens in a variety of ways. Observing something is being causally influenced by it in certain ways. If the causal potentialities involved in the possession of a property are such that there is a fairly direct causal connection between the possession of it by an object and the sensory states of an observer related to that object in certain ways, e.g., looking at it in good light, we say that the property itself is observable. If the relationship is less direct, e.g., if the property can affect the sensory states of the observer only by affecting the properties of something else which the observer observes, a scientific instrument, say, we speak of inferring that the thing has the property from what we take to be the effects of its possession. In other cases we conclude that something has a property because we know that it has other properties which we know from other cases to be correlated with the one in question. But the latter way of knowing about the properties of things is parasitic on the earlier ways; for unless the instantiation of the property had, under some circumstances, effects from which its existence could be concluded, we could never discover laws or correlations that would enable us to infer its existence from things other than its effects.

Suppose that the identity of properties consisted of something logically independent of their causal potentialities. Then it ought to be possible for there to be properties that have no potential whatever for contributing to causal powers, i.e., are such that under no conceivable circumstances will their possession by a thing make any difference to the way the presence of that thing affects other things or to the way other things affect it. Further, it ought to be possible that there be two or more different properties that make, under all possible circumstances, exactly the same contribution to the causal powers of the things that have them. Further, it ought to be possible that the potential of a property for contributing to the production of causal powers might change over time, so that, for example, the potential possessed by property A at one time is the same as that possessed by property B at a later time, and that possessed by property B at the earlier time is the same as that possessed by property A at the latter time. Thus a thing might undergo radical change with respect to its properties without undergoing any change in its causal powers, and a thing might undergo radical change in its causal powers without undergoing any change in the properties that underlie these powers.

The supposition that these possibilities are genuine implies, not merely (what might seem harmless) that various things might be the case without its being in any way possible for us to know that they are, but also that it is impossible for us to know various things which we take ourselves to know. If there can be properties that have no potential for contributing to the causal powers of the things that have them, then nothing could be good evidence that the overall resemblance between two things is greater than the overall resemblance between two other things; for even if A and B have closely resembling effects on our senses and our instruments while C and D do not, it might be (for all we know) that C and D share vastly more properties of the causally impotent kind than do A and B. Worse, if two properties can have exactly the same potential for contributing to causal powers, then it is impossible for us even to know (or have any reason for believing) that two things resemble one another by sharing a single property. Moreover, if the properties and causal potentialities of a thing can vary independently of one another, then it is impossible for us to know (or have any good reason for believing) that something has retained a property over time, or that something has undergone a change with respect to the properties that underlie its causal powers. On these suppositions, there would be no way in which a particular property could be picked out so as to have a name attached to it; and even if, *per impossibile*, a name did get attached to a property, it would be impossible for anyone to have any justification for applying the name on particular occasions.

It may be doubted whether the view under attack has these disastrous epistemological consequences. Surely, it may be said, one can hold that it is a contingent matter that particular properties have the causal potentialities they have, and nevertheless hold, compatibly with this, that there are good theoretical reasons for thinking that as a matter of fact different properties differ in their causal potentialities, and that any given property retains the same potentialities over time. For while it is logically possible that the latter should not be so, according to the contingency view, the simplest hypothesis is that it is so; and it is reasonable to accept the simplest hypothesis compatible with the data.

Whatever may be true in general of appeals to theoretical simplicity, this one seems to me extremely questionable. For here we are not really dealing with an explanatory hypothesis at all. If the identity of properties is made independent of their causal potentialities, then in what sense do we explain sameness or difference of causal potentialities by positing sameness or difference of properties? There are of course cases in which we explain a constancy in something by positing certain underlying constancies in its properties. It is genuinely explanatory to say that something retained the same causal power over time because certain of its properties remained the same. And this provides, *ceteris paribus*, a simpler, or at any rate more plausible, explanation of the constancy than one that says that the thing first had one set of underlying properties and then a different set, and that both sets were sufficient to give it that particular power. For example, if the water supply was poisonous all day long, it is more plausible to suppose that this was due to the presence in it of one poisonous substance all day rather than due to its containing cyanide from morning till noon and strychnine from noon till night. But in such cases we presuppose that the underlying property constancies carry with them constancies in causal potentialities, and it is only on this presupposition that positing the underlying constancies provides the simplest explanation of the constancy to be explained. Plainly this presupposition cannot be operative if what the 'inference to the best explanation' purports to explain is, precisely, that sameness of property goes with sameness of causal potentialities. It is not as if a property had the causal potentialities in question as a result of having yet *other* causal potentialities, the constancy of the latter explaining the constancy of the former. This disassociation of property identity from identity of causal potentiality is really an invitation to eliminate reference to properties from our explanatory hypotheses altogether; if it were correct then we could, to use Wittgenstein's metaphor, 'divide through' by the properties and leave the explanatory power of what we say about things untouched.

It might be objected that even if my arguments establish that the causal potentialities of a genuine property cannot change over time, they do not establish that these causal potentialities are essential to that property, in the sense of belonging to it in all possible worlds. The immutability of properties with respect to their causal potentialities, it might be said, is simply a consequence of the immutability of laws—of the fact that it makes no sense to speak of a genuine law holding at one time and not at another. And from the fact that the laws governing a property cannot change over time it does not follow, it may be said, that the property cannot be governed by different laws in different possible worlds.

Let me observe first of all that in conceding that the immutability of the causal potentialities of genuine properties is a consequence of the immutability of laws, the objection concedes a large part of what I want to maintain. It is not true in general of mere-Cambridge properties that their causal potentialities cannot change over time; for example, this is not true of *grueness* on the Barker–Achinstein definition of *grue*, where something is grue just in case it is green and the time is before T (say A.D. 2000) or it is blue and the time is T or afterwards.[11] That genuine properties are marked off from mere-Cambridge properties by their relation to causal laws (and that it is nonsense to speak of a world in which it is the mere-Cambridge properties rather than the genuine ones that are law-governed in a way that makes their causal potentialities immutable) is a central part of my view.

There is, moreover, a *prima facie* case for saying that the immutability of the causal potentialities of a property does imply their essentiality; or in other words, that if they cannot vary across time, they also cannot vary across possible worlds. Most of us do suppose that *particulars* can (or do) have different properties in different possible worlds. We suppose, for example, that in some possible worlds I am a plumber rather than a philosopher, and that in some possible worlds my house is painted yellow rather than white. But it goes with this that particulars can change their properties over time. It is possible that I, the very person who is writing this essay, might have been a plumber, because there is a possible history in which I start with the properties (in this case relational as well as intrinsic) which I had at some time in my actual history, and undergo a series of changes which result in my eventually being a plumber. If I and the world were never such that it was then possible for me to *become* a plumber, it would not be true that I might have been a plumber, or (in other words) that there is a possible world in which I am one. There is, in short, a close linkage between identity across time and identity across possible worlds; the ways in which a given thing can be different in different possible worlds depend on the ways in which such a thing can be different at different times in the actual world. But now let us move from the case of particulars to that of properties. There is no such thing as tracing a property through a series of changes in its causal potentialities— not if it is a genuine property, i.e., one of the sort that figures in causal laws. And so there is no such thing as a possible history in which a property starts with the set of causal potentialities it has in the actual world and ends with a different set. To say the least, this calls into question the intelligibility of the suggestion that the very properties we designate with words like 'green', 'square', 'hard', and so on, might have had different causal potentialities than they in fact have.

---

[11] See S. F. Barker and P. Achinstein, 'On the New Riddle of Induction', *The Philosophical Review*, 69 (1960), 511–22. The definition given there is not equivalent to that originally given by Goodman, in *Fact, Fiction and Forecast*, 3rd edition (Indianapolis: Bobbs-Merrill, 1975), p. 74, and it is the latter which is employed elsewhere in the present essay.

However, this last argument is not conclusive. My earlier arguments, however, if sound, establish that there is an intimate connection between the identity of a property and its causal potentialities. But it has not yet been decisively established that *all* of the causal potentialities of a property are essential to it. The disastrous epistemological consequences of the contingency view would be avoided if for each property we could identify a proper subset of its causal potentialities that are essential to it and constitutive of it, and this would permit some of a property's causal potentialities, those outside the essential cluster, to belong to it contingently, and so not belong to it in some other possible worlds. There would, in this case, be an important difference between the trans-world identity of properties and that of particulars—and it is a difference which there is in my own view as well. If, as I believe, the assertion that a certain particular might have had different properties than it does in the actual world (that in some other possible world it does have those properties) implies that there is a possible history 'branching off' from the history of the actual world in which it acquires those properties, this is because there is, putting aside historical properties and 'identity properties' (like being identical to Jimmy Carter), no subset of the properties of such a thing which constitutes an individual essence of it, i.e., is such that, in any possible world, having the properties in that subset is necessary *and sufficient* for being that particular thing. To put this otherwise, the reason why the possible history in which the thing has different properties must be a branching-off from the history of the actual world is that the individual essence of a particular thing must include historical properties. Now I am not in a position to object to the suggestion that properties differ from particulars in having individual essences which do not include historical properties and which are sufficient for their identification across possible worlds; for I hold that the totality of a property's causal potentialities constitutes such an individual essence. So a possible alternative to my view is one which holds that for each property there is a proper subset of its causal potentialities that constitutes its individual essence. Such a view has its attractions, and is compatible with much of what I say in this essay; in particular, it is compatible with the claim that within any possible world properties are identical just in case they have the same causal potentialities. But I shall argue in section 9 that this view is unworkable, and that there is no acceptable alternative to the view that all of the causal potentialities of a property are essential to it.

6

As was intended, my account of properties does not apply to what I have called mere-Cambridge properties. When my table acquired the property of being such that Gerald Ford is President of the United States, which it did at the time Nixon resigned from the presidency, this presumably had no effect on its causal powers. Beds that were slept in by George Washington may command a higher price than those that lack this historical property, but presumably this is a result, not of any causal potentialities in the beds themselves, but of the historical beliefs and interests of those who buy and sell them. And grueness, as defined by Goodman, is not associated in the way greenness and blueness are with causal potentialities. (In this sense, which differs from that invoked in section 5, something is grue at a time just in case it is green at that time and is first examined before T, say, A.D. 2000, or is blue at that time and is not first examined before T.) It can happen that the only difference between something that is grue and something that is not is that one of them has and the other lacks the historical property of being (or having been) first examined before the time T mentioned in Goodman's definition of *grue*; and presumably this does not in itself make for any difference in causal potentialities. It can also happen that two things share the property of being grue in virtue of having properties that have different potentialities—that is, in virtue of one of them being green (and examined before T) and the other being blue (and not so examined).

There is an epistemological way of distinguishing genuine and mere-Cambridge properties that is *prima facie* plausible. If I wish to determine whether an emerald is green at t, the thing to do, if I can manage it, is to examine the emerald at t. But examination of a table will not tell me it is such that Gerald Ford is President of the United States, or whether it is fifty miles south of a burning barn. And if I am ignorant of the date, or if t is after T (the date in Goodman's definition), examination of an emerald will not tell me whether it is grue. Likewise, while scrutiny of a bed may reveal a plaque claiming that it was slept in by George Washington, it will not tell me whether this claim is true. Roughly, if a question about whether a thing has a property at a place and time concerns a genuine nonrelational property, the question is most directly settled by observations and tests in the vicinity of that place and time, while if it concerns a mere-Cambridge property it may be most directly settled by observations and tests remote from that place and time, and observations and tests made at that place and time will either be irrelevant (as in the case of the property of being

such that Jimmy Carter is President) or insufficient to settle the question
(as in the case of grue).

It would be difficult to make this into a precise and adequate criterion
of genuineness of property, and I do not know whether this could be done.
But I think that to the extent that it is adequate, its adequacy is explained
by my account of properties in terms of causal powers. Properties reveal
their presence in actualizations of their causal potentialities, a special case
of this being the perception of a property. And the most immediate and
revealing effects of an object's having a property at a particular place and
time are effects that occur in the immediate vicinity of that place and time.
To be sure, we cannot rule out on purely philosophical grounds the
possibility of action at a spatial and/or temporal distance. And the more
prevalent such action is, the less adequate the proposed epistemological
criterion will be. But there do seem to be conceptual limitations on the
extent to which causal action can be at a spatial or temporal distance. It is
doubtful, to say the least, whether there could be something whose causal
powers are *all* such that whenever any of them is activated the effects of its
activation are spatially remote from the location of the thing at that time,
or occur at times remote from the time of activation.

Causation and causal powers are as much involved in the verification of
ascriptions of mere-Cambridge properties as in the verification of ascriptions of genuine ones. But in the case of mere-Cambridge properties some
of the operative causal powers will either belong to something other than
the object to which the property is ascribed, or will belong to that object at
a time other than that at which it has that property. Thus if I verify that a
man has the property of being fifty miles south of a burning barn, it will be
primarily the causal powers of the barn, and of the intervening stretch of
land (which, we will suppose, I measure), rather than the causal powers of
the man, that will be responsible for my verifying observations.

7

It will not have escaped notice that the account of properties and property
identity I have offered makes free use of the notion of a property and the
notion of property identity. It says, in brief, that properties are identical,
whether in the same possible world or in different ones, just in case their
coinstantiation with the same properties gives rise to the same powers.
This is, if anything, even more circular than it looks. For it crucially
involves the notion of sameness of powers, and this will have to be
explained in terms of sameness of circumstances and sameness of effects,

the notions of which both involve the notion of sameness of property. And of course there was essential use of the notion of a property in my explanation of the notion of a conditional power.

It is worth observing that there is a distinction between kinds of powers that corresponds to the distinction, mentioned earlier, between genuine and mere-Cambridge properties.[12] Robert Boyle's famous example of the key can be used to illustrate this.[13] A particular key on my key chain has the power of opening locks of a certain design. It also has the power of opening my front door. It could lose the former power only by undergoing what we would regard as real change, for example, a change in its shape. But it could lose the latter without undergoing such a change; it could do so in virtue of the lock on my door being replaced by one of a different design. Let us say that the former is an intrinsic power and the latter a mere-Cambridge power. It is clear that in my account of properties the word 'power' must refer only to intrinsic powers. For if it refers to mere-Cambridge powers as well, then what seems clearly to be a mere-Cambridge property of my key, namely being such that my door has a lock of a certain design, will make a determinate contribution to its having the powers it has, and so will count as a genuine property of it. But it seems unlikely that we could explain the distinction between intrinsic and mere-Cambridge powers without making use of the notion of a genuine change and that of a genuine property. And so again my account of the notion of a property in terms of the notion of a power can be seen to be circular.

How much do these circularities matter? Since they are, I think, unavoidable, they preclude a reductive analysis of the notion of a property in terms of the notion of causality. But they by no means render my account empty. The claim that the causal potentialities of a property are essential to it, and that properties having the same causal potentialities are identical, is certainly not made vacuous by the fact that the explanation of the notion of a causal potentiality, or a conditional power, must invoke the notion of a property. As I see it, the notion of a property and the notion of a causal power belong to a system of internally related concepts, no one of which can be explicated without the use of the others. Other members of the system are the concept of an event, the concept of similarity, and the concept of a persisting substance. It can be worthwhile, as a philosophical exercise, to see how far we can go in an attempt to reduce one of these concepts to others—for both the extent of our success and the nature of

---

[12] This was called to my attention by Nicholas Sturgeon.
[13] See Boyle, 'The Origins and Forms of Qualities', in *The Works of the Honourable Robert Boyle*, 5 volumes (London: A. Millar, 1744), volume II, pp. 461 ff.

our failures can be revealing about the nature of the connections between the concepts. But ultimately such attempts must fail. The goal of philosophical analysis, in dealing with such concepts, should not be reductive analysis but rather the charting of internal relationships. And it is perfectly possible for a 'circular' analysis to illuminate a net-work of internal relationships and have philosophically interesting consequences.

8

According to the theory of properties I am proposing, all of the causal potentialities possessed by a property at any time in the actual world are essential to it and so belong to it at all times and in all possible worlds. This has a very strong consequence, namely that causal necessity is just a species of logical necessity. If the introduction into certain circumstances of a thing having certain properties causally necessitates the occurrence of certain effects, then it is impossible, logically impossible, that such an introduction could fail to have such an effect, and so logically necessary that it has it. To the extent that causal laws can be viewed as propositions describing the causal potentialities of properties, it is impossible that the same properties should be governed by different causal laws in different possible worlds, for such propositions will be necessarily true when true at all.

It is not part of this theory, however, that causal laws are analytic or knowable *a priori*. I suppose that it is analytic that flexible things bend under suitable pressure, that poisonous things cause injury to those for whom they are poisonous, and so on. But I do not think that it is analytic that copper is an electrical conductor, or that knife-shaped things, if knife-sized and made of steel, are capable of cutting butter. Nor does it follow from the claim that such truths are necessary that they are analytic. Kripke has made a compelling case for the view that there are propositions that are necessary *a posteriori*, that is, true in all possible worlds but such that they can only be known empirically.[14] And such, according to my theory, is the status of most propositions describing the causal potentialities of properties. The theory can allow that our knowledge of these potentialities is empirical, and that it is bound to be only partial. But in order to show how, in the theory, such empirical knowledge is possible, I must now bring out an additional way in which the notion of causality is involved in the notion of a property.

---

[14] See Saul Kripke, 'Naming and Necessity', in *Semantics of Natural Language*, edited by D. Davidson and G. Harman (Dordrecht: Reidel, 1972), 253–355.

One of the formulations of my theory says that every property is a cluster of conditional powers. But the converse does not seem to me to hold; not every cluster of conditional powers is a property. If something is both knife-shaped and made of wax, then it will have, among others, the following conditional powers: the power of being able to cut wood conditionally upon being knife-sized and made of steel (this it has in virtue of being knife-shaped), and the power of being malleable conditionally upon being at a temperature of 100°F (this it has in virtue of being made of wax). Intuitively, these are not common components of any single property. By contrast, the various conditional powers a thing has in virtue of being knife-shaped—for example, the power of being able to cut wood conditionally upon being knife-sized and made of steel, the power of being able to cut butter conditionally upon being knife-sized and made of wood, the power of having a certain visual appearance conditionally upon being green, the power of having a certain other visual appearance conditionally upon being red, and so on—are all constituents of a single property, namely the property of being knife-shaped. The difference, I think, is that in the one case the set of conditional powers has, while in the other it lacks, a certain kind of causal unity. I shall now try to spell out the nature of this unity.

Some subsets of the conditional powers which make up a genuine property will be such that it is a consequence of causal laws that whatever has any member of the subset necessarily has all of its members. Thus, for example, something has the power of leaving a six-inch-long knife-shaped impression in soft wax conditionally upon being six inches long if and only if it has the power of leaving an eight-inch-long knife-shaped impression in soft wax conditionally upon being eight inches long. Now some conditional powers will belong to more than one property cluster; thus, for example, there are many different shape properties that give something the power of being able to cut wood conditionally upon being made of steel. But where a conditional power can be shared by different properties in this way, it will belong to a particular property cluster only if there is another member of that cluster which is such that it is a consequence of causal laws that whatever has that other member has the conditional power in question. And at the core of each cluster there will be one or more conditional powers which are such that as a consequence of causal laws whatever has any of them has all of the conditional powers in the cluster. For example, if something has, conditionally upon being made of steel, the power of leaving a knife-shaped impression in soft wax, then it cannot fail to be knife-shaped, and so cannot fail to have all of the other conditional powers involved in being knife-shaped. I suggest, then, that conditional powers X and Y belong to the same property if and only if it is a consequence of causal laws that either (1) whatever has either of them has the other, or (2) there is some third conditional power such that whatever has it has both X and Y.

Returning now to the conditional power of being able to cut wood conditionally upon being made of steel and the conditional power of being malleable conditionally upon being at a temperature of 100°F, it seems to me that these do not qualify under the proposed criterion as belonging to a common property. It is obviously not true that whatever has one of them must have the other. And it does not appear that there is any third conditional power which is such that whatever has it must have the two conditional powers in question.

If I am right in thinking that the conditional powers constituting a property must be causally unified in the way indicated, it is not difficult to see how knowledge of the causal potentialities of properties can develop empirically. The behavior of objects, that is, the displays of their powers, will reveal that they have certain conditional powers. Once it is discovered that certain conditional powers are connected in a lawlike way, we can use these to 'fix the reference' of a property term to the cluster containing those conditional powers and whatever other conditional powers are related to them in the appropriate lawlike relationships.[15] And we can then set about to determine empirically what the other conditional powers in the cluster are.

9

As I observed earlier, my theory appears to have the consequence that causal laws are logically necessary, and that causal necessity is just a species of logical necessity. While to some this may be an attractive consequence, to many it will seem counterintuitive. It does seem to most of us that we can conceive of possible worlds which resemble the actual world in the kinds of properties that are instantiated in them, but differ from it in the causal laws that obtain. My theory must maintain either that we cannot really conceive of this or that conceivability is not proof of logical possibility.

Anyone who finds both of these alternatives unacceptable, but is persuaded by the arguments in section 5 that the identity of properties is determined by their causal potentialities, will look for ways of reconciling that conclusion with the view that there can be worlds in which some of the

[15] For the notion of 'reference fixing', see Kripke, 'Naming and Necessity', pp. 269–75.

causal laws are different from, and incompatible with, those that obtain in the actual world. I want now to consider two ways in which one might attempt to achieve such a reconciliation. First, it might be held that while propositions describing the causal potentialities of properties are necessarily true if true at all, there are other lawlike propositions, namely those asserting lawlike connections between conditional powers, which are contingent and so true in some possible worlds and false in others. According to this view, when we seem to be conceiving of worlds in which the same properties are governed by different laws, what we are really conceiving of are worlds in which the same conditional powers stand one to another in different lawlike connections than they do in the actual world, and so are differently clustered into properties. Second, it might be held that my condition for the identity of properties across possible worlds is too strict. The theory I have advanced might be called the 'total cluster theory'; it identifies a property with a cluster containing all of the conditional powers which anything has in virtue of having that property, and maintains that in any possible world anything that has that property must have all of the members of that cluster. One might attempt to replace this with a 'core cluster theory', which identifies the property with some proper subset of the conditional powers something has in virtue of having that property. On this theory, it is only some of the causal potentialities possessed by a property in the actual world, namely those constituted by the conditional powers in its core cluster, that are essential to it—so it is possible for the same property to have somewhat different causal potentialities in different possible worlds, because of different laws relating the conditional powers in its core cluster with other conditional powers.

I do not believe, however, that either of these attempted reconciliations is successful. The first involves the suggestion that it is at least sometimes a contingent matter whether two conditional powers belong to the same property, and hence that there could be a world in which some of the same conditional powers are instantiated as in this world, but in which, owing to the holding of different laws, these are differently clustered into properties. The difficulty with this is that the specification of a conditional power always involves, in two different ways, reference to properties that are instantiated in our world and which, *ex hypothesi*, would not be instantiated in the alternative world in question. It involves reference to the properties on which the power is conditional, and also to the properties in the instantiation of which the exercise of the power would result. For example, one of the conditional powers in the property of being knife-shaped is the power, conditionally upon being made of steel, of leaving a knife-shaped impression if pressed into soft wax and then withdrawn. This conditional power, although not by itself identical to the property of being knife-shaped, could not be exercised without that property being instantiated. Neither could it be exercised without the property of being made of steel being instantiated. And a conditional power could not be instantiated in a world in which the causal laws would not allow an exercise of it. So in general, a conditional power could not be instantiated in a world in which the causal laws did not permit the instantiation of the properties whose instantiation would be involved in its instantiation or in its exercise.

Nothing I have said precludes the possibility of there being worlds in which the causal laws are different from those that prevail in this world. But it seems to follow from my account of property identity that if the laws are different then the properties will have to be different as well. And it does not appear that we have the resources for describing a world in which the properties that can be instantiated differ from what I shall call the 'actual world properties', that is, those that can be instantiated in the actual world. We have just seen that we cannot do this by imagining the conditional powers that exist in this world to be governed by different laws, and so to be differently grouped into properties.

It might seem that we can at least imagine a world in which *some* of the properties that can be instantiated are actual world properties while others are not. But a specification of the causal potentialities of one property will involve mention of other properties, a specification of the causal potentialities of those other properties will involve mention of still other properties, and so on. If there could be a world in which some but not all of the actual world properties can be instantiated, this could only be because those properties were causally insulated, as it were, from the rest—that is, were such that their causal potentialities could be fully specified without reference to the rest and vice versa. It seems unlikely that any proper subset of the actual world properties is causally insulated in this way—and any that are insulated from all properties we know about are thereby insulated from our knowledge and our language. But could there be a world in which the properties that can be instantiated include all of the actual world properties plus some others? This would be possible only if the two sets of properties, the actual world properties and the properties that cannot be instantiated in the actual world, were causally insulated from one another. And because of this, it would be impossible for us to say anything about the properties that cannot be instantiated in the actual world; for what we can describe is limited to what can be specified in terms of properties that can be so instantiated. What we could describe of such a world would have to be compatible with the laws that specify the causal potentialities of the actual world properties and, what we have found to be inseparable from these, the laws describing the lawlike connections between the conditional powers that constitute these properties.

Now let us consider the second attempt to reconcile the claim that the identity of a property is determined by its causal potentialities with the apparent conceivability of worlds in which the causal laws that obtain are different from, and incompatible with, those that obtain in the actual world. This involves the proposal that we adopt a 'core cluster theory' in place of the 'total cluster theory', and make the identity of a property dependent on a proper subset, rather than on the totality, of the causal potentialities it has in the actual world. Like the first attempted reconciliation, this involves the idea that at least some of the lawlike connections between conditional powers hold only contingently; it is this that is supposed to make it possible for the composition of the total cluster associated with a property to differ from one possible world to another, owing to different conditional powers being causally linked with the conditional powers in the property's essential core cluster. But it would seem that the lawlike connections between those conditional powers included in the essential core cluster will have to hold of logical necessity, i.e., in all possible worlds. For if they held only contingently, then in some possible worlds they would not hold. In such a world, the individual conditional powers which in the actual world constitute the essential core of the property could be instantiated, but the property itself could not be instantiated. Even if these conditional powers could be instantiated together in such a world, their coinstantiation would not count as the instantiation of a property, and so of that property, since the requisite causal unity would be lacking. But I have already argued, in discussing the first attempted reconciliation, that it is not possible that there should be a world in which conditional powers that are instantiated in the actual world can be instantiated while actual world properties cannot be instantiated.

But if, as I have just argued, the lawlike connections between conditional powers within the essential core cluster will have to hold of logical necessity, then we are faced with a problem. Some lawlike connections between conditional powers will hold contingently (according to the core cluster theory), while others will hold as a matter of logical necessity. How are we to tell which are which? It does not appear that we can distinguish these lawlike connections epistemologically, i.e., by the way in which they are known. For if, as I am assuming, there are truths that are necessary a posteriori, the fact that a connection is discovered empirically is no guarantee that it does not hold necessarily. Nor can it be said that we identify the necessary connections by the fact that they hold between conditional powers belonging to some property's essential core cluster; for this presupposes that we have some way of identifying essential core clusters, and how are we to do this if we do not already know which connections between conditional powers are necessary and which are contingent?

It might be suggested that what constitutes a set of conditional powers as constituting an essential core cluster is just its being a lawlike truth that whatever has any of its members has all of them, and that it is by discovering such lawlike truths that we identify essential core clusters. Given that the lawlike connections between members of essential core clusters hold of logical necessity, this would amount to the claim that if two conditional powers are so related that the possession of either of them is both causally necessary and causally sufficient for the possession of the other, then the lawlike connection between them holds as a matter of logical necessity, while if the possession of one is causally sufficient but not causally necessary for the possession of the other then the lawlike connection may be contingent. I have no knockdown argument against this view, but it seems to me implausible. If it is possible for it to be a contingent fact that the possession of one conditional power is causally sufficient for the possession of another, then it seems to me that it ought to be possible for it to be a contingent fact that the possession of one conditional power is both causally necessary and causally sufficient for the possession of another; that is, it ought to be possible for it to be contingently true of two conditional powers that the possession of either of them is causally sufficient for the possession of the other. So if we deny that the latter is a possibility, we should also deny that the former is.

It may be suggested that it is our linguistic conventions that make certain causal potentialities essential to a property, and so determine the makeup of a property's essential core cluster. But this cannot be so. It may in some cases belong to the conventionally determined sense of a property word that the property it designates has certain causal potentialities; while I think there is no need for property words to have such Fregean senses, and think that such words often function much as Kripke thinks natural kind terms do, I have no wish to deny that a property word can have a conventionally determined sense. But there is only so much that linguistic conventions can do; and one thing they cannot do is to dictate to reality, creating lawlike connections and *de re* necessities. Having discovered that certain conditional powers necessarily go together, and so are appropriately related for being part of an essential core cluster, we can lay down the convention that a certain word applies, in any possible world, to those and only those things having those conditional powers. But this leaves open the question of how we know that the conditional powers in question are appropriately related—that they must go together in any world in which either can be instantiated. And here appeal to convention cannot help us.

It begins to appear that if we hold that some lawlike connections are contingent, there is no way in which we could discover which of the lawlike connections between conditional powers are logically necessary and which are logically contingent, and so no way in which we could identify the essential core clusters of properties. This means that when we conceive, or seem to be conceiving, of a possible world in which the actual world properties are governed by somewhat different laws, there is no way in which we can discover whether we are conceiving of a genuine possibility. All that any of our empirical investigations can tell us is what lawlike connections obtain in the actual world; and without some way of telling which of these connections are contingent and which necessary, this gives us no information about what can be the case in other possible worlds. This makes all talk about what logically might be and might have been completely idle, except where questions of logical possibility can be settled *a priori*. If the core cluster theory makes the modal status of causal connections, their being necessary or contingent, epistemologically indeterminate in this way, it does not really save the intuitions which lead us to resist the total cluster theory, according to which all such connections are necessary. Unless we are prepared to abandon altogether the idea that there is a 'fact of the matter' as to whether there are logically possible circumstances in which a given property would make a certain contribution to the causal powers of its subject, I think we must accept the total cluster theory and its initially startling consequence that all of the causal potentialities of a property are essential to it.

10

If, as my theory implies, there are no situations that are logically but not causally possible, how is it that we are apparently able to conceive or imagine such situations? Saul Kripke has suggested one answer to a very similar question.[16] He holds that it is a necessary truth that heat is molecular motion, but recognizes that it seems as if we can imagine heat turning out to be something other than this. According to Kripke, this appearance of conceivability is something to be explained away, and he explains it away by claiming that the seeming conceivability of heat turning out not to

[16] 'Naming and Necessity', pp. 331–42.

be molecular motion consists in the actual conceivability of something else, namely of sensations of a certain sort, those that we in fact get from heat, turning out to be caused by something other than molecular motion. The latter really is conceivable, he holds, and for understandable reasons we mistake its conceivability for the conceivability of something that is in fact not conceivable.

But if conceivability is taken to imply possibility, this account commits one to the possibility that the sensations we get from heat might standardly be caused by something other than molecular motion (and so something other than heat); more than that, it commits one to the possibility that this might be so and that these sensations might be related to other sensations and sense-experiences in all the ways they are (or have been to date) in the actual world. And since the property of having such sensations is one that is actualized in this world, this would commit one, in my view, to the claim that it is compatible with the laws of nature that prevail in the actual world that these sensations should be so caused and so related to other experiences. Now this claim may be true—if 'may be' is used epistemically. But it is hard to see how we are entitled to be confident that it is. For might there not be laws, unknown to us, that make it impossible that the standard cause of these sensations should be anything other than it is, given the way they are related to the rest of our experience? If the seeming conceivability of heat turning out to be something other than molecular motion does not prove the actual possibility of this, why should the seeming conceivability of certain sensations being caused by something other than molecular motion prove the actual, and so causal, possibility of that? And if seeming conceivability no more proves possibility in the latter case than in the former, there seems little point in distinguishing between conceivability and seeming conceivability; we may as well allow that it is conceivable (and not just seemingly conceivable) that heat should turn out to be molecular motion, and then acknowledge that conceivability is not conclusive proof of possibility. We could use the term 'conceivable' in such a way that it is conceivable that P just in case not-P is not provable *a priori*. Or we could use it in such a way that it is conceivable that P just in case it is epistemically possible that it is possible that P should be the case—that is, just in case P's being possible is compatible, for all we know, with what we know. These uses of 'conceivable' are not equivalent, but on both of them it is possible to conceive of what is not possible.

11

Although many of the implications of the account I have advanced are radically at odds with Humean views about causality, it does enable us to salvage one of the central tenets of the Humean view, namely the claim that singular causal statements are 'implicitly general'. As I see it, the generality of causal propositions stems from the generality of properties, that is, from the fact that properties are universals, together with the fact which I began this essay by pointing out, namely that causal relations hold between particular events in virtue of the properties possessed by the constituent objects of those events, and the fact, which I have tried to establish in the essay, that the identity of a property is completely determined by its potential for contributing to the causal powers of the things that have it. If I assert that one event caused another, I imply that the constituent objects of the cause event had properties which always contribute in certain ways to the causal powers of the things that have them, and that the particular episode of causation at hand was an actualization of some of these potentialities. I may of course not know what the relevant properties of the cause event were; and if I do know this, I may know little about their causal potentialities. This is closely related to the now familiar point that in claiming to know the truth of a singular causal statement one is not committed to knowing the laws in virtue of which it holds.[17] Moreover, a single causal statement does not commit one to the claim that the instantiation of the relevant properties in relevant similar circumstances always produces the effect that it did in the case at hand; for the laws governing these properties may be statistical, the powers to which the properties contribute may, accordingly, be statistical tendencies or propensities, and the causation may be nonnecessitating. Also, the claim that singular causal statements are implicitly general does not, as here interpreted, imply anything about how such statements are known—in particular, it does not imply the Humean view that causal relationships can only be discovered *via* the discovery of regularities or 'constant conjunctions'. But where the present theory differs most radically from theories in the Humean tradition is in what it claims about the modality of the general propositions, the laws, that explain the truth of singular causal propositions; for whereas on the Humean view the truth of these propositions is contingent, on my view it is logically necessary. I thus find myself, in what I once would have regarded as reactionary company,

---

[17] See, for example, Donald Davidson, 'Causal Relations', *The Journal of Philosophy*, 64 (1967), 691–703.

defending the very sort of 'necessary connection' account of causality which Hume is widely applauded for having refuted.

POSTSCRIPT

(The following was appended to the original publication of this essay as a 'Note Added in Proof'.)

Richard Boyd has offered the following as a counter example to the account of properties proposed in this essay. Imagine a world in which the basic physical elements include substances A, B, C, and D. Suppose that X is a compound of A and B, and Y is a compound of C and D. We can suppose that it follows from the laws of nature governing the elements that these two compounds, although composed of different elements, behave exactly alike under all possible circumstances—so that the property of being made of X and the property of being made of Y share all of their causal potentialities. (This means, among other things, that it follows from the laws that once a portion of X or Y is formed, it cannot be decomposed into its constituent elements.) It would follow from my account of properties that being made of X and being made of Y are the same property. And this seems counterintuitive. If, as appears, X and Y would be different substances, the property of being composed of the one should be different from the property of being composed of the other.

I think that this example does show that my account needs to be revised. I propose the following as a revised account which is still clearly a causal account of properties: for properties F and G to be identical, it is necessary *both* that F and G have the same causal potentialities *and* (this is the new requirement) that whatever set of circumstances is sufficient to cause the instantiation of F is sufficient to cause the instantiation of G, and vice versa. This amounts to saying that properties are individuated by their possible causes as well as by their possible effects. No doubt Boyd's example shows that other things I say in the essay need to be amended.

XVI

PROPERTIES AND PREDICATES

D. H. MELLOR

INTRODUCTION

I share David Armstrong's realism about universals.[1] I agree with him that properties and relations exist, just as the particulars exist which have those properties and relations. I also agree with him that universals are not to be understood semantically as the meanings, references, or extensions of predicates.[2] This does not of course prevent there being obvious connections between universals and predicates. For example, to every property there obviously corresponds a possible predicate applying to all and only particulars with that property. But it does not follow from this, and is not obviously true, that to every actual predicate there corresponds a single property or relation. Perhaps 'given a predicate, there may be none, one or many universals in virtue of which the predicate applies [and] given a universal, there may be none, one or many predicates which apply in virtue of that universal'.[3] So the questions remain: how do universals relate in general to our predicates, and how in particular do they relate to what those predicates mean?[4]

First published in the author's *Matters of Metaphysics* (Cambridge: Cambridge University Press, 1991), 170–82, and reprinted by permission of Cambridge University Press. A few minor corrections and other changes have been made to the text and references of this paper as originally published. None affects the argument.

[1] D. M. Armstrong, *Universals and Scientific Realism*, 2 volumes (Cambridge: Cambridge University Press, 1978)—hereafter *USR*—and *Universals: An Opinionated Introduction* (Boulder, Colorado: Westview Press, 1989).

[2] *USR*, Introduction.

[3] *USR*, volume 2, p. 9.

[4] Besides the works referred to, my answers to these questions have been considerably influenced by J. L. Austin, 'Are There *A Priori* Concepts?', *Philosophical Papers*, 2nd edition (Oxford: Oxford University Press, 1939), 32–54, Mark Wilson, 'Predicate Meets Property', *Philosophical Review*, 91 (1982), 549–89, and an unpublished paper by Greg McCulloch. Earlier versions of this paper were discussed at a Conference on Truth and Reference held at the Inter-University Centre in Dubrovnik in September 1990 and at the Cambridge University Moral Sciences Club in November 1990. Its subsequent revision for publication was much indebted to comments made in those discussions, especially by Alexander Bird, Jeremy Butterfield, Mike Martin, Greg McCulloch and Roger Teichman, and also to comments made later by Jeremy Butterfield, Tim Crane, Alex Oliver and Peter Weatherall.

In order to tackle these questions I shall make some assumptions which I shall defend only briefly if at all. Some are uncontroversial, some merely terminological. Others are more serious, but I shall not argue for them at length because, although I do believe them, my main interest here is in what they entail.

First of all, although for brevity I shall refer only to properties, I shall take it for granted that what I say also applies *mutatis mutandis* to relations. On the other hand, I shall not assume that what I say applies to all properties, and specifically not to apparently necessary properties of abstract particulars like numbers and sets, such as the oddness of the number 3. I am interested here only in contingent properties of so-called 'concrete' particulars: i.e. roughly, particulars which have causes and/or effects and are more or less localized in space and time. 'Concrete', however, is a bad name for them, since the particulars that concern me may well include events (such as explosions) and processes (such as fires and long walks) as well as material objects (such as planets and people). Whether particulars of all these kinds exist and, if so, how they are related to each other are of course contentious questions, but fortunately not ones I need to tackle here. What matter here are contingent properties, not how many or what kinds of particulars have those properties.

Next, I take existence, and the having of properties, to be tenseless but not modal. In other words, I restrict them to the actual world, but not to the present as opposed to the past or future. This assumption too is contentious, and it does affect some of my conclusions, but only in obvious and uninteresting ways that anyone who disagrees with it can easily work out. In what follows, therefore, I shall take it for granted that the class of real people does not, for example, contain the merely possible Danish Prince Hamlet, but does contain all the human ancestors and all the as-yet-unconceived human descendants of everybody alive today.

And as for all these actual human beings, so for the property (if any) of being human which they all share. As a realist about universals, I take the actual properties of actual past, present, and future particulars to exist, and to do so whether or not they ever have been or ever will be conceived of by us or by any other thinkers. That is, I reject both nominalism and conceptualism about universals, although again I shall not discuss my reasons for doing so, nor for adopting any specific version of realism about universals. What I am going to discuss is what properties there actually are—an open question for realists, just as what particulars there are is an open question for nominalists—and what if anything those properties contribute to the meanings of our predicates.

PROPERTIES

I shall start by elaborating on my rejection of the obvious answer to these questions: namely, that properties just are (or are given by) the meanings of our predicates. One reason for denying this is of course that, if they were, they could not *give* our predicates their meanings, any more than particulars could give the meanings of names or other singular terms if that was all they were. But of course they are not. No one thinks the Planet Mars just is, or is part of, or defined by, the meaning of the word 'Mars' which we use to refer to it. We may indeed give a referential account of that word's meaning, i.e. one which takes the planet Mars to be a part or all of what the word 'Mars' means. But what makes this a serious thesis about the meaning of that word is precisely that it takes for granted the planet's independent existence and identity: we are using the planet Mars to give the meaning of the word 'Mars', not the other way round.

Similarly with our predicate 'is red'. We might take the property of being red to be part or all of what 'is red' means. But this again will be a serious thesis about the meaning of that word only if it takes for granted the property's independent existence and identity, i.e. if it uses the property to give the meaning of the predicate rather than the other way round.

We may of course reject these accounts. We may deny that Mars itself is any part of what our word 'Mars' means, perhaps because we think its meaning is given by a definite description (such as 'the red planet') which any planet might satisfy. But this will not make us deny Mars's existence or query its identity. There is more to Mars than its semantic role, and we have more than semantic reasons to believe in its existence. Indeed that is an understatement. The planet Mars does not depend on its semantic role at all, either for its identity or for its existence: which is why a referential account of the meaning of the word 'Mars', whatever else may be wrong with it, is neither trivial nor viciously circular.

Similarly, I maintain, for the property, if any, of being red. But not everyone will agree. Some philosophers still think that properties, unlike particulars, do depend on their semantic roles: that a property is nothing if not all or part of what some predicate means. Unless the meaning of 'is red' is, includes, or entails a corresponding property, then no such property exists. And if it does exist, its identity is given by its role in the meaning of the predicate, not the other way round.

I, like Armstrong, disagree. I think that in this respect properties are just like planets. We have good non-semantic reasons for believing in them, and there is more to them than their semantic roles. Indeed I think that is another understatement. A contingent universal's existence, like that of Mars, does not depend on its having any semantic role, and its identity does not depend on what that role is. Which is why accounts that invoke properties to give the meanings of predicates, whatever else may be wrong with them, are also neither trivial nor viciously circular.

But what then are the non-semantic reasons for believing in contingent universals, and what, if not the meanings of predicates, fixes their identity? I take the main reasons for believing in contingent universals to be the roles they play in causation and in laws of nature, and those laws are what I take to give those universals their identity.

Now one might think that causation needs universals just because it is one: namely, as Davidson and others maintain, a relation between particular events, as in 'The explosion *caused* the fire'.[5] I do not think that, because I think that what the causation in such cases primarily links are facts, not particulars.[6] So I would rather report this example of singular causation by saying 'There was a fire *because* there was an explosion', which represents the causation not by a predicate ('caused') but by a connective ('because'). This of course is yet another contentious claim, but again it is not one I need to defend here: since even if causation is not a universal, it will still need universals. For just as Davidson thinks that causation only links particulars with properties that make them instantiate laws of nature, so I think it only links facts which have just such properties as constituents. And if so, then causation will need universals anyway, and we need not discuss whether it itself is one.

But is this so, and if so, why? Why must causes and effects have, or contain, properties that figure in laws? I think the reason is that singular causation entails physical probabilities, or chances. Suppose for example the causation in this case is deterministic, so that in the circumstances an explosion is both sufficient and necessary for a fire. This means that in the circumstances the chance of a fire occurring is 1 with an explosion and 0 without one. But this, I have argued elsewhere,[7] entails that in sufficiently similar circumstances (i) anything sufficiently like the actual explosion would always produce something like the actual fire and (ii) nothing else would ever do so. And this I take to be an existential proposition, entailing that these sufficient similarities exist: in other words, that there are properties C, F, and G, of which the actual circumstances, explosion, and fire respectively are instances, such that it is a law of nature that in C-circumstances, all and only F-events are followed by G-events.

    [5] D. Davidson, 'Causal Relations', *Causation*, edited by E. Sosa and M. Tooley (Oxford: Oxford University Press, 1967), 75–87.
    [6] D. H. Mellor, *The Facts of Causation* (London: Routledge, 1995), chapter 9.
    [7] *The Facts of Causation*, chapter 3, §§1,4.

That, briefly, is why I think causation always instantiates laws. Again the argument is contentious, but again I need not defend it. For all I need is its conclusion, which is much less contentious—and even that contention I shall now try to disarm by disclaiming some common but contentious claims about causation and laws which I do not accept and to which nothing here will commit me.

First, I am not committed to physicalism. Nothing I have to say about causation and laws, or about the particulars and properties involved in them, requires them to be physical. Nor does it require them not to be. Nothing in what follows will entail either physicalism or its negation.

Next, I am not committed to causal determinism. Causation does not entail deterministic laws, because its connotations do not require causes to be either sufficient or necessary for their effects. I do think they require causes to raise their effects' chances, but they need not raise them to 1, and they need not raise them from 0.[8] So although individual circumstances, causes, and effects will always need some properties C, F, and G to make them instantiate laws, those laws need not be deterministic: they need only entail, for example, that in normal circumstances (e.g. in the presence of oxygen and inflammable material and the absence of other causes of fires) fires have a greater chance of occurring when explosions do than when they do not.

Finally, I am not committed to laws having or entailing any kind of necessity, natural or otherwise—except of course in the common but trivial sense in which calling something naturally or physically necessary just means that it is entailed by a law, or has a chance of 1.

So much for what I am not committed to. What I am committed to is a distinction between laws and statements of laws.[9] This distinction is easily, and often, overlooked: as when Humeans say that laws are just true generalisations, like the statement 'All Fs are Gs'. But they could equally well say that all it takes to make this generalisation state a law is the fact that all actual Fs are Gs, and call that fact the law. Now whether we think of laws as true statements (or sentences or propositions) or as the facts, Humean or otherwise, that make those statements state laws often does not matter, which is no doubt why the difference is often overlooked. But here it does matter, because what law statements contain are predicates (or their meanings), whereas what the relevant facts contain are properties. And clearly what causation needs are the facts, with their constituent properties, not the statements with their predicates. That is

[8] See my 'On Raising the Chances of Effects', in my *Matters of Metaphysics* (Cambridge: Cambridge University Press, 1988), 225–34.

[9] See D. M. Armstrong, *What is a Law of Nature?* (Cambridge, Cambridge University Press, 1983), p. 8.

why in what follows it is the facts, and not the statements, which I shall call laws.

I do not of course deny the close connection between the properties that laws contain and the predicates we use to state those laws. On the contrary, that connection is, as we shall see, much closer than it is between properties and most other predicates. But this is not because the predicates that occur in law statements define the corresponding properties. It is the other way round. For the fact is that we have no semantic (or any other *a priori*) criterion of identity for the contingent properties that laws contain, any more than we have for contingent particulars. The most we can say *a priori* is this: for F and F^* to be the same property, the predicates 'is F' and 'is F^*' must be coextensive in all possible worlds—since otherwise whether some possible particular is F will depend on which predicate we use to say that it is F, which is absurd.

But this modest *a priori* truth will not enable us to identify F, or any other contingent property. Properties are identified *a posteriori* by scientific theories, construed as Ramsey sentences: i.e., as saying for example that *there are* properties C, F, and G such that in C-circumstances all F-events have such-and-such a chance of being followed by G-events. If that statement is true, then there are such properties, and there is such a law, of which those properties are constituents. And being a constituent of some such laws is, as I argue elsewhere,[10] all there is to being a property. There is no more to temperatures than the thermodynamic and other laws they occur in; no more to masses and forces than the laws of motion and of motion's gravitational and other causes; and so on. In other words, if we stated all the laws there are in a single Ramsey sentence Σ, the properties Σ would quantify over are all the properties there are.

And this means that, with one possible exception, Σ would provide a definite description of all actual contingent properties. The exception (pointed out to me by Jeremy Butterfield) would be a pair of symmetrically related properties P and P^*—like being left- and right-handed—identifiable only by ostension. Whether two properties could really differ like this without entering differently into *some* law is not clear to me; but even if they did, Σ would still quantify over both of them. So even then the contingent properties there are could still be just those Σ quantifies over; and that from now on is what I shall assume they are. So our question now becomes: how do these properties relate to the meanings of our predicates?

---

[10] *The Facts of Causation*, chapter 15.

PREDICATES

Suppose I see that some thing, a, is red, i.e. that the predicate 'is red' applies to it. What has happened? Clearly something about a has caused me to believe this. But what? In particular, is it just the fact that a has the property of being red?

But what does this question mean? What is it for a to have the property of being red? What is it indeed for there to be such a property? If actual properties are those that our Ramsey sentence Σ quantifies over, what makes one of them the property of being red? Well, suppose that anything which anyone sees to be rightly called red always has a certain property P, and that its being P is what causes them to see that. Whether there is any such property P is, as we shall see, a very moot point. But suppose for the moment there is. Then clearly, if anything is the property of being red, P is.

But how, if it is, does P contribute to the meaning of 'is red'? Suppose we agree to start with that to the predicate 'is red' there corresponds a singular term, 'Red', referring to the property (if any) that all and only red particulars share: as in 'Red is a warm colour'. Then if 'Red' refers to anything, it refers to P. So suppose it does refer to P—and does so even though no one knows which property P is, because no one knows enough laws of nature to distinguish P from all other properties.

Some philosophers may deny this possibility because it conflicts with what Gareth Evans calls Russell's Principle, namely 'that a subject cannot make a judgment about something unless he knows which object his judgment is about' (p. 89).[11] But this principle is false. We can easily make judgments about (and hence refer to) things without anyone knowing which they are. For example, I can easily judge that it is raining now without anyone knowing what time it is, i.e. which time my token 'now' refers to. Similarly, when I measure an object's temperature T, I judge in advance that T is what my thermometer will say it is: so I refer to T even before I know which temperature it is, and even if my thermometer fails me and no one ever knows which it is. But if we can use 'now' and 'T' as singular terms to refer to times and temperatures without anyone knowing which times or temperatures they are, we can certainly use 'Red' as a singular term to refer to P without anyone knowing which property P is.

So let us suppose we do that. How does our use of 'Red' to refer to P relate to our use of the predicate 'is red'? In particular, how does it relate to that predicate's extension, i.e. to the particulars it applies to. Obviously they cannot *be* the property P, since they are many and P is one. Nor can P

---

[11] G. Evans, *The Varieties of Reference* (Oxford: Clarendon Press, 1982), p. 89.

be the set of all P-things. For since P is a contingent property, there could be more or fewer P-things, and hence more or fewer red things things, than there actually are. But if P were its own extension, and hence that of 'is red', there could not be: so it isn't.

Indeed P can obviously not be any set of P-things, precisely because being P is what *makes* things members of such sets. What P, like any other universal, is, I maintain, is a constituent of atomic facts, like the fact that a is P,. I admit of course that what this amounts to—and especially what links a and P—are hard and long-standing questions: to which I can only respond here by asserting, with Armstrong,[12] that they do have answers, and that those who deny that facts have universal constituents face even harder questions.

But those are not the questions I want to discuss here. The question here is this. If 'Red' refers to P, and this is what makes 'is red' apply to all and only P-things, then what makes 'Red' refer to P? In particular, if 'Red' refers to P by having a *sense* which makes it do so, what gives 'Red' that sense?

The obvious answer is that 'Red' gets its sense from a kind K of visual sensation which P-things give us when they make us call them red, so that 'Red' refers to the property of things which causes us to get sensations of a kind K: namely, P. But although this could be how we apply 'is red' it notoriously need not be. We can learn to see when to apply 'is red' without the P-things it applies to giving all of us sensations of the same kind. Being P must make a difference to how things look to us, but the difference need not be the same for everyone. I can learn to apply 'is red' by learning to associate it with whatever kind of visual sensations I get from the things which existing users tell me are called red. It is this learned use of the predicate that fixes which kind (or kinds) of sensation this will be for me, not the other way round. And what fixes this learned use, and hence the extension of 'is red', is the property P: since instances of P are in fact what we learn to respond to by calling them red.

But this makes P look less like a referent than a sense, the sense of the predicate 'is red': namely, that which fixes its extension. But if it is, then again it cannot be necessary for us, or any authority we defer to, to know what or which sense this is. For as we have seen, P can fix the extension of 'is red' in this way without anyone knowing which property P is. But this no more stops P being a sense than it stops it being a referent: since we no more need to know which senses our words have than we need to know which things they refer to. For suppose the sense of 'is red' was in fact given by sensations of a certain kind K, which it certainly could be, even if it isn't. This would not require us to know which kind of sensation K is. It would only require us to respond reliably to K-sensations by applying 'is red' to the things that caused them. But if that is enough to make K the sense of 'is red', then P can also be the sense of 'is red'. For all it takes for P to fix the extension of 'is red' is for our eyes to make us respond reliably to P-things by calling them red.

Now 'sense' is of course a term of philosophic art, and for some Fregean artists it takes more than this for a word to have a sense.[13] But if it does, then 'is red' needs no sense. Yet something about us will still fix the extension of this predicate as we use it: namely, our having learned to let a thing's being P cause us to call it red. So I prefer to stick to the minimal sense of 'sense' as that which fixes the reference or extension of our words, and let P be the sense of 'is red' even though no one knows which property P is.

Suppose then that some property P is, in this minimal sense, the sense of 'is red'. How much of that predicate's meaning does this fix? Not much, and certainly not enough to give us our *concept* of red. For even with words linked as closely to our perceptions as colour predicates are, there is more to understanding them than being able to apply them. To know what 'is red' means it is not enough to know when something is red. We must be able to draw some inferences from that: 'is red' has connotations, if only 'is coloured' and 'is not green'. How does P help to provide them?

The short answer is that it does not, at least not directly. a's being P can make us call a red without inclining us to infer anything from that fact. For as we have seen, P can enable us to apply 'is red' without our knowing any of the laws in which P figures. We need not even know the laws of reflection that make P the property which causes us to call things red, let alone the laws of chemistry that determine what chemical properties will make things P and therefore red. P need not give 'is red' any connotations at all.

But P will constrain its connotations. For we do want our inferences to preserve truth, and when we see that they do not, we give them up. So the inferences we persist in, and eventually make part of the meanings of our predicates, will mostly preserve truth—or at least, they will when their premises and conclusions can be verified by our senses. So at least the verifiable connotations of 'is red' will not contradict the laws that P figures in. Indeed the fact that these connotations generally do preserve truth will generally follow from some of those laws. The connotations of 'is red' will therefore certainly be constrained to some extent by the laws that make P the property it is.

[13] E.g. Evans, *The Varieties of Reference*, chapter 1.

But they will equally certainly not be constrained enough to make P part of our concept of red. For even if a single property P is in fact what makes us apply 'is red' as we do, this fact is obviously not one of that predicate's connotations. It is no part of our concept of red that all red things share any one property (in my non-semantic sense), let alone the property P. And rightly so, since there need be no one such property that all red things share. For laws need not, and mostly do not, take the simple form 'In C-circumstances, all and only Fs are (followed by) Gs', where C, F, and G are single properties. In particular, the laws on which our senses rely when we use them to apply predicates like 'is red' will almost always have much more complicated antecedents. At the very least, they may easily make things need a negation ($\sim P$), or a disjunction ($P \vee Q$), or a conjunction ($P \& Q$) of properties to make us call them red—and $\sim P$, $P \vee Q$, and $P \& Q$ will not be properties on my account, since the Ramsey sentence Σ that quantifies over P and Q will not also quantify over them.

But maybe I should allow the existence of complex properties like $\sim P$, $P \vee Q$, and $P \& Q$. For even if a and b need only be P or Q to be red, it still seems to follow from their both being red that there is something they both are. But that something cannot be P or Q, since a may be P but not Q and b Q but not P. So it looks as if the complex property $P \vee Q$ must exist to be the something that both a and b are. But not so: any more than an actual person (Nobody) must exist in order to be what two empty rooms c and d both contain. The only sense in which it obviously follows that there is something that a and b both are is substitutional: they are both truly called red, just as c and d are both truly said to contain nobody. But on an objectual interpretation of the existential quantifier, it no more obviously follows that there is an actual property which a and b share than that there is an actual occupant whom c and d share.

Yet even if it does not follow, it may still be true. It is less obvious that there are no such properties as $\sim P$, $P \vee Q$, and $P \& Q$ than that there is no such person as Nobody. But there really are no such complex properties, as the following argument shows.[14] For suppose there are, i.e. that there are properties U, V, and W such that $\sim P = U$, $P \vee Q = V$, and $P \& Q = W$. Then Ua and $\sim Pa$, for example, are the very same fact. But they cannot be, because they have different constituents: the first containing U but not P, the second P but not U. And similarly for Va and $Pa \vee Qa$, and for Wa and $Pa \& Qa$. So there are no such properties as U, V, and W—which is not of course to deny the existence of the predicates 'U', 'V', and 'W'.

Armstrong, however, while agreeing that there are no negative or disjunctive properties like $\sim P$ and $P \vee Q$, does think there are conjunctive ones

---

[14] Taken from F. P. Ramsey, 'Universals', [chapter IV of this volume], pp. 61–2

like $P\&Q$.[15] And conjunctive properties are indeed more credible than disjunctive and negative ones, just because they do sustain the existential inference: a and b being P and Q does entail that a and b share a property—indeed two properties, namely P and Q. But this hardly shows that they share a third property $P\&Q$. Nor does Armstrong succeed in showing that. His claim that 'it is logically and epistemically possible that all properties are conjunctive properties'[16] just begs the question, while the intuition behind it (that nature may be infinitely complex, so that, for example, there may be no limit to the small-scale structure of matter) needs no complex properties: since there need be no limit to the number or complexity of laws of nature, nor hence to the number of properties over which Σ has to quantify. And Armstrong's only other argument is a *non sequitur*.[17] The fact that $Pa\&Qa$ may have effects which do not follow from those of Pa and Qa does not show that $P\&Q$ is a property, merely that laws of the form 'All $P\&Q$s are ...' need not follow from laws of the forms 'All Ps are ...' and 'All Qs are ...'.

I conclude then that there really are no complex properties, and therefore that there need be no one property that all red things share. And once we see that there need be no such property, it is obvious that in fact there is not. For the property or properties of light that make it red will clearly differ from all the other equally different properties of objects that make them respectively reflect, transmit, and emit red light. So our application of 'is red' must in fact rely on at least four laws, with the same consequents—the forming of a belief that something is red—but different antecedents, involving four properties $(P_1 \ldots P_4)$ of light and of reflecting, transmitting, and emitting objects respectively, which in four corresponding kinds $(C_1 \ldots C_4)$ of observational circumstances make them cause such a belief.

There is thus no such property as Red, i.e. no property that all red things share. No one property gives 'is red' its sense in even the minimal sense of fixing its extension, let alone in any more substantial sense of fixing its connotations and hence our concept of red. Even the minimal extension-fixing sense of 'is red' must be at least a disjunction $P_1C_1 \vee \ldots \vee P_4C_4$, of four conjunctions, of the properties of the four different kinds of red things that make us call them red with those of the circumstances in which they do so. But this does not make the predicate 'is red' ambiguous. For since, as we have seen, we need not know what the sense of 'is red' is that fixes its extension, we need not know, or even think, that it is disjunctive. Our concept of red no more requires red things to differ in their relevant properties than it requires them to be the same.

Nor will the lack of a property that all red things share make it any harder

---

[15] *USR*, chapter 15.1.   [16] p. 32.   [17] p. 35.

for us to learn how to apply 'is red'. It obviously will not if what makes us call things red is that they all give us sensations of some kind, even if that kind varies from person to person. For then it is the similarity of those sensations that makes us call all the different things that cause them red, not that of the properties which make those things give us those sensations. So if this is what makes us call things red, it obviously does not matter whether all red things share a property or not. But it does not matter anyway, even if this is not what makes us call things red. We can still learn to respond reliably to instances of a complex combination of properties like $P_1C_1 \lor \ldots \lor P_4C_4$ just as easily as to instances of a single property P. For as we have seen, our calling things red is not an inference from our seeing them to be P, or $P_1C_1 \lor \ldots \lor P_4C_4$: it is a direct effect that we learn to let those things have on us in those circumstances. And however complex the combination of properties involved, we can learn to be affected in this way without having any prior concept either of red or of those properties. For we can learn by example, being corrected by existing users of the predicate, just as the network of parallel distributed processors described by Churchland can learn by example to use sonar to tell underwater mines from rocks.[18] And just as Churchland's network can learn without containing any representation either of mines or of the properties by which it learns to detect them, so we can learn what to call red without having or acquiring any concept either of red or of the properties to which we learn to respond by calling the things that have them red.

Nothing therefore in our learning or use of 'is red' requires it to correspond to any one property of the things we apply it to. And as for 'is red', so for almost all our predicates—except some of those we use to state laws of nature. For if, as I have argued, actual properties are those quantified over by the Ramsey sentence Σ that states all laws, then predicates corresponding to Σ's predicate variables will in turn correspond to properties. And this gives us reason to think that the simple predicates we use in our law statements—e.g. those ascribing masses, temperatures, energies, chemical and biological kinds, mental states and kinds of sensation—correspond to properties. We may of course be wrong: not only because our supposed law statements may be false, but because discovering more laws may convince us that predicates we thought were simple (like 'chlorine') are really complex. But even when a predicate 'is P' really is simple, the property P will still not give us its connotations. For even if Σ identifies P, P does not identify Σ. The laws of nature are contingent: they are not entailed by even the totality of properties they contain, let alone by any one of them. And

[18] P. M. Churchland, *Matter and Consciousness*, revised edition (Cambridge, Mass.: MIT Press, 1988), chapter 7.5.

although, as we have seen, the laws that contain P will somewhat constrain the connotations of 'is P', they certainly will not provide them. For not only do we not know all those laws (and probably never will), but even if we did, that would still not determine which of them we do or should build into the meanings of the predicates involved.

In short, contingent universals contribute little to the meanings even of the scientific predicates we use to identify them. And to the meanings of most other predicates they contribute even less: not even their extensions. Thus what Wittgenstein said of 'is a game' may well be true of every ordinary predicate: no one property is shared by everything it applies to. But that does not dispose, as some have thought, of universals and hence of the problems they present: it provides no excuse for nominalism or conceptualism in either metaphysics or semantics. What it does show is the need to recognise how much our concepts, and the meanings of our predicates, differ from the actual properties and relations of things, but also how much, and in what complex ways, they depend on them.

NOTES ON THE CONTRIBUTORS

D. M. Armstrong was, until his retirement, Challis Professor of Philosophy at the University of Sydney. Among his books are *Perception and the Physical World* (1961), *A Materialist Theory of the Mind* (1968), *Belief, Truth and Knowledge* (1973), *Universals and Scientific Realism*, 2 volumes (1978), *What is a Law of Nature?* (1983) and *A Combinatorial Theory of Possibility* (1989).

Keith Campbell is Challis Professor of Philosophy at the University of Sydney. He is the author of *Body and Mind* (1970), *Metaphysics: An Introduction* (1976) and *Abstract Particulars* (1990).

Chris Daly is Lecturer in Philosophy at Keele University. He has published articles on metaphysics.

Michael Devitt is Professor of Philosophy at the University of Maryland. His publications include *Realism and Truth* (1984; 2nd edition, 1991) and *Coming To Our Senses* (1996).

Gottlob Frege (1848–1925) taught mathematics at the University of Jena. He is now regarded as the principal founder of modern mathematical logic. His works include *Begriffsschrift* (1879), *Grundlagen der Arithmetik* (1884) and the two-volume *Grundgesetze der Arithmetik* (1893, 1903).

Frank Jackson is Professor of Philosophy in the Research School of Social Sciences of the Australian National University. His publications include *Perception: A Representative Theory* (1977) and *Conditionals* (1987). He is the editor of *Conditionals* (1991) in the present series.

David Lewis is Professor of Philosophy at Princeton University. His publications include *Convention* (1969), *Counterfactuals* (1973), *On the Plurality of Worlds* (1986) and *Parts of Classes* (1991). Two volumes of his collected essays have appeared: *Philosophical Papers*, Volume I (1983) and Volume II (1986).

D. H. Mellor is Professor of Philosophy at the University of Cambridge and a Fellow of Darwin College. He is the author of *The Matter of Chance* (1974), *Real Time* (1981) and *The Facts of Causation* (1995). A volume of some of his essays, *Matters of Metaphysics*, was published in 1991.

Alex Oliver is University Assistant Lecturer in Philosophy at the University of Cambridge and a Fellow of Queens' College. He has published articles on the metaphysics of sets and properties, and the philosophy of mathematics.

W. V. Quine is Edgar Pierce Professor of Philosophy, Emeritus, at Harvard University. He has published more than twenty books on mathematical logic, philosophy of language and philosophy of science, including *From a Logical Point of View* (1953), *Word and Object* (1960), *Ontological Relativity and Other Essays* (1969), *Theories and Things* (1981) and *From Stimulus to Science* (1995).

F. P. Ramsey (1903–1930) was University Lecturer in Mathematics at the University of Cambridge and a Fellow of King's College. He wrote ground-breaking papers in economics, logic, mathematics and philosophy. His philosophical papers have been reprinted in *F. P. Ramsey: Philosophical Papers*, edited by D. H. Mellor (1990).

Bertrand Russell (1872–1970) was one of the great figures of twentieth-century philosophy. A prolific writer, his philosophical inventions and discoveries include his paradox, theory of types, and theory of descriptions. He was awarded the Nobel Prize for Literature in 1950.

Sydney Shoemaker is Susan Linn Sage Professor of Philosophy at Cornell University. His publications include *Self-Knowledge and Self-Identity* (1963) and *Identity, Cause, and Mind* (1984), which is a collection of his own essays. He has also co-edited *Knowledge and Mind* (1982) with Carl Ginet and co-authored *Personal Identity* (1984) with Richard Swinburne.

Donald C. Williams (1899–1983) was Professor of Philosophy at Harvard University and wrote on metaphysics and epistemology. His works include *The Ground of Induction* (1947) and his collected papers, *The Principles of Empirical Realism* (1966).

SELECT BIBLIOGRAPHY
(Not including material in this volume.)

We have grouped items under salient topics. Readers are also advised to consult the contents and bibliographies of the following two anthologies:

Loux, M. J., editor, *Universals and Particulars: Readings in Ontology* (Garden City, New York: Doubleday, 1970).

Schoedinger, A. B., editor, *The Problem of Universals* (Atlanta Highlands, New Jersey: Humanities Press, 1992).

For an overview of recent work and a detailed discussion of the so-called problem of universals:

Oliver, A., 'The Metaphysics of Properties', *Mind*, 105 (1996), 1–80.

FREGE: PROPERTIES AS FUNCTIONS

Currie, G., 'Frege's Metaphysical Argument', *Philosophical Quarterly*, 34 (1984), 329–42.

Dudman, V. H. '*Bedeutung* for Predicates', *Studien zu Frege, Volume III*, edited by M. Schirn (Stuttgart–Bad Cannstatt: Frommann–Holzboog, 1976), 71–84.

Dummett, M., *Frege: Philosophy of Language*, 2nd edition (London: Duckworth, 1981), chapters 7–8.

Frege, G. (1892), 'On Concept and Object', *Translations from the Philosophical Writings of Gottlob Frege*, edited by P. T. Geach and M. Black, 3rd edition (Oxford: Blackwell, 1980), 42–55.

Wiggins, D., 'The Sense and Reference of Predicates: A Running Repair to Frege's Doctrine and a Plea for the Copula', *Philosophical Quarterly*, 34 (1984), 311–28.

RUSSELL: PROPERTIES AS UNIVERSALS

Marcus, R. B., 'On Some Post-1920s Views of Russell on Particularity, Identity, and Individuation', in her *Modalities: Philosophical Essays* (New York: Oxford University Press, 1993), 177–88.

Quine, W. V., 'Russell's Ontological Development', *Theories and Things* (Cambridge, Mass.: Harvard University Press, 1966), 73–85.

Russell, B. (1911), 'On the Relations of Universals and Particulars', in his *Logic and Knowledge*, edited by R. C. Marsh (London: George Allen & Unwin, 1956), 105–24.

—— (1918), 'The Philosophy of Logical Atomism', in his *Logic and Knowledge*, edited by R. C. Marsh (London: George Allen & Unwin, 1956), 177–281.

Urmson, J. O., 'Russell on Universals', *Philosophers Ancient and Modern*, edited by G. Vesey (Cambridge: Cambridge University Press, 1986), 245–58.

RAMSEY ON THE PARTICULAR/UNIVERSAL DISTINCTION

Dummett, M., *Frege: Philosophy of Language*, 2nd edition (London: Duckworth, 1981), chapter 4.

Geach, P. T., *Reference and Generality* (Ithaca, New York: Cornell University Press, 1962), chapter 2.

—— 'Names and Identity', *Mind and Language*, edited by S. Guttenplan (Oxford: Oxford University Press, 1975), 139–58.

Simons, P., 'Ramsey, Particulars and Universals', *Theoria*, 57 (1991), 150–61.

Strawson, P. F. (1953–4), 'Particular and General', in his *Logico-Linguistic Papers* (London: Methuen, 1971), 28–52.

—— (1970), 'The Asymmetry of Subjects and Predicates', in his *Logico-Linguistic Papers* (London: Methuen, 1971), 96–115.

QUINE'S CRITERION OF ONTOLOGICAL COMMITMENT AND HIS ANIMADVERSIONS ON PROPERTIES

Alston, W. P., 'Ontological Commitments', *Philosophical Studies*, 9 (1958), 8–17.

Armstrong, D. M., *Nominalism and Realism: Universals and Scientific Realism Volume I* (Cambridge: Cambridge University Press, 1978), chapter 6.

Pap, A., 'Nominalism, Empiricism and Universals: I', *Philosophical Quarterly*, 9 (1959), 330–40.

Quine, W. V. (1950), 'Identity, Ostension and Hypostasis', *From a Logical Point of View*, 2nd edition, revised (Cambridge, Mass.: Harvard University Press, 1980), 65–79.

—— (1953), 'Logic and the Reification of Universals', *From a Logical Point of View*, 2nd edition, revised (Cambridge, Mass.: Harvard University Press, 1980), 102–29.

—— (1975), 'On the Individuation of Attributes', *Theories and Things* (Cambridge, Mass.: Harvard University Press, 1981), 100–12.

UNIVERSALS

Aune, B., 'Armstrong on Universals and Particulars', *D. M. Armstrong*, edited by R. J. Bogdan (Dordrecht: Reidel, 1984), 161–9.

Armstrong, D. M., *Nominalism and Realism: Universals and Scientific Realism Volume I* (Cambridge: Cambridge University Press, 1978).

—— *A Theory of Universals: Universals and Scientific Realism Volume II* (Cambridge: Cambridge University Press, 1978).

—— 'In Defence Of Structural Universals', *Australasian Journal of Philosophy*, 64 (1986), 85–8.

—— *Universals: An Opinionated Introduction* (Boulder, Colorado: Westview Press, 1989).

Fox, J. F., 'Truthmaker', *Australasian Journal of Philosophy*, 65 (1987), 188–207.

Goldstein, L., 'Scientific Scotism—The Emperor's New Trousers or Has Armstrong Made Some Real Strides?', *Australasian Journal of Philosophy*, 61 (1983), 40–57.

Jubien, M., 'On Properties and Property Theory', *Properties, Types and Meaning, Volume 1*, edited by G. Chierchia *et al.* (Dordrecht: Kluwer, 1989), 159–75.

Lewis, D., 'Against Structural Universals', *Australasian Journal of Philosophy*, 64 (1986), 25–46.

—— 'Comment on Armstrong's "In Defence of Structural Universals" and Forrest's "Neither Magic nor Mereology"', *Australasian Journal of Philosophy*, 64 (1986), 92–3.

Mortensen, C., 'Arguing for Universals', *Revue Internationale de Philosophie*, 41 (1987), 97—111.

TROPES

Armstrong, D. M., *Universals: An Opinionated Introduction* (Boulder, Colorado: Westview Press, 1989), chapter 6.

Bacon, J., *Universals and Property Instances: The Alphabet of Being* (Oxford: Blackwell, 1995).

Campbell, K., *Abstract Particulars* (Oxford: Blackwell, 1990).

Martin, C. B., 'Substance Substantiated', *Australasian Journal of Philosophy*, 58 (1980), 3–10.

Mulligan, K. *et al.*, 'Truth-Makers', *Philosophy and Phenomenological Research*, 44 (1984), 287–321.

Simons, P., 'Particulars in Particular Clothing: Three Trope Theories of Substance', *Philosophy and Phenomenological Research*, 54 (1994), 553–7.

Stout, G. F., 'The Nature of Universals and Propositions', *Proceedings of the British Academy*, 10 (1921–3), 157–72.

—— 'Are the Characteristics of Particular Things Universal or Particular? II', *Aristotelian Society Supplementary Volume*, 3 (1923), 114–27.

Williams, D. C., 'On the Elements of Being: II', *Review of Metaphysics*, 7 (1953), 71–92.

—— (1959), 'Universals and Existents', *Australasian Journal of Philosophy*, 64 (1986), 1–14.

NATURAL PROPERTIES

Fodor, J. A., *The Language of Thought* (New York: Crowell, 1975), Introduction.

Goodman, N., 'Seven Strictures on Similarity', *Experience and Theory*, edited by L. Foster and J. W. Swanson (London: Duckworth, 1970), 19–29.

Hirsch, E., *Dividing Reality* (New York: Oxford University Press, 1993), chapter 3.

Putnam, H. (1970), 'On Properties', in his *Mathematics, Matter and Method: Philosophical Papers, Volume 1*, 2nd edition (Cambridge: Cambridge University Press, 1979), 305–22.

Quine, W. V., 'Natural Kinds', in his *Ontological Relativity and Other Essays* (New York: Columbia University Press, 1969), 114–38.

Quinton, A., *The Nature of Things* (London: Routledge & Kegan Paul, 1973), chapter 9.

Shoemaker, S. (1979), 'Identity, Properties and Causality', in his *Identity, Cause and Mind* (Cambridge: Cambridge University Press, 1984), 234–60.

—— 'On What There Are', *Philosophical Topics*, 16 (1988), 201–23.

Sober, E., 'Evolutionary Theory and the Ontological Status of Properties', *Philosophical Studies*, 40 (1981), 147–76.

Taylor, B., 'On Natural Properties in Metaphysics', *Mind*, 102 (1993), 81–100.

PROPERTIES: CAUSATION AND LAWS

Armstrong, D. M., *What is a Law of Nature?* (Cambridge: Cambridge University Press, 1983).

Bennett, J., *Events and their Names* (Oxford: Clarendon Press, 1988).

Bigelow, J. and Pargetter, R., *Science and Necessity* (Cambridge: Cambridge University Press, 1991), chapters 5–6.

Carroll, J. W., 'Ontology and the Laws of Nature', *Australasian Journal of Philosophy*, 65 (1987), 261–76.

Dretske, F., 'Laws of Nature', *Philosophy of Science*, 44 (1977), 246–68.

Kim, J., 'Events as Property Exemplifications', *Action Theory*, edited by M. Brand and D. Walton (Dordrecht: Reidel, 1976), 159–77.

Lewis, D., 'Events', in his *Philosophical Papers. Volume 2* (New York: Oxford University Press, 1986), 241–69.

Mellor, D. H. (1980), 'Necessities and Universals in Natural Laws', in his *Matters of Metaphysics* (Cambridge: Cambridge University Press, 1991), 136–53.

—— *The Facts of Causation* (London: Routledge, 1995).

Menzies, P., 'A Unified Account Of Causal Relata', *Australasian Journal of Philosophy*, 67 (1989), 59–83.

Swoyer, C., 'The Nature of Natural Laws', *Australasian Journal of Philosophy*, 60 (1982), 203–23.

Tooley, M., 'The Nature of Laws', *Canadian Journal of Philosophy*, 7 (1977), 667–98.

—— *Causation: a Realist Approach* (Oxford: Clarendon Press, 1987).

van Fraassen, B. C., *Laws and Symmetry* (Oxford: Clarendon Press, 1989), chapter 5.

PROPERTIES IN SEMANTICS

Armstrong, D. M., *A Theory of Universals: Universals and Scientific Realism Volume II* (Cambridge: Cambridge University Press, 1978), chapter 13.

Barwise, J. and Perry, J., *Situations and Attitudes* (Cambridge, Mass.: MIT Press, 1983).

Bealer, G., *Quality and Concept* (Oxford: Clarendon Press, 1982).

Davidson, D. (1977), 'The Method of Truth in Metaphysics', *Inquiry into Truth and Interpretation* (Oxford: Clarendon Press, 1984), 199–214.

Montague, R. (1969), 'On the Nature of Certain Philosophical Entities', in his *Formal Philosophy: Selected Papers of Richard Montague*, edited by R. Thomason (New Haven: Yale University Press, 1974), 148–87.

Schiffer, S., *Remnants of Meaning* (Cambridge, Mass.: MIT Press, 1987), chapter 3.

Wilson, M., 'Predicate Meets Property', *Philosophical Review*, 91 (1982), 549–89.

The following works deal with aspects of properties not covered in this volume.

PROPERTIES AND THE METAPHYSICS
OF MATHEMATICS

Armstrong, D. M., 'Classes Are States of Affairs', *Mind*, 100 (1991), 189–200.

Bealer, G., *Quality and Concept* (Oxford: Clarendon Press, 1982), chapter 5.

Bigelow, J., *The Reality of Numbers* (Oxford: Clarendon Press 1988).

—— 'Sets are Universals', *Physicalism in Mathematics*, edited by A. D. Irvine (Dordrecht: Kluwer, 1990), 291–305.

Jubien, M., 'Straight Talk About Sets', *Philosophical Topics*, 17 (1989), 91–107.

Maddy, P., *Realism in Mathematics* (Oxford: Clarendon Press, 1990), chapter 3.

Oliver, A., 'The Metaphysics of Singletons', *Mind*, 101 (1992), 129–40.

Shapiro, S., 'Mathematics and Reality', *Philosophy of Science*, 50 (1983), 523–48.

PROPERTIES AND THE METAPHYSICS OF MODALITY

Armstrong, D. M., *A Combinatorial Theory of Possibility* (Cambridge: Cambridge University Press, 1989).

Bigelow, J. and Pargetter, R., *Science and Necessity* (Cambridge: Cambridge University Press, 1991), chapters 3–4.

Forrest, P., 'Ways Worlds Could Be', *Australasian Journal of Philosophy*, 64 (1986), 5–24.

Lewis, D., Critical Notice of D. M. Armstrong's *A Combinatorial Theory of Possibility, Australasian Journal of Philosophy*, 70 (1992), 211–24.

Skyrms, B., 'Tractarian Nominalism', *Philosophical Studies*, 40 (1981), 199–206.

Stalnaker, R. C., 'Anti-Essentialism', *Midwest Studies in Philosophy, Volume IV: Studies in Metaphysics*, edited by P. A. French *et al.* (Minneapolis: University of Minnesota Press, 1979), 343–55.

—— *Inquiry* (Cambridge, Mass.: MIT Press, 1984), chapter 3.

INDEX OF NAMES

(not including entries in the Select Bibliography)

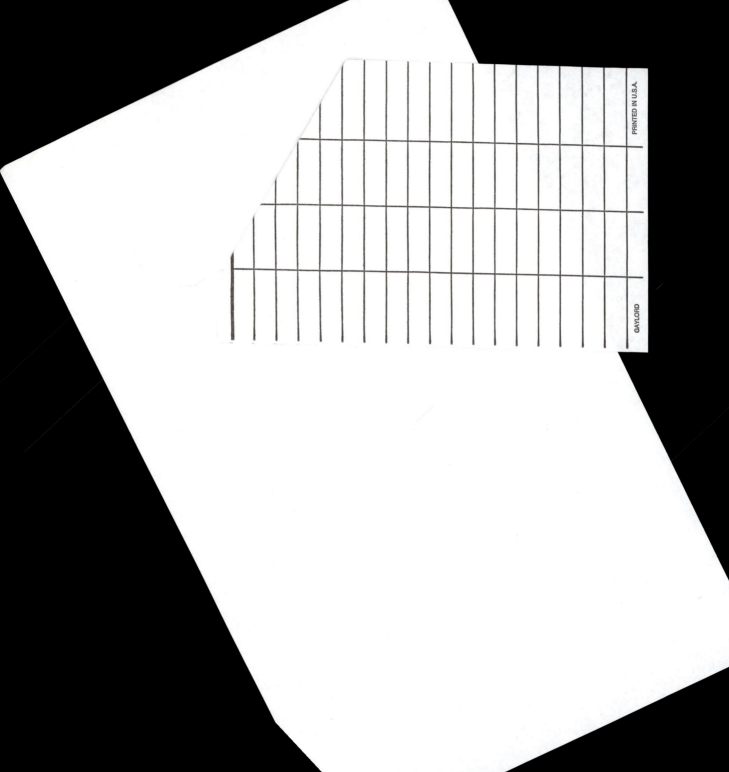